FOOD SUPPLY CHAIN MANAGEMENT

Food Supply Chain Management: Economic, Social and Environmental Perspectives was written to give supply chain partners, policymakers, researchers, students and food enthusiasts a deep understanding of how food is grown, processed, manufactured, distributed and sold to American consumers. *Food Supply Chain Management* also explores the interplay between domestic and global food supply and demand. Throughout this text, the two primary approaches to meeting the world's food needs—traditional agricultural and the sustainability approach—are assessed. Readers of this book should develop an informed platform for dialoguing about the global food supply chain—today and in the future—and for making informed food decisions.

Madeleine Pullman is an Associate Professor of Operations Management at Portland State University in Portland, Oregon. She earned her PhD in Business Administration at the University of Utah in 1997. She previously taught in Graduate and Executive programs at Cornell University, London Business School, Southern Methodist University, Colorado State University, the University of Colorado and the University of Utah. Her articles have appeared in various journals including the *Journal of Operations Management, Decision Sciences, Production and Operations Management,* the *Journal of Service Research,* the *International Journal of Service Industry Management,* the *Cornell Hotel and Restaurant Administration Quarterly, Omega* and the *Journal of Product Innovation Management.*

Zhaohui Wu is an Associate Professor of Supply Chain and Operations Management at Oregon State University in Corvallis, Oregon. He is currently teaching and conducting research on supply networks, buyer–supplier relationships and environmental management strategy in supply chain operations. Zhaohui worked as a buyer at Lord Corporation, a US aerospace company, and as a project manager at CMEC, a Chinese international trade company.

FOOD SUPPLY CHAIN MANAGEMENT

Economic, Social and Environmental Perspectives

Madeleine Pullman and Zhaohui Wu

Routledge
Taylor & Francis Group

NEW YORK AND LONDON

First published 2012
by Routledge
711 Third Avenue, New York, NY 10017

Simultaneously published in the UK
by Routledge
2 Park Square, Milton Park, Abingdon, Oxon OX14 4RN

Routledge is an imprint of the Taylor & Francis Group, an informa business

Library of Congress Cataloging-in-Publication Data
Pullman, Madeleine, 1957-
Food supply chain management : economic, social and environmental
perspectives / Madeleine Pullman, Zhaohui Wu.
p. cm.
Includes bibliographical references and index.
1. Food industry and trade. 2. Food supply. 3. Sustainable agriculture.
I. Wu, Zhaohui, 1968- II. Title.
HD9000.5.P85 2011
338.1'9–dc22   2011006333

ISBN: 978-0-415-88588-1 (hbk)
ISBN: 978-0-415-88589-8 (pbk)
ISBN: 978-0-203-80604-3 (ebk)

Typeset in Baskerville
by Glyph International
Printed and bound in the United States of America on acid-free paper by
Edwards Brothers, Inc.

SUSTAINABLE FORESTRY INITIATIVE
Certified Fiber Sourcing
www.sfiprogram.org

CONTENTS

FIGURES AND TABLES

Figures

Tables

ABOUT THE AUTHORS

Madeleine (Mellie) Pullman is the Willamette Industries Professor of Supply Chain Management at Portland State University. She received her BS (1980) from Evergreen State College and her MS in Mechanical Engineering (1984), MBA (1993) and PhD in Business Administration (1997) from the University of Utah. Before joining Portland State, she taught in graduate and executive programs at Cornell University, London Business School, Bainbridge Graduate Institute, Southern Methodist University, Colorado State University, the University of Colorado and the University of Utah.

Prior to becoming a professor, Pullman worked as a quality manager for Black Diamond Equipment, a brew-master and consultant at Hops Brewery and Schirf Brewing Company, a landscape designer and contractor and a test engineer at Litton Industries. Additionally, she spent her formative years working in the restaurant and catering industry as a manager, chef and cook, in addition to other humbling positions.

Her major research interests include sustainability and supply chain management, sustainable food and beverage supply chains and experiential service design. In addition to authoring books on service operations management (*Successful Service Operations Management, 1st and 2nd editions*), her articles have appeared in various journals and periodicals including the *Journal of Operations Management, Decision Sciences, Production and Operations Management*, the *European Journal of Operations Research*, the *Journal of Supply Chain Management*, the *Journal of Service Research*, the *International Journal of Service Industry Management*, the *Cornell Hotel and Restaurant Administration Quarterly, Omega*, the *Journal of Management Inquiry* and the *Journal of Product Innovation Management*.

Pullman has served on many food-related non-profit boards including the City of Portland's Food Policy Council, the City of Portland's Sustainable Food Purchasing Committee, Food Alliance, Upstream Health and Slow Food Wallowa County. She is an avid food and beverage enthusiast and writes for several local magazines including Beer Northwest and Sustainable Business Oregon.

Zhaohui Wu is an Associate Professor of Supply Chain Management at Oregon State University. He received his BA from Xian Foreign Language Institute (1990, China), his MBA from Bowling Green State University (1997) and his PhD in Supply Chain Management from Arizona State University (2003).

Prior to his academic career, Wu worked as a project manager for China Machinery and Equipment Import and Export Corporation (China) and a commodity manager for Lord Corporation (US). He is currently teaching and conducting research on supply networks, supply management, and environmental management strategy in supply chain operations. He works with and researches companies in a variety of industries including aerospace, automotive, telecommunication, pharmaceuticals, food service and food manufacturing. He has received research grants from the National Science Foundation, the AT&T Fellowship of Industrial Ecology and the Institute for Supply Management.

His articles have appeared in various journals including the *Journal of Operations Management*, the *Journal of Supply Chain Management*, the *Journal of Cleaner Production, IEEE Transactions on Engineering Management*, the *Journal of Business Research, Business Horizon*, the *Journal of Business-to-Business Marketing*, the *Journal of Purchasing and Supply Management* and the *International Journal of Integrated Supply Management*. Currently Wu serves as an associate editor for the *Journal of Operations Management*. He also serves on the advisory board of PACCESS Inc.

PREFACE

Food supply chain management is today consistently garnering the attention of the media, the public and government policymakers. While the economic interests of the food industry have traditionally been business' dominant focus, today the public wants to know how food businesses are affecting society and the environment, and how they manage a multitude of safety concerns. Thus, owners and managers of food-related businesses today must frequently address numerous social, environmental and safety stakeholder groups and topics. This challenge is compounded by the competitive and relatively low margin nature of the food industry.

The food supply chain requires many natural resources to function properly. With the exception of the energy industry, no other industry will face as many demands from the growing world population as the food industry. We wrote this book because we believe that it is important for current and future food managers and policymakers to understand the current system, structure, institutions and economic, social and environmental forces at play in each sector. We have attempted to be as comprehensive as possible but given the huge array of issues, this is certainly not an exhaustive coverage of every possible topic. We do attempt to cover multiple perspectives and provide examples of companies trying to move beyond a solely economic focus to balance the bottom line with social and environmental needs. We believe that most food companies will eventually head in this direction. As we highlight some of today's innovators as examples.

Purpose of the Book

The purpose of this book is to describe the current US food supply chain and its management practices from multiple perspectives. At the time of writing this first edition, no comprehensive book on US food supply chain management and the different issues faced by each sector exists. As university professors teaching in this area, we wanted and needed a comprehensive book for our classes, and, in the past, resorted to case studies, articles, readings and popular press books to introduce students to the subject. This book is an attempt to remedy that situation and as such it is designed for students, food enthusiasts, potential and current managers, researchers and policymakers working in the food arena. It provides an overview of how each sector of the food chain functions and it introduces the economic, social and environmental issues that each sector is currently facing. Those who want a detailed or specialist perspective on a specific sector will need to go beyond this book, although we do believe it provides a thorough introduction.

Chapter Overviews

Chapter One introduces the food supply chain, its economic significance, changes in the agricultural structure of the United States in recent decades, consumer and policy trends affecting food supply and demand, and the proposed solutions of the mainstream agriculture system versus the sustainable agricultural movement.

Chapter Two covers food safety. It highlights the scope of the problem, details the role of the government agencies responsible for food safety, introduces the industry systems and practices that work to ensure safe food production, and summarizes key food safety concerns on a food-by-food basis.

Chapters Three through Five describe animal protein, commodity crop and fruit and vegetable supply chains, respectively. Each chapter discusses the importance of the crop, summarizes current production methods in the United States, details the supply chain structure and summarizes significant players and public policy, social and environmental issues.

Chapter Six describes food regulation and verification mechanisms. We explain the concept of credence attributes, describe various types of credence attribute claims and the methods used to convey claims to consumers. We also examine the claims regulated by the government and verified by industry and nonprofit organizations. We look specifically at the United States Department of Agriculture's role in regulating food quality and information claims. The chapter also explores the food certifications that have gained a significant market presence worldwide.

Chapters Seven through Nine provide an overview of food service, manufacturing and retailing activities. Each chapter explains the economic importance of the sector, details their supply chain structure, lists significant players and assesses relevant social and environmental issues. Additionally, distribution, purchasing and logistics are discussed where applicable.

Chapter Ten provides an overview of hunger relief supply chain management. As a growing area of interest in food supply chain management, this chapter explores the difference between development aid and hunger relief, and provides examples of how traditional supply chain management ideas are being applied to food crises today.

Chapter Eleven concludes the book by summarizing the challenges we face in creating a food system that addresses the numerous environmental, economic and social justice needs and concerns that exist today. We look at food security issues and describe emerging solutions that address these challenges from a global perspective.

Each chapter herein also provides a short, illustrative example of the subject matter at hand, either an issue analysis or a producer profile. Two detailed case studies are also featured in this book, each exemplifying the complicated range of supply chain issues that producers face today as they attempt to meet their business needs in a socially responsible manner.

ACKNOWLEDGMENTS

We would like to acknowledge the individuals who have made this book possible. First, we wish to thank our student support teams at Portland State and Oregon State Universities for their professional research support, editing and graphic talents, patience, commitment and key insights for improving the book: Allison McManus, Maty Sauter and Ryan Owens, all MBA students at Portland State; Yinyin Cao, Maggie McClaran, Krista Spike and Kurt Christensen, all students at Oregon State. We also wish to thank Fred Kepler for his insights and editing of several of the chapters, and Bill Rankin, Phil Howard, U.S. Wheat Associates and Fulton Provision Company for the use of several significant graphics.

Second, we would like to thank the people and organizations that helped fund this project: the Loacker Faculty Research Grant program at Portland State, PACCESS and the Summer Research Fellowship at Oregon State University. Additionally, we would like to thank the leadership at our respective business schools for encouraging sustainability research: Scott Dawson, Darrell Brown and Scott Marshall at Portland State; Ilene Kleinsorge and Jack Drexler at Oregon State.

Third, we thank John Szilagyi and Sara Werden from Routledge Publishing for supporting the project.

Finally, we give our special thanks to our spouses, Tim and Maya, and other family members and friends, who encouraged and supported us throughout this effort.

January 2011
Mellie Pullman, Portland, Oregon
Zhaohui Wu, Corvallis, Oregon

ABBREVIATIONS

ACA	Accredited Certifying Agent
CAFO	Concentrated Animal Feeding Operation
CAS	Controlled Atmosphere Stunning
CBP	US Customs and Border Protection Agency
CDC	Centers for Disease Control and Prevention
COS	Canadian Organic Standards
CSA	Community Supported Agriculture
C-TPAT	Customs Trade Partnership Against Terrorism
DSR	Distributor Sales Representative
ECR	Efficient Consumer Response
EDI	Electronic Data Interchange
EPA	US Environmental Protection Agency
FAO	Food and Agriculture Organization of the United Nations
FAST	Free and Secure Trade Program
FDA	US Food and Drug Administration
FEMA	US Federal Emergency Management Agency
FIFO	First-In-First-Out
FLO	Fairtrade Labelling Organization
FSIS	USDA Food Safety and Inspection Service
GAP	Good Agricultural Practices
GHP	Good Handling Practices
GMO	Genetically modified organisms
GSA	US General Services Administration
HACCP	Hazard Analysis and Critical Control Points system
IFRC	International Federation of the Red Cross
IP systems	Identity Preservation systems
IPM	Integrated Pest Management
ISO	International Organization for Standardization
JAS	Japanese Agricultural Standard
LIFO	Last In First Out
MAP	Modified Atmosphere Packaging

MSC	Marine Stewardship Council
NAFTA	North American Free Trade Agreement
NCBA	National Cattlemen's Beef Association
NOP	USDA National Organic Program
NSBP	National School Breakfast Program
NSLP	National School Lunch Program
OFPA	Organic Foods Production Act
PTI	Produce Traceability Initiative
RFID	Radio Frequency Identification
RPCs	Reusable Plastic Containers
SAN	Sustainable Agriculture Network
SKUs	Stock Keeping Units
3PL	Third Party Logistics
UNJLC	United Nations Joint Logistics Centre
USAID	US Agency for International Development
USDA	US Department of Agriculture
VOCs	Volatile Organic Compounds
WFP	United Nations World Food Program

1

INTRODUCTION TO FOOD SUPPLY CHAIN MANAGEMENT

Today's global food supply chain feeds over 310 million Americans and almost 7 billion more people around the world. Farms and ranches produce raw food products—grains, fruits, vegetables, meats and dairy—which then move by truck, rail or sea through a complicated distribution network that links processors, manufacturers, retailers, food service establishments and consumers, as illustrated in Figure 1.1. While food may be a relatively unremarkable aspect of most Americans' lives, the food production process is actually deeply complex, influencing and influenced by natural, economic, cultural and political factors that are both national and international in scope. Comprehending these factors is critical to developing an informed opinion about the way we eat today, and the way we will produce food in the future as domestic and global populations increase.

What Do We Eat?

Today, most Americans enjoy a relatively high standard of living compared to people in developing countries. The average American consumes just under 2,000 pounds of food per year, including 630 pounds of dairy products, 413 pounds of vegetables, 273 pounds of fruit, 230 pounds of meat and non-dairy animal products, 192 pounds of grain-based products, 142 pounds of sweeteners and 85 pounds of fat. Perhaps not surprisingly, these numbers include a substantial amount of French fries, pizza and ice cream—29, 23 and 24 pounds, respectively. The estimated average lifetime consumption of food products for a person living in the developed world is illustrated in Figure 1.2.

In contrast, people in developing countries eat less than those in developed countries; i.e., they have fewer average per capita calories available to them each day—around 2,700, as opposed to the developing world's 3,200 calories. Their eating patterns are also different, as they consume far more carbohydrates and starches and far fewer animal proteins and fats, which are expensive and resource-intensive to produce. While the overall supply of food in the world is, so far, adequate to meet caloric needs, vast discrepancies in food access exist—created primarily by poverty—resulting in substantial undernourishment

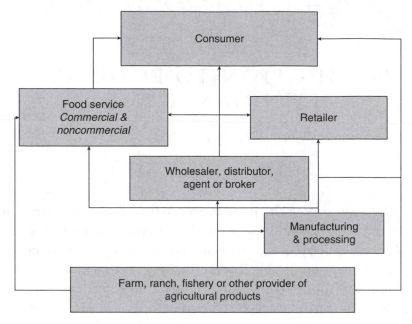

Figure 1.1 **The food supply chain**

and malnourishment in some populations. An estimated 925 million people in the world today are undernourished, meaning their caloric intake falls below minimum dietary requirements on a consistent basis. About 36 million people die each year due to malnourishment, or a lack of adequate nutrition.

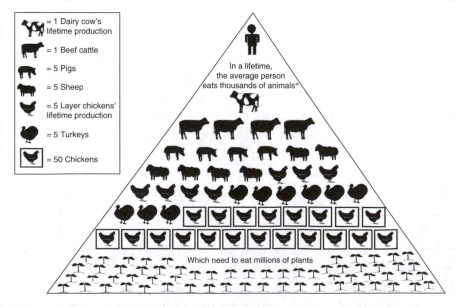

Figure 1.2 **Food consumption in the developed world**
*Not applicable to non-meat eaters or those that choose not to eat specific meats for religious reasons (Source: Compassion in World Farming)

The US population is expected to reach 440 million people by 2050. Global population is projected to reach over 9 billion in the next 40 years. Thus, food needs are going to increase as population expands. At the same time, the resources available to grow and produce food are going to decline, due to the inherent, non-farming related needs of human beings—land to live on, water to drink, fuel to drive, etc. It is estimated that for every person added to the US population, approximately one acre of land is lost due to urbanization and highway construction alone. At this rate, only 0.6 acres of farmland will be available to grow food for each American by 2050, as opposed to the 1.8 acres per capita that is available today. Other resource and cost implications associated with population growth are listed in Table 1.1.

The estimated carrying capacity of land—i.e., the estimated amount of land required to maintain current American dietary standards with current production practices—is 1.2 acres. Therefore, Americans will either need to significantly decrease or alter our food intake, change our food production practices, or pay more for food in the coming decades. Even with changes to consumption and production practices, food prices are projected to increase three- to five-fold by 2050. This will dramatically influence our existing quality of life and social balance, as Americans are used to spending a very small amount of our income on food—approximately 15%. In contrast, people in other developed countries spend 30% to 50% of their income on food, and those in developing countries spend, on average, 50% to 60% of their income on food.

If existing consumption and land use trends continue, researchers have also forecast that the United States will likely cease to be a food exporter by 2025, as all food grown in the United States will be needed for domestic consumption.

Table 1.1 **Resource and Cost Implications for US Food Production**

	Current Population	*2050 Population*
	309 million	520 million*
Resource Availability Per Capita		
Arable Land	1.8 acres	0.6 acres
Pasture Land	2.3 acres	1.1 acres
Forest Land	2.2 acres	1.0 acres
Fresh Water	1,300 gallons	700 gallons
Energy	2,500 gal. oil equivalents	1,600 gal. oil equivalents
Food Exports	$155	$0
Other Impacts		
Diet Proportions	69% plant, 31% animal	85% plant, 15% animal
Food Costs	N/A	3- to 5-fold increase

* Note that the 2050 population projection was recently adjusted by the US Census Bureau, to 440 million. Source: D. Pimentel and M. Giampietro.

Other countries that were once self-sufficient or were food exporters are already facing this problem. China, for example, used to produce enough corn and cereal products to meet its own demands. Today, however, it must import many commodities to meet demand. As America is one of the biggest agricultural producers in the world and a major food exporter, a halt to US food exports could dramatically reduce world food supplies—particularly staple crops, like grains—and increase global food costs, furthering nutritional inequality and instability in the world. It could also negatively influence our economic security, as our trade deficit will increase if not offset in some other way.

Food is big business in America. Feeding our own population generates an estimated $1 trillion in consumer sales each year. The food industry accounts for 17% of the worker population, and 12% of gross national product. Approximately 20% of the agricultural products grown in America are exported, comprising 9% of US exports valued at about $115 billion each year. In addition to international trade, we supply vast quantities of food to humanitarian service organizations, who directly distribute surplus commodities to disaster- and poverty-stricken people throughout the world. Clearly, finding a way to meet our own and others' food needs in the future is a critical domestic and global priority. The question for many is how this is best achieved.

Schools of Thought

Today, several opposing schools of thought exist, each striving to answer the question of how to best feed the world. Some argue that the problem of global scarcity is best addressed by continuing to industrialize. In this model, the focus is on increasing yields, or increasing food supplies through more intensive farming and the application of biotechnologies. Others feel that the entire food production system needs to be reconceptualized—from the agricultural process to food distribution and waste management—in order to address the numerous environmental and economic issues that are currently resulting from the industrialized food production model. Both approaches have merits, and both have possible drawbacks that, if they come to fruition, could have negative consequences for the food supply, and thus, humanity.

The industrial perspective's primary merit is that it is already in play and has momentum; the vast majority of agricultural lands are already being farmed using an industrialized model, and this model has proven to be effective, so far, in producing sufficient calories to meet global demand. Its drawbacks, however, are numerous, and include significant ecological destruction, such as topsoil loss and water contamination; an increasing reliance on nonrenewable resources, like petroleum-based fertilizers, to enhance agricultural yields; and, in all likelihood, increasing reliance on genetically modified organisms (GMOs) to help manage impending resource constraints—e.g., drought-resistant seeds.

This latter issue is further problematic as GMO crops are already having a delete-rious impact on plant diversity and the ecosystem, due to cross-pollination with wild plants. GMOs also increase the dependency of individual farmers, and thus the entire food supply, on the few companies that create GMO seeds, since GMO seeds are patented and must be repurchased each year, as opposed to being saved for free use in future harvests.

The alternative to the industrial perspective is the sustainability school of thought, which is emerging and still taking shape, but demonstrating the poten-tial to meet global food needs while better managing some of the environmen-tal and social issues addressed poorly by the industrial food production model. Sustainable agriculture practices call for increasing plant and animal diversity at an agricultural facility so that the outputs from one system (decaying plant matter, animal manure) become the inputs for another in a continual process, negating the need for vast nonrenewable chemical inputs to boost yields. Sustainable agriculture also seeks to restore and improve the ecosystem services that benefit human beings and animals—i.e., water and soil quality—through more natural farming methods like geographically appropriate crop selection, crop rotation and cover crop planting. In essence, in the sustainability model, researchers and practitioners are considering how the carrying capacity of agricultural lands and the overall ecosystem can be rebuilt and possibly improved. An additional key focus of most sustainability advocates is enhancing support for small- and midsized food producers.

Proponents of the industrialized agricultural model claim that the sustain-able agriculture concept cannot address the growing food needs of the planet. If current dietary patterns and food consumption rates are maintained, this may indeed be true. However, others argue that reducing discretionary food consumption could allow sustainable agriculture to adequately feed the world. The most obvious way to reduce discretionary consumption is to reduce people's consumption of inefficient food products, such as processed foods, dairy and meat. Animal products in particular are at the end of a long food chain, each phase of which requires numerous inputs that increase animal products' input to energy conversion ratio. In contrast, food products with a short food chain, such as grains and vegetables, have a much lower input to energy conversion ratio, making them more sustainable. Reducing discretionary food consump-tion may also help address the obesity epidemic in America, and stave off impending obesity epidemics elsewhere.

This book presents both the industrial and the sustainable agriculture per-spective as it walks through the food supply chain, as both are relevant and important in today's growing world. In presenting these perspectives, this book strives to help consumers understand the environmental, social and economic impact of their food choices so that they can make informed eating decisions.

Key Food Industry Trends

Several trends have been influencing the food industry for decades, and therefore surface repeatedly as themes in this book. First among these is a change in industry structure—primarily consolidation and concentration, the results of which are partially illustrated in Table 1.2. A second major trend is a shift in the basic food supply chain, which has globalized, giving consumers year-round access to a vast array of interesting food products. Simultaneously, consumer interest in modes of agricultural production that improve personal and environmental health have encouraged the emergence of local food supply chains, which differ markedly from global supply chains and pose unique challenges to all supply chain partners. Lastly, new food industry technologies have emerged that are enhancing food safety and accountability efforts. These major trends are detailed below.

Table 1.2 **Basic US Food Supply Chain Statistics**

	Farmers and Producers	Manufacturers and Processors	Wholesalers and Distributors	Food Service Vendors	Retailers
Number of entities	>2.1 million	>26,000	>33,000	>580,000	>210,000
Sales Revenue	$375 billion	$540 billion	$600 billion	$580 billion	$548 billion
Structure	125,000 farms control 75% of US agricultural production value	100 firms control 75% of production; 4 meat firms control 70% of slaughter production	50 firms control 50% of sector value	3 companies control most food service management contracts in the US	20 firms control 60% of sector; Wal-Mart controls 20% of sector; 75% of retailers are chains
Focus	• 650,000 cattle farmers and ranchers • 500,000 hay farmers • 330,000 grain and oilseed farmers • 100,000 fruit and nut farmers	• 19% meat • 17% bakery • 14% fruits and vegetables • 11% dairy	• 46% wholesale • 54% agents and brokers	• 40% full service restaurants • 37% limited service restaurants • 6.1% education vendors • 4.4% hotels	• 90% grocery • 6% convenience • 4% specialty

Note: Does not include beverage manufacturers.
Source: Author.

Changes in Agricultural Production and Industry Structure

Increased farm productivity and enhanced global trade have given American consumers a wide selection of interesting food, often available year-round. However, these charges have come at a cost. The share of food sale revenue that goes to farmers today is much smaller than that received by other members of the food supply chain. Figures 1.3 and 1.4 illustrate the breakdown of the

Figure 1.3 **Breakdown of a dollar spent on food** (Source: R.A. Cook).

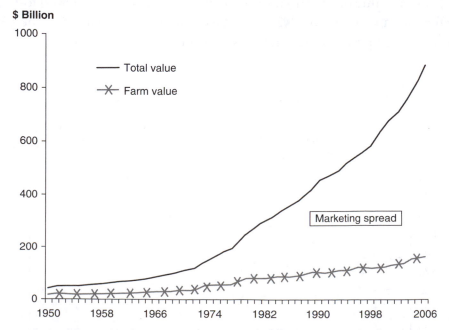

Figure 1.4 **Marketing spread for domestically-produced food products, 1950–2006** (Source: R.A. Cook).

average dollar spent on food in the United States, and the marketing spread—or the difference between the total value of a food product and the amount received by the farmer. While the consolidation of farm product suppliers has tended to keep costs down, increased food marketing expenditures have significantly outweighed those benefits and continued to drive overall prices up. These trends have reduced revenues for the average farmer, particularly small- and midsized farmers in the United States.

Consequently, the number of US farms has declined almost every year since World War II, and there are now just over 2.2 million farms in America. Interestingly, just under 300,000 new farms have launched in the United States since 2002, and between 2002 and 2007 there was a net increase of 75,810 farms. Compared to existing farms, these new farms tend to have more diversified production, fewer acres, lower sales and younger operators, who also work off-farm to gain supplementary income. However, while the number of farms has increased slightly in recent years, farmland decreased by 2% between 2002 and 2007. Today, 922.1 million acres of farmland exists in the United States.

Changes in farm ownership patterns are also occurring in America. The most recent agricultural census indicates that the smallest and largest farms are increasing in number while midsized farms are decreasing. Between the last two census periods, the number of farms with sales of less than $2,500 increased by 74,000 while those with sales of more than $500,000 grew by 46,000. Agricultural production is also becoming more concentrated, with 125,000 farms responsible for 75% of the value of US agricultural production in 2007, compared to 144,000 farms for the same share in 2002. Gross farm income is increasing in the United States, keeping up with production costs, as illustrated in Figure 1.5.

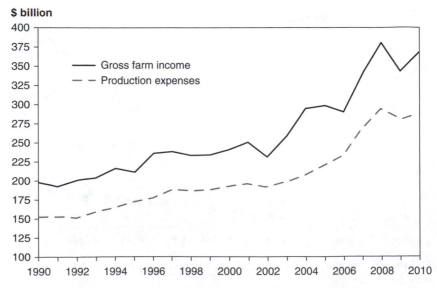

Figure 1.5 **US gross farm income and production costs, 1990–2010** (Source: USDA ERS).

This shift in production structure—more big and small farms and fewer midsized farms—reflects an overall shift in the rest of the food supply chain, as well. Consumer and public policy support is emerging for smaller farms, which are served by "boutique" supply chain variations, such as farmers' markets, while the existing industrialized and consolidated supply chain serves the larger, generally corporate farms that produce the food consumed by the vast number of people in America and the world.

Consumer Response and Food Supply Chain Shifts

Consumers today are paying attention to voices from both the industrialized and alternative food camps as the popular press discusses issues related to food supply chains. Many consumers appear genuinely interested in supporting healthier food systems and rural economies, often via supply chain models that directly support small and midsized farms. Farmers' markets, Community Supported Agriculture arrangements (CSAs) and Farm to School initiatives are examples of these new supply chain models.

Interestingly, these smaller players are driving other supply chain innovations such as mobile processing facilities that enable on-site meat processing, fruit cooling and beverage bottling; cooperative or shared processing facilities that increase the capacity of individual producers, like those in the wine and dairy industries; and scannable labels that convey a farm or ranch's story to the end consumer via personal hand held devices or websites.

Larger producers are aiming to improve the quality and efficiency of their supply chains through partnerships with manufacturers, wholesalers and brokers. Technology innovations such as Efficient Consumer Response and case tracking systems help large producers meet consumer demand with higher service levels and lower inventory and waste costs.

Unfortunately, midsized farms are getting squeezed in between these two systems. Midsized farms are defined as small commercial farms with annual sales of $50,000 to $99,999, with annual returns averaging $17,000; and moderately sized commercial farms are those with annual sales of $100,000 to $249,999, with annual returns average $40,000. While midsized farms are often too big to benefit from direct sales models such as CSAs or farmer's markets, they are also too small to build partnerships with larger supply chain partners. Thus, declines in this sector are not expected to change without policy interventions.

Technology Innovations

The food system has been revolutionized throughout time by technological innovation. Historically, innovations have developed around yield-improving production technologies, such as tractors, combines and hybrid seeds; raw material processing, such as milling and hulling; and perishability reduction, i.e., refrigeration. With today's intense focus on food safety, innovation is now honing in on issues like bacterial growth inhibition, micro-element pollutant detection, food stabilization and general contaminant prevention. Other technologies are aiming to improve product quality, traceability and resource use. Examples of these technologies include bar codes, radio frequency identification tags (RFID) and scanning technologies that can be tied into the Internet. Global positioning systems are also being used to track products through the logistics system, and to increase precision when seeding fields.

On the sustainability side, innovations include the development of methods and products to rebuild topsoil, such as direct seeding into field stubble, which prevents erosion as there is no tilling. Dairies and other animal facilities are experimenting with bio-digesters to convert animal and plant wastes into useful fuels on the farm. Researchers and innovators such as Temple Grandin have developed animal housing that respects animal welfare needs, animal handling solutions and many other socially and environmentally friendly crop and animal production systems. Other innovations include certification standards and labels for ensuring that various social, environmental and quality practices are followed and conveying this information to the consumer via labeling and marketing campaigns.

Conclusion

This chapter has introduced the focus of this book—the food supply chain. The remainder of this book focuses on specific aspects of the food supply chain and the significant food products consumed worldwide. Clearly, food supply chain management will continue to garner consumer and media attention as the world's population grows, and will be a challenging arena for both managers and policymakers in future years. Thus, this book is an attempt to improve the reader's comprehension of the many issues and possibilities in food supply chain management from a variety of important and relevant perspectives.

Discussion Questions

1. What are the significant differences between the industrial and sustainable focused food production and supply chain models? Is there potential for middle ground between these concepts? If so, what is that middle ground?
2. What is discretionary food consumption? What are some examples of discretionary food consumption and how might reducing discretionary food consumption impact public and ecological health?
3. What is happening to midsized farmers in the United States? Why should US policymakers be concerned about the loss of midsized farms?

4. What are some of the food supply chain technology innovations that you have witnessed? How do they work, and why are they interesting to you?

Additional Readings and Links

- A national initiative has formed to study agricultural issues related to midsized farming, ranches and related agrifood enterprises. Research and several case studies are available on the Agriculture of the Middle project website: http://www.agofthemiddle.org/
- A detailed study of population growth and its relationship to agriculture, "Food, Land, Population and the US Economy" was used as a source in this chapter. The full copy of the report is interesting and is available from the Carrying Capacity Network: 2000 P Street NW, Suite 240 Washington, D.C. 20036; (202) 296-4548.
- The Food and Agriculture Organization of the United Nations studies global food production, consumption and hunger trends. Numerous interesting charts on these topics are available for free online: http://www.fao.org/economic/ess/chartroom-and-factoids/chartroom/en/

2

FOOD SAFETY

On February 24, 2009 the Nebraska Department of Health and Human Services identified an outbreak of *Salmonella* serotype Saintpaul. More than 125 people fell ill, reporting symptoms that included abdominal cramps, headaches, fever and diarrhea. Health officials in Nebraska and Iowa conducted a case-control study to identify whether the outbreak could be associated with a particular food item or restaurant. While case-control studies do not prove cause and effect, they can characterize a relationship, and thus provide information regarding disease etiology and disease patterns within a population. Analysis of this data can therefore help health officials identify possible point sources or contaminating agents.

Of the 64 case-control study participants, 73% of the afflicted case-patients reported they had eaten alfalfa sprouts. Because the epidemiological process is slow, it took nearly a month to ascertain the source of the problem, but the investigation eventually isolated a single company as the source: CW Sprouts of Omaha. However, the company reported it had followed Food and Drug Administration (FDA) guidelines for reducing microbial hazards in sprouted seeds.

These guidelines included soaking the seeds for 15 minutes in a 2% chlorine solution, rinsing the seeds and germinating them in water. Forty-eight hours after sprouting and draining, CW Sprouts cultured and tested its water for both *Salmonella* and *E. coli* pathogens. The company's records indicated that no positive test results had been generated in January or February of 2009 using this process. Nonetheless, the company conducted a voluntary recall on March 3, 2009. By March 19, the outbreak had spread to six states and 186 people were ill.

A second outbreak was identified in mid-April. Sprouts linked to this outbreak came from companies in Michigan, Minnesota and Pennsylvania. Further investigation pointed to the actual seeds as the cause of contamination. In fact, all of the seeds in both outbreaks came from a single supplier: Caudill Seed in Louisville, Kentucky.

There are several ways the seeds could have been tainted, including the use of contaminated water, the use of improperly composted manure as fertilizer, fecal contamination from domestic or wild animals, contaminated runoff from animal processing facilities or improperly-cleaned harvesting and processing equipment. It is also possible the seeds were contaminated during conditioning or distribution, or were improperly stored.

Ultimately, 228 people in 13 states fell ill. Because of the multitude of possible contamination sources and the number of people afflicted, it is likely that litigation and lawsuits for damages and compensation will continue for many years.

Introduction

This chapter explores the issue of food safety in America. We begin by assessing the overall scale and impact of the issue. We then assess the role of the government agencies responsible for food safety. We review the basic industry practices designed to reduce food safety risks, and assess general food safety concerns related to animal products, grains, nuts and produce. We conclude by evaluating intentional threats to the US food supply—i.e., tampering and terrorism.

Issue Overview

The Centers for Disease Control and Prevention (CDC) estimate that foodborne illnesses make 48 million people sick and cause 3,000 deaths in the United States each year. Food can be contaminated at any stage in the production process, from planting and harvest to poor storage of finished products. While food safety problems are typically thought of as biological in nature, contamination can also come from chemical or physical sources. For instance, certain substances found in the environment, such as oil, solvents and industrial chemicals, can pose a danger to consumers if they make their way into the food or water supply. Ironically, many agents used to combat food contamination, such as insecticides, fungicides, herbicides and other chemicals used in farming and food processing, can also be toxic in large amounts.

The CDC defines an outbreak of foodborne illness as two or more illnesses resulting from consumption of the same food product. The total number of outbreaks in the United States has remained steady for more than a decade, at about 1,200 per year. That number may actually be much larger as mild cases of

Table 2.1 **Recent Multi-State Outbreaks, 2006–2009**

Year	Pathogen Type and Food Source
2006	• *E. coli* O157:H7 and bagged spinach • *E. coli* O157:H7 and shredded lettuce (restaurant chain A) • *E. coli* O157:H7 and shredded lettuce (restaurant chain B) • Botulism and commercial pasteurized carrot juice • *Salmonella* and fresh tomatoes
2007	• *E. coli* O157:H7 and frozen pizza • *Salmonella* and peanut butter • *Salmonella* and a vegetarian snack food • *Salmonella* and dry dog food • *Salmonella* and microwaveable pot pies • *Salmonella* and dry puffed rice breakfast cereal • *E. coli* O157:H7 and ground beef • Botulism and canned chili sauce
2008	• *Salmonella* and cantaloupe • *E. coli* O157:H7 and ground beef • *Salmonella* and fresh produce items
2009	• *Salmonella* and peanut butter containing foods • *Salmonella* and imported white and black pepper • *Salmonella* and alfalfa sprouts • *E. coli* O157:H7 and raw cookie dough

Source: Robert V. Tauxe.

foodborne illness—often caused by poor handling or sanitation in homes and restaurants—frequently go unreported to officials. The number of large, multistate outbreaks is on the rise. Table 2.1 presents a partial list of recent, multistate outbreaks in the United States.

As implied, outbreaks can be local or dispersed, depending on how they start and spread. Local outbreaks impact several people in a small area, and are typically caused by a food handling error. The afflicted group frequently self-identifies the problem, and if notified, local jurisdictions deal with the responsible person or vendor. Dispersed outbreaks impact many people in a wide geographical area and can result from a range of food products. Therefore, they are more difficult to identify and manage. Common pathogens that link afflicted individuals and food products are identified through lab testing, and the source of contamination is identified through epidemiological investigation. Dispersed outbreaks are typically caused by contamination during the food production process.

Globalization has limited transparency in the food production process. Food is no longer necessarily grown close to home, so food sources may not be readily apparent to consumers or easy to track down for public health officials. Likewise, a food product today typically has many handlers, from harvesters to processors to distributors, which can make it difficult to trace individual ingredients back to their origin, particularly after they have been combined into multi-ingredient products. The contamination source and culpability of any one handler in a contaminated food's supply chain may therefore be difficult to ascertain. Disease outbreaks and recalls in recent years have drawn the public's attention to these and other food safety issues, improving some aspects of the problem. Nonetheless, issues remain.

As noted, large, multistate outbreaks appear to be on the rise. This is due in part to improvements to analytical tools, which are enabling epidemiologists to better see links between seemingly disparate outbreak events. Another reason, however, is an increase in centralized food production. Large plants are handling ever-increasing volumes of food, and then shipping that food regionally, nationally and globally. Contamination in a base product at one facility can therefore contaminate many food products at a mass scale worldwide. Differing laws and safety systems in source countries can further complicate safety management in the United States.

Government's Role in Food Safety

Ensuring the safety of the US food supply falls to numerous federal, state and local agencies, as noted in Table 2.2. Chief among them are two federal agencies, the United States Department of Agriculture (USDA) and the FDA. The USDA and the FDA share responsibility for inspecting and regulating the

Table 2.2 **US Regulatory and Public Health Agencies**

Agency	Affiliation/Authority	Responsibility
United States Department of Agriculture (USDA)	Executive Office of the President via Article Two of the US Constitution	Regulates beef, pork, poultry and egg processing; regulates food advertising and claims labeling (e.g., organic labels); responsible for many other agriculture-related activities, including meat and shell egg grading
Food and Drug Administration (FDA)	Department of Health and Human Services	Regulates all food products not regulated by the USDA, including shell eggs; responsible for informational food labeling (e.g., nutritional data and ingredients)
Centers for Disease Control (CDC)	Department of Health and Human Services	Provides foodborne illness outbreak surveillance and epidemiological management services; coordinates PulseNet
State and Local Public Health Departments	Varies	Provide foodborne illness outbreak surveillance and epidemiological management and on-the-ground services; regulate inspection of food service establishments

Source: Author.

production, distribution and sale of food in the United States, particularly food that is sold across state lines. Most state agriculture departments inspect dairies, in addition to non-meat commodities that are particularly relevant to a state's agricultural base. For example, the Idaho Department of Agriculture inspects hops. Some state agriculture departments also inspect meat that is produced and sold only in-state.

Government agencies also provide food-related public health services, like restaurant inspections, pathogen subtyping and traceback investigations. These services are as essential in ensuring consumer safety as are regulatory agencies. While regulatory agencies generally aim to prevent foodborne illnesses, public health agencies provide critical analyses that can staunch an outbreak in process or prevent an outbreak from occurring again. The CDC is the lead public health agency in the United States. The CDC works in conjunction with state public health departments, which in turn work with local public health agencies to manage outbreak events.

Several international organizations also work to promote global food safety. The World Health Organization (WHO) coordinates global outbreak surveillance activities and develops policy recommendations at the international level. The Food and Agriculture Organization of the United Nations (FAO) assesses the safety of food and animal feed worldwide. Codex Alimentarius, a subsidiary of WHO and FAO, develops standards and codes of practice for the safe handling of commodities.

The USDA and the FDA

At the federal level, the USDA has jurisdiction over meat, poultry and pasteurized processed egg products. The FDA is responsible for all other foods. The two departments share jurisdiction for food labeling, with the FDA responsible for informational labeling and the USDA protecting consumers from misbranding and fraudulent claims. The USDA and the FDA have very different budgets, enforcement authority and regulatory approaches. The USDA has more resources and therefore uses continuous inspection and prior approval methods to ensure safe food production. The FDA relies on random inspection and enforcement in the marketplace. Detailed explanations of the USDA's and FDA's missions and activities are provided below.

USDA

The USDA's main purpose is to serve and promote the interests of agriculture. In this regard, it provides inspection services for meat, poultry and select egg products, but is also responsible for farmer assistance, food marketing, agricultural research and the administration of supplemental nutrition benefits in America. The USDA also has responsibility for rural development and natural resource management activities, primarily the administration of the US Forest

Service and the Natural Resources Conservation Service. The USDA is a large department. Its annual budget in 2010 was $134 billion, the majority of which went to nutrition assistance programs.

The Food Safety and Inspection Service agency of the USDA (FSIS) conducts daily inspections of slaughterhouses and poultry processing plants, supports state agency inspections of similar establishments, runs the Public Health Information System to improve safety outcomes in the meat and poultry industries, and evaluates foreign food safety systems. FSIS employees are located at over 6,000 slaughterhouses, processors and import houses nationwide, and at other federally regulated facilities that produce non-food products, like cotton and lumber. FSIS's budget in 2010 was just over $1 billion.

FDA

The FDA is a branch of the US Department of Health and Human Services, and is responsible for monitoring about 80% of the food supply in America. The FDA regulates non-meat and poultry processing activities, enforces certain labeling laws—including those related to ingredients, nutrition, allergens and some marketing claims—and protects the US food supply from malicious, criminal and terrorist activities. In addition to its food safety purview, the FDA is responsible for regulating drugs, medical devices, biologics (e.g., blood, vaccines, tissues), animal products and services, cosmetics, radiation-emitting products and tobacco products. The FDA's total requested budget in 2010 was $3.2 billion, a 19% increase over its 2009 budget. Of that, $259 million was allocated to protecting the US food supply.

Despite the FDA's extensive scope, the agency did not have the authority to order a food recall until early 2011. Prior to this, recalls for food products regulated by the FDA were voluntary, their performance effectively mandated by the market and the threat of lawsuits. The Food Safety and Modernization Act, signed by President Barack Obama in January 2011, gave the FDA this authority, and strengthened its inspection capabilities. Although it is too early to see how its expanded authority will impact actual food safety, it is anticipated that the FDA will take a more proactive approach to preventing foodborne illness as a result of this law. Sources of funding for the $1.4 billion legislation are not yet known. Food recalls for products regulated by the USDA remain voluntary.

The CDC and Public Health Agencies

CDC

The CDC is the lead public health agency in the United States. Its Food Safety Office holds primary responsibility for leading epidemiological teams during multi-state and international food illness outbreaks. In this role, the CDC coordinates teams to identify and investigate the cause of a major foodborne illness. Beyond this leadership role, the CDC is responsible for enhancing the capacity of state and local health agencies via training and consultation, and for distributing tools, data and educational materials about foodborne illnesses to other government agencies and the public. The CDC also conducts research on preventing foodborne illness. In 2010, the CDC's budget for food safety activities was about $27 million.

PulseNet is a national network of laboratories coordinated by the CDC. This network has been instrumental in identifying pathogens during large outbreaks for nearly two decades. PulseNet performs DNA subtyping ("fingerprinting") of bacteria through pulsed-field gel electrophoresis (PFGE). PFGE distinguishes different strains of organisms to the degree that bacterium with the same fingerprint can be assumed to have originated from the same source. However, actually identifying that source involves a lengthy traceback investigation, which in turn requires numerous interviews and inspections. These interviews and inspections are typically performed by state and local health departments.

STATE AND LOCAL HEALTH DEPARTMENTS

The activities of state and local health departments vary widely, depending on their size, mandates and available budget. Some state health departments, such as the Iowa Department of Public Health, focus primarily on leadership, management and consulting during an outbreak event, while local health departments carry out the majority of on-the-ground investigatory tasks, such as data and sample collection, interviews, cause identification and hypothesis development. Other state health departments own more of the investigation process. For instance, local health departments in California have first responder responsibilities during a food illness event, but the Food and Drug Branch of the California Department of Public Health takes the lead in the investigation process. Most local health departments also play a critical role in illness prevention by licensing and inspecting food establishments.

Inter-Agency Coordination and Collaboration

Because contamination can occur anywhere in the food supply chain—from farming to the cooking and serving process—and because responsibility for protecting the food supply in America is fragmented across levels and areas of expertise in government, inter-agency coordination and collaboration are essential. Collaboration is common between the USDA and the FDA; the CDC, the USDA and the FDA; the CDC and state health departments; and state and local health departments. A list of other federal agencies that may be involved in food safety efforts is provided in Table 2.3.

As an example of collaboration, the USDA and the FDA work together to issue the Good Agricultural Practices (GAP) and Good Handling Practices

Table 2.3 **Other Federal Agencies with Food Safety Roles**

Agency	Affiliation/Authority	Responsibility
Fish and Wildlife Service (FWS)	Department of the Interior	Manages freshwater fisheries and hatcheries
Bureau of Land Management (BLM)	Department of the Interior	Issues permits and controls livestock grazing on approximately 160 million acres of federal land
Environmental Protection Agency (EPA)	Independent; derives authority from the Federal Insecticide, Fungicide, and Rodenticide Act (FIFRA)	Registers and regulates more than 18,000 pesticides; designates labeling and "restricted" or "general use" classification

Source: Author.

(GHP) guidelines. These guidelines outline recommended practices for farmers and food processors to reduce hazards in the produce industry. The USDA and the FDA also routinely collaborate on lab testing and data distribution, training and food terrorism prevention initiatives.

An example of public health collaboration is the work that the CDC does with USDA and FDA inspectors to identify the source of a food-related outbreak. USDA and FDA representatives help trace the origins of a respective food product, and may provide lab assistance to identify contaminants. The USDA and the FDA also coordinate recalls and initiate regulatory actions against producers, if warranted and allowed by law, after the CDC and other public health entities identify the source and cause of an outbreak event.

Numerous examples of successful coordination between government agencies—as well as good individual agency performance—exist with regard to food safety. Indeed, the US food supply has become exponentially safer in the last century, since the initiative to regulate food production first began. However, the safety net designed to protect consumers can fail. Criticisms of regulatory agencies are particularly fervent. Stories of filthy food manufacturing facilities at the source of a product recall, or stories of processors that are routinely cited for safety violations and yet not shut down fuel consumer discontent.

These violations of public trust occur because regulatory agencies are tasked with balancing the public's right to a safe food supply with a company's right to do business. Critics often comment that in striving to achieve this balance, agencies like the USDA have demonstrated a bias in favor of industry, as the USDA has shifted much of the burden of safety enforcement and improvement to industry itself in the last decade. Critics further levy that agencies like the USDA favor large-scale agricultural producers, as the costs to develop, refine and maintain required safety plans have proven too great for many small- and mid-sized processors, many of whom perceive their risks as more limited given their much lower production volumes.

While these critiques are based in fact and reflect legitimate concerns, the small agency budgets allocated to regulating the majority of the $1 trillion US food supply clearly enable only limited government involvement in any food safety effort. Moreover, in the past decade, the courts have demonstrated a preference for allowing companies to stay in business—despite safety concerns.

For instance, in 2003, the government ruled against the USDA in a suit brought by Supreme Beef Processors of Texas, who contended that because *Salmonella* pathogens are not, by themselves, a danger to consumers (they are only a danger if combined with inadequate cold storage and cooking procedures), the USDA had no authority to establish safety thresholds for the bacteria in beef processing plants. In effect, the courts suspended the USDA's ability to force a plant shut down due to *Salmonella* contamination. Although the USDA still has the ability to force a plant shut down due to a variety of other issues, the example illustrates the nature of the debate. In recent years, industry has demanded—and thus today holds—primary responsibility for ensuring the safety of the US food supply.

Industry's Role in Food Safety

Although government is responsible for regulating some aspects of food safety, and for determining the source of contamination when it occurs, food companies do the actual work of making facilities and processes safe. To do this, food producers and distributors follow basic safety programs that are mandated, but not designed, by government. They may also leverage longstanding manufacturing concepts—such as Total Quality Management and Six Sigma—to achieve very high safety and quality standards.

Here we introduce the primary safety program in the food industry: the Hazard Analysis and Critical Control Points (HACCP) program. We also detail the "Six Ts" that comprise general, good industry practice: traceability, transparency, testability, time, trust and training. While the "Six Ts" are not regulated or mandated by any government agency, they can be useful in guiding the development of mandated safety programs, as well as the implementation of robust quality improvement processes, like Six Sigma, as noted in Table 2.4.

HACCP

In 1959, NASA commissioned Pillsbury to create food for its space program. The strict requirements for space food meant that Pillsbury's traditional food safety procedures were inadequate, as they allowed for too much contamination. Pillsbury adapted one of NASA's engineering protocols—its "identify, test,

Table 2.4 **The "Six Ts" and DMAIC**

Define	The project team is formed, project deliverables are defined and the team trained. *Traceability* (being able to "map" the supply chain) is an input to this phase. *Training* is an outcome, as supply chain managers need to be trained on the practices required to ensure a high-quality product and suppliers need to be trained on those same expectations and standards.
Measure	The team identifies the key metrics related to quality, implements the plans required to collect data and obtains a baseline. In this phase, *testability* must be an outcome, as tests must be implemented to allow measurement at each necessary point in the supply chain.
Analyze	The team gathers data and determines root causes of any gaps in performance. *Transparency* of procedures and norms is necessary to begin this process. Root cause analysis can also help improve buyer-supplier trust throughout the supply chain.
Improve	Covers all key metrics. For the Six T's it should include *traceability* of inputs, *testability* of products, *transparency* and *time*. Reducing time in the supply chain reduces the risk of many types of quality failures, such as those related to perishability, and adds to the bottom line.
Control	Any improvements made in *time, testability, transparency* and/or *traceability* need to be shared through system-wide *training*. In this phase, continuous process improvement and discussion help to increase the level of *trust* in the global supply chain.

Source: Author.
Note: For an organization trying to improve the quality of the products it sources through a global supply chain, the Six T's can serve as both necessary inputs and desired outputs in each phase of the Define, Measure, Analyze, Improve, Control (DMAIC) cycle of the Six Sigma process.

control" process—to help it identify potential points of failure in its manufacturing processes, test for quality at these points and, by refining production processes, control outcomes. In so doing, Pillsbury created the first industry version of HACCP. By 1972, the federal government was advocating for HACCP to be used in food production facilities nationwide.

HACCP plans give managers and line workers a way to evaluate and improve their food production processes, from receiving to distribution. HACCP calls for an identification of hazards—i.e., places where biological, chemical or physical contamination can occur. Critical control points, or physical locations or stages of production where specific controls can be applied to prevent food safety problems, are then identified. The production process is monitored with specific controls in effect—intended to improve outcomes—and corrective actions are taken if a deviation occurs. The process requires extensive verification and record keeping to ensure that a company's HACCP plan is being adhered to, and to enable continuous improvement.

HACCP manages for specific process hazards. However, HACCP does not address the overall operating condition of a food manufacturing or

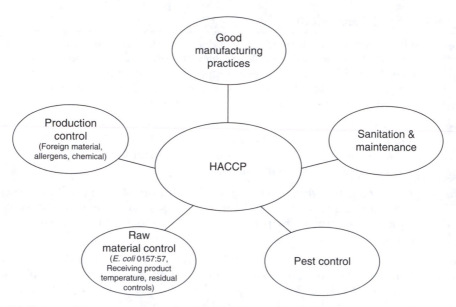

Figure 2.1 **Prerequisite programs and HACCP** (Source: USDA FSIS).

processing environment. Prerequisite programs do this, creating the foundation for HACCP's implementation. Examples of prerequisite programs are
Good Manufacturing Practices, Sanitation Control Procedures and Sanitation
Standard Operating Procedures. The relationship between prerequisite programs and HACCP is illustrated in Figure 2.1.

Both prerequisite programs and individual HACCP plans are closely monitored by USDA and FDA inspectors to ensure that companies are in compliance
with their safety goals. Because the economic consequences of a plant shutdown can be disastrous for food manufacturers, however, the USDA and the
FDA typically opt to work with producers to make safety improvements in lieu
of forcing a shutdown, if and when violations occur. Additionally, as already
noted, the regulatory authority of the USDA and the FDA to suspend operations at a plant that is in violation of its safety program or plan is limited in some
instances.

The "Six Ts"

The "Six Ts" are a set of principles that encourage good, safe practices in the
food industry. While not a specific rule set, like HACCP, the principles remind
food industry managers to build quality into their sourcing, production and
distribution processes. The "Six Ts" are described below.

TRACEABILITY

Traceability is the ability to track a product through its supply chain, and
back again. It is of fundamental importance when food safety issues arise,

as investigators need to know how a food product was handled and from where it came. This type of traceability is termed regulatory traceability. Traceability is also an important marketing concept, as products with credence attributes need to be managed separate from the processes used to grow and manufacture similar products that lack the distinguishing attribute (e.g., organic versus nonorganic tomato sauce). This type of traceability is termed value traceability.

Traceability requires good information exchange between all participants in a supply chain. However, this can be difficult to do. As ingredients are processed through multiple channels and combined, information on the origin and handling of individual ingredients can become harder to maintain. Thus, traceability efforts become more demanding and expensive. Investment in information tracking systems such as bar codes and radio frequency identification (RFID) tags and readers, along with the training necessary in their use, can be effective, but these are beyond the reach of many small producers. For those that can make the investment, however, tracking systems have much to offer, including improved regulatory compliance, increased quality control, better inventory management and higher margins due to loss reductions.

TRANSPARENCY

Transparency is the thorough and systematic provision of information to consumers about production and processing activities. A globalized market makes transparency difficult. For example, supplier countries like China have thousands of small farms operating just above the subsistence level. Products coming from these farms are frequently sold on a cash basis, leaving no paper trail. A lack of transparency creates opportunities for corruption and deceptive practices in the supply chain. Although country-of-origin labeling laws now exist, details about the animal feed, fertilizers and pesticides used during the production process in a foreign country are often impossible to obtain. Large buyers of imported products can impose certification regimes on suppliers, but without an independent third-party inspection, the value of the certification is unknown. In such an opaque environment, labels that claim a product is "Made in the USA" or a "Product of Canada" are often just marketing tools.

TESTABILITY

Testability is the ability to detect a certain attribute through analysis, and routine testing for certain negative attributes, such as pathogens at control points. It is critical in ensuring a safe food supply. However, testing has its drawbacks, thus it should not be relied on as the only control process in a food supply chain. For one, food inspections are generally destructive, meaning that tested samples are no longer fit for consumption. Testing for the myriad things that can go wrong with food is also impractical. In addition, minor deviations from even the best processes can lead to problems that are unidentifiable through short-term testing; e.g., shelf life.

TIME

Time refers to the duration of a specific process. In terms of supply chain management, it can refer to how long a product is in transit, the difference between the time a problem is discovered and reported, and a producer or industry's recovery time after a supply disruption. In all cases, less is better: fresh produce, frozen foods and baked goods are highly susceptible to spoilage and need to be transported quickly; outbreaks need to be detected and staunched quickly to protect the public's health; and industry needs to minimize downtime so as to maximize profits.

TRUST

Trust is the expectation that buyers and sellers will behave in accordance with expressed or implied commitments. One obstacle to trust in the global market is a lack of shared values. For instance, American consumers and overseas food producers often have different attitudes toward cleanliness and food safety. While integrity may exist on both sides, trust may be hindered by a lack of clarity about expectations and commitments. Recent food recalls also show that even in countries with shared values, trust alone is inadequate to ensure a safe food supply. For example, in 2010, 550 million eggs were recalled after outbreaks of *Salmonella Enteritidis* sickened dozens of people across the country. All the eggs were produced by two Iowa facilities; the owner of one had a history of health, safety and labor violations dating back as far as 1975. These examples underscore the vulnerability of the food supply to unscrupulous suppliers.

TRAINING

Training refers to the development of the knowledge, skills and attitudes needed by workers to maintain food safety and quality. Training is the best way to overcome the cultural differences inherent in a globalized supply chain. Its scope ranges from adopting good agricultural practices to training in how to use a sophisticated tracking system.

Category-Specific Concerns

This section discusses specific safety risks associated with animal products, grains, nuts and produce. Common methods used to reduce pathogens and contaminants in these food types are explained. Risks associated with imported foods are also assessed herein.

Animal Products

According to the CDC, raw foods of animal origin are the most likely to be contaminated. Animal products are particularly susceptible to microbial contamination because of their high moisture and protein content, which create an
ideal environment for pathogen growth, and because animals produce fecal
matter that can contaminate the production process. Of particular concern are
commingled animal products. For example, one ground beef patty may contain
the meat of several hundred cows because of the way beef is processed. A pathogen present in one animal could therefore contaminate an entire batch of processed product. Because of their susceptibility to contamination, animal
products are a highly regulated and inspected food category. Substantial funding goes toward securing animal product food safety via continuous inspection
by the USDA.

After processing begins, animal products must be chilled for the duration of
their supply chain. Because bacterial growth (and spoilage) could occur if
chilled temperatures are not maintained, their supply chains are therefore
often referred to as cold chains. To kill bacteria, fresh meat and poultry products can be irradiated with gamma, electron or x-ray energy. Irradiated foods
sold in the United States carry the "radura" symbol, and have packaging labeled
with "treated by irradiation" or "treated with irradiation." Most dairy products
are pasteurized to kill bacteria. Despite the irradiation and pasteurization
processes, the cold chain must be maintained if pathogens are to be kept at bay.

Meat products regulated by the USDA receive an inspection stamp after processing and testing. Meat cannot be stamped until it passes inspection, and it
cannot be sold in the United States until it is stamped. The term "USDA
Inspected" should therefore not be considered a marketing attribute for meat
products. Note that beef grading (e.g., "prime," "choice," etc.) is also done by
the USDA, but that is a separate, optional aspect of quality management for
which beef processors pay a fee. The testing and stamping process for ground
beef is illustrated in Figure 2.2.

Figure 2.2 **Ground beef testing and inspection stamp** (Source: Photos courtesy of Fulton
Provision Company).

Dairy products are regulated by the FDA, but most dairy inspection services are provided by state agriculture departments. Thus, laws about dairy products vary. For instance, raw milk products cannot be sold across state lines, but some states may allow the sale of raw milk products in-state. The ease with which contamination can spread in fluid milk makes dairy products amenable to tampering. FDA guidelines therefore suggest that dairies limit access to shipping, processing and receiving areas and lock or seal the milk house and access points to bulk milk. FDA recommendations also suggest using inventory logs to track products and ingredients in storage, using production logs to record activity during a given day or shift, tracking shipments and deliveries and creating a quality control log to track mandatory and voluntary testing results.

Because animal products have such different laws and guidelines, safety training is essential, both in industry and in government inspection agencies. Managers, supervisors and employees must be fluent in all hygiene and sanitation regulations that are relevant to their particular product so that they can assess risks accurately and take effective preventative and corrective measures when needed. Inspectors need to be well-versed in the pathogens common to animal products, and able to understand what environments and situations put food safety most at risk.

Grains and Nuts

Grains are much less susceptible to pathogen growth than are animal products and produce. However, physical contamination, such as the infestation of raw and milled grain products by rodents and insects, is a problem. To alleviate physical contamination, cleanliness is very important. Equipment and facilities involved in grain production, processing and distribution activities need to be cleaned and disinfected regularly. Physical and chemical means of reducing rodent and insect populations may also be employed by processors, but the misuse of chemical means—i.e., rodenticides—can introduce new contaminants into the grain supply chain.

Contact with moisture can encourage bacterial and fungal growth in grain products. To avoid this type of contamination, grain should be stored in cool and dry conditions. New trends in food manufacturing, in which grains are combined with wet products and yet not fully cooked before sale, have created new avenues for microbial contamination in the market. Examples include refrigerated pastas and raw cookie doughs, often sold in the deli section at supermarkets.

Because of their small size, grains are always commingled—i.e., harvested, stored, processed and transported in bulk. Because they are commingled, isolating and finding the source of a contaminated product can be extremely difficult. Traceability in the grain supply chain is also difficult as grain products are commonly combined with other ingredients during the production process. For instance, flour may consist of several varieties of wheat. US food regulations allow for the irradiation of grain and grain products, which can help kill pathogens and insects. Note that nuts are not a grain, but as their supply chains are similar, they share many food safety vulnerabilities.

Produce

Along with animal products, fruits and vegetables are the main source of food-borne illness in the United States. Outbreaks in recent years have been traced to alfalfa sprouts, bagged spinach, cantaloupe and tomatoes, among others. Because fruits and vegetables are used in many processed foods, produce contamination can impact a wide range of finished goods. Like animal products, fresh produce requires a cold chain to prevent pathogen growth and spoilage. Disruption at any point in the cold chain can create a food safety issue.

The use of dirty, contaminated water at some point in the production process is the most common reason for produce contamination. Thus, irrigation, cooling and processing are all vulnerable points in the produce supply chain. Poor temperature control after harvest, and during packing and shipping, can exacerbate an existing pathogen problem. Consumer handling in the retail environment can also contaminate produce. Chapter 5 provides extensive information on cold chain management in the produce industry. Chapter 8 discusses food processing and manufacturing safety in detail, which has extensive application to the produce industry.

Imported Foods

Imported foods are popular in the American diet. For instance, year-round demand for fresh produce has created an extensive counter-seasonal fruit trade, bringing foods like grapes to the United States in winter. Although we eat large amounts of imported foods, they are not regulated by US agencies, the exception being country-of-origin labeling laws, which are regulated and enforced by the FDA and the Department of Homeland Security (DHS), and foreign meat processors, which are regulated by the USDA. Rather, imported foods are regulated in their country of origin.

Because most imported foods are not regulated by US agencies, there is no uniform program of testing for chemical or microbial contamination of foreign food. Importers can bring foods into the United States so long as they are registered with the FDA, and so long as the FDA receives notice that a shipment is incoming. Imported food products are subject to FDA inspection when it is offered at a US port of entry. The FDA may detain import shipments if the shipments are found to be out of compliance with US requirements. US importers can also impose contractual obligations on foreign suppliers, but it is up to the importer to verify compliance. Thus, the safest approach toward imported food is to practice due diligence at home.

Tampering and Terrorism

In addition to inadvertent contamination, the intentional, malicious contamination of food is a threat for which private companies and government must always be prepared. Examples of tampering are numerous, and range from obnoxious pranks committed by individuals to true safety threats that have resulted in consumer death. Thankfully, examples of extreme food tampering, i.e., food terrorism, are very rare, although WHO in 2007 identified food terrorism as a key public health threat for the world in the twenty-first century, in part due to globalization.

With the widespread adoption of tamper-resistant packaging in the United States in the past two decades, post-production tampering is more difficult to accomplish than it once was. Therefore, most tampering today occurs during the food production process. WHO's study of tampering and terrorism also indicates that the points in the supply chain where food changes hands are the most vulnerable to sabotage. Indeed, government and private industry efforts to increase the safety of the US food supply primarily focus on enhancing safety in food production and distribution, particularly international production and distribution.

For example, the Customs-Trade Partnership Against Terrorism (C-TPAT) is a voluntary initiative designed to enhance the safety of imported foods. It involves importers, licensed customs brokers, carriers, consolidators and manufacturers, along with the US Customs and Border Protection agency (CPB). Through C-TPAT, CBP encourages businesses to verify the security practices of their supply chain partners and to certify their own security practices. Once validated and certified, C-TPAT participants receive tangible benefits, including streamlined inspection services. A side benefit is improved loss prevention due to enhanced security.

The Free and Secure Trade program (FAST) is similar to C-TPAT. It features a clearance system for low-risk truck shipments entering the United States from Canada and Mexico. FAST participants have dedicated lanes at border crossings, and receive expedited inspections.

The CDC has also assessed threats to the US food supply, assessing and ranking various foodborne pathogens to determine their potential for use in terrorist attacks. The most dangerous—Category A agents—include *Bacillus anthracis (anthrax)* and *Clostridium botulinum (botulism)*, both of which can cause death if consumed. However, most foodborne pathogens are classified as Category B agents, such as *Salmonella* spp., *Shigella dysenteriae* and *E. coli* O157:H7. These agents are easier to disseminate than the Category A agents, but will cause low

Issue Analysis: Peanut Corporation of America

On November 25, 2008, the CDC began an epidemiological assessment of a cluster of *Salmonella Typhimurium* after an outbreak surfaced the previous month. After investigation and analysis, the CDC determined the origin of the contamination to be King Nut peanut butter, produced by the Peanut Corporation of America (PCA) at its Blakely, Georgia facility. The company processed only 2.5% of America's peanuts, but supplied its products to over 200 food processors and manufacturers, widely dispersed in the United States and in 23 countries and non-US territories worldwide. The impact of the contamination was therefore widespread, with extensive human and economic consequences.

Outbreak Timeline

As early as November 10, 2008, PulseNet identified the first multi-state cluster of *Salmonella Typhimurium* infections—13 cases in 12 states. The CDC began to monitor for additional cases surfacing with the same DNA fingerprint. On November 24, a second cluster was identified and an epidemiological assessment began. By December 28, the Minnesota Department of Health determined that a number of the afflicted patients ate in one of three facilities: two long-term care facilities and one elementary school. A review of the menus and invoices at these facilities showed that all of the institutions had one menu item in common: King Nut creamy peanut butter. A few weeks later, the Minnesota Department of Health found *Salmonella* in an open container of King Nut peanut butter, confirming the suspected source of the outbreak.

King Nut, a maker and distributor of fruit and nut specialty products, was a distributor of peanut butter made by PCA. Consequently, the FDA and the Georgia Department of Agriculture investigated PCA's facility in Blakely; an epidemiologist from the CDC also joined the team. One week later, the Connecticut Department of Public Health also found the *Salmonella* strain in a sealed container of King Nut peanut butter. PCA then commenced a recall of its peanut butter and peanut paste.

This recall directly affected the companies that used PCA peanut products in their manufacturing process. For instance, Kellogg's had to recall its Austin and Keebler brands of peanut butter crackers, as both brands were made at a plant that used peanut paste from PCA. The CDC and the FDA also issued an advisory regarding specific peanut butter and peanut butter products to alert other manufacturers and consumers. On January 21, the FDA expanded the scope of its review, launching an investigation into PCA's Plainview, Texas facility. Shortly after that, PCA expanded its recall and a tanker truck carrying peanut paste was cultured and tested positive for *Salmonella Typhimurium.*

Since some of the peanut products had already been used in food production, investigators knew that contamination was likely already widespread. Indeed, soon after the tanker truck was cultured, Oregon's public health department confirmed the strain in contaminated dog treats. Within 48 hours, the Texas Department of State Health Services ordered PCA to stop production and distribution at its Texas facility and to recall all products it had manufactured since January 1, 2007. A week later, the strain was again confirmed in fresh ground peanut butter distributed at a Colorado health food chain, and in ground peanut meal sourced from the Plainview facility. Finally, on February 20, PCA issued a statement informing its customers to cease distribution and use of all products from both its Georgia and Texas plants.

Supply Chain Consequences

In the PCA case, as can occur in ingredient-driven outbreaks, contaminated ingredients spread relatively undetected throughout the supply chain before being used and consumed in various settings. Peanut butter and peanut paste are common ingredients in cereal, cookies, crackers, ice cream, candy, pet treats and other foods. However, although the risk of such an incident occurring was relatively equal for all of PCA's manufacturing and retail clients, the capacity, experience and preparation of PCA's commerical buyers to manage such a crisis varied significantly. In short, the consequences for PCA's supply chain partners were greater for smaller companies than for larger companies.

For example, large manufacturers such as Kellogg's, Kraft and General Mills had the supply chain management and logistics expertise to handle PCA's ingredient crisis. They were able to quickly track their suppliers and their suppliers' sources, and manage information going to retailers and others down the chain. These large companies also had experienced legal departments that could navigate the complicated recall stipulations. They also had the benefit of public relations and advertising departments to help the affected brands rebound after the recall, and the economic resources to afford the recall's costs and float operations during brand downtime.

To the contrary, the PCA recall had serious ramifications for some smaller companies with much more limited expertise and resources. Deeply impacted were a small health food chain in Colorado, a Las Vegas manufacturer of protein bars, a Connecticut packager of nuts and dried fruits, a cannery in Montana and an ice cream manufacturer in New York. When PCA announced on February 20, 2009 that it had filed for Chapter 7 bankruptcy, it was no longer able to communicate with its commerical customers about its recalled products, leaving them in the lurch financially, and with damaged reputations. The small food manufacturers had no recourse, except to wait for the conclusion of bankruptcy proceedings, and to hope there might be reimbursement or recompense in the future.

There were notable exceptions to this pattern. For example, as part of its quality control program, a small, Iowa-based cookie dough factory, Aspen Hills, had prepared itself for such an event by practicing mock recalls every six months. When the feigned crisis happened, Aspen Hills tracked every single unit of "contaminated" product, and then promptly notified each of its customers. Needless to say, this company was better able to manage the crisis than its unprepared counterparts.

Other Consequences

Legal evidence against PCA was straightforward, and thus its negligence appeared clear. The findings of a February 2, 2009 plant investigation revealed open passageways for rodents to access manufacturing equipment, rodent excrement and dead rodents in manufacturing areas. Filters were contaminated with feathers, lint, dust and miscellaneous foreign debris. Birds' nests were observed in the manufacturing facility, although bird droppings are a known source of *Salmonella* contamination. Such observations made it difficult to conceive that PCA had no knowledge of the risks they were taking, and the potential effect of those risks for consumers.

By March 2009, 714 people in 46 states and Canada had been infected, and nine people had died. In addition to the human toll, more than 2,100 processed and packaged foods were recalled because they contained ingredients from PCA. The outbreak cost the US economy an estimated $1.5 billion.

mortality and only moderate morbidity if spread through the food supply—i.e., impacts similar to that of an ordinary outbreak.

Discussion Questions

1. What are the roles and responsibilities of the various regulatory agencies in safeguarding the US food supply? Who manages public health responsibilities associated with food safety in the United States?

2. How has globalization impacted food safety in the United States? Where relevant, use the "Six Ts" to structure your discussion.

3. Research a recent foodborne illness outbreak. What factors contributed to the outbreak? How quickly was it caught? How did the event impact the producer, its partners in the supply chain and consumers? What could have been done to prevent the outbreak?

4. Some have argued that locally produced foods, in addition to foods produced by small-scale growers and processors, do not need the safety infrastructure created by robust programs and plans, like HACCP. Assess the merits of this argument.

Additional Readings and Links

*   Moss, Michael. October 3, 2009. "The Burger that Shattered Her Life." *New York Times.* Interesting article that walks readers through the epidemiological process during an outbreak.

*   The website www.foodsafety.gov posts information from the CDC, the FDA and the USDA on recalls and alerts, and provides safety tips for meat, fish and produce.

*   The Food Safety Project at Iowa State University Extension (www.extension.iastate.edu/foodsafety) provides tips on food preparation; information on picnic and take-out food safety; food safety news; and information on food irradiation and the shelf-life of various products.

*   The Partnership for Food Safety Education (www.fightbac.org) recommends safe food-handling tips, and provides information on recalls and a food safety glossary.

3

ANIMAL PROTEIN SUPPLY CHAINS

Today, almost all major fast food chains are establishing standards and policies for animal handling in their protein supply chains. McDonald's and Wendy's are among those starting to make changes. Their efforts related to pork, eggs and poultry are described below.

For pork, the two chains are encouraging suppliers to adopt a comprehensive plan to eliminate sow gestation stalls (small crates housing a single sow and its piglets). Cargill Pork, McDonald's biggest supplier, is working with its contracted pig farms to achieve this goal. Today, 50% of Cargill's contractors have eliminated their use of the crates. Wendy's incentivizes the transition through preferential buying. Currently, 10% of Wendy's pork products meet the standard; the company's goal is to have 20% of its suppliers eliminate the crates.

The housing systems for laying hens are also receiving attention, although debates exist about the need to transition from battery cages to cage-free or free range systems. Wendy's egg program has been in place since 2001 and today 2% of their eggs come from cage-free hens. They have also indicated they will consider increasing this goal based on "animal science and best industry practices," noting that they are a low volume purchaser of eggs and therefore do not have enough clout to deeply influence industry practices. McDonald's does not have a transition goal and is waiting for conclusive evidence that cage-free systems are more humane than other environments.

Both chains have also evaluated controlled atmosphere stunning (CAS) of poultry. In 2007, McDonald's Global Poultry Board completed an assessment of the various stunning methods used by McDonald's suppliers. The study examined the trade-offs between animal welfare, safety, quality, cost and the environment. Based on its analysis, the Poultry Board recommended that McDonald's continue to support its suppliers' use of both CAS and electrical stunning, while advocating for continuous improvement in animal welfare for both systems. Wendy's is taking a similar approach.

Introduction

In this chapter, the significant domesticated animal protein supply chains will be described with a focus on the primary products from cows (beef and dairy), pigs (pork) and chickens (eggs and poultry). Because this chapter focuses on the significant domesticated animal protein chains, lamb and seafood products will not be discussed. The chapter concludes with a discussion of food safety and sustainability issues related to animal protein production practices.

Industry Overview

The animal protein sector is the fastest growing food category in the world due to the combined effects of population growth, rising incomes and urbanization. As incomes increase, consumption of meat, eggs and milk typically increases, often at the expense of traditional staple foods. Additionally, while rural communities tend to have simple diets, urbanizing communities tend to demand a diet rich in animal proteins and fats. As a result, the developing world has more than doubled its per capita meat consumption in the last 30 years and is forecast to aggressively grow the category over the next 20 years relative to the industrialized world, where flat to 10% growth is expected. In total, the World Health Organization (WHO) predicts that annual meat production will increase by more than 50% to 376 million tons by 2030.

Consuming more high-value protein will improve the nutritional status of the vast majority of people in the world. Because of its nutritional benefits, animal protein—meat in particular—has long been considered a high-status food in most cultures. However, excessive consumption of animal products can pose health risks. Key concerns include an increased risk of cancer and higher rates of cardiovascular disease, such as hypertension. Excessive consumption of animal protein occurs mainly in developed countries and high socioeconomic sectors.

The United States and other industrialized countries have the highest meat and dairy consumption rates but their patterns of consumption have shifted over time. As shown in Figure 3.1, beef has always been popular in the United States, with demand peaking in the late 1970s. However, beef has gradually lost ground due to health concerns and pricing. Chicken has gradually replaced beef as the meat of choice while pork has made gradual inroads and lamb has stagnated. These trends are expected to continue for the next 20 years with chicken continuing to make the most gains, followed by pork and then beef. Additionally, the US export market is expected to continue to grow to meet increasing demand in developing countries, as illustrated in Figure 3.2.

Meat production has the lowest energy conversion ratio (inputs to outputs, i.e., feed to meat) of all agricultural growing practices, thus requiring significantly

Pounds

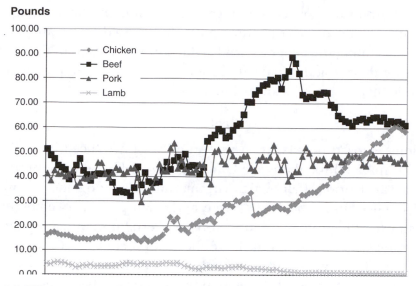

Figure 3.1 **US per capita consumption of meats, 1909–2005** (Source: USDA ERS).

more land and water than plant-based products. For example, on an annual basis one hectare of land can supply enough beef to feed one person, or enough potatoes to feed 22 people. As increasing worldwide demand for animal protein necessitates more large-scale, industrial production facilities, demands on natural resources will therefore intensify.

It is also anticipated that more animal production facilities will end up located close to urban areas due to urban sprawl, thereby increasing public health risks. Thus, health, trade, agricultural and environmental policies will need to address

Billion pounds

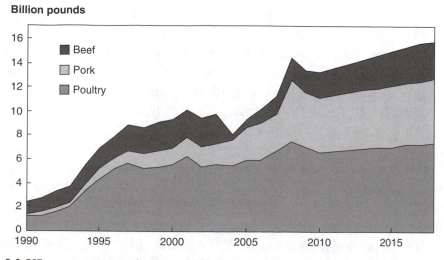

Figure 3.2 **US meat export projections, 1990–2019**

a confluence of issues concerning meat production in the coming years. The current locations of meat production in the United States are shown in Figure 3.3, illustrating the geographically concentrated nature of the industry. Table 3.1 summarizes additional attributes of the animal supply chains discussed in this chapter, and key animal metrics.

Beef

Beef has long enjoyed popularity in the Americas. Introduced by Columbus, cattle quickly spread throughout the United States and became highly concentrated in Texas, Florida, California, Virginia and New England. As western rangeland opened up in the 1890s, large and small producers emerged and shifted most US cattle production to regional western hubs, with a supply chain centered on railroad development. Here the main focus was four to five-year-old steers, raised on rangeland and shipped from local loading stations to railroad stockyard hubs typically located in the Midwest. The harvest season for cattle was June to November.

Stockyards served as accumulation points for sorting and distribution to packers. At this time, stockyards did not focus on feeding cattle, the exception being Midwestern farmers who raised corn and pigs and who often fed surplus corn to their cattle. Packers were also concentrated at the rail centers, where different types of animals were slaughtered and packed for sale to small, local butcher shops or turned into mixed loads (beef quarters, boxes of ham and bacon, lamb carcasses), which were then shipped by refrigerated rail to eastern markets.

Today, the cattle and beef supply chain has six major components, depicted in Figure 3.4. Cow/calf operators (ranchers) raise cows and their young calves. Born after a 283-day gestation period, the calves receive mother's milk and are weaned at six to ten months; the weaned calves then graze on pasture and rangeland. Some ranchers sell these weaned calves (400–600 pounds each) to stocker operators whose purpose is to add more weight to the calves by grazing or concentrated feeding in feedlots. For the commodity beef market, full-grown calves (600–800 pounds) are sold to feedlots in the Midwest (Iowa and Illinois) or the high plains (Texas to Nebraska). Typically, cattle producers sell their livestock through local or remote auctions conducted by video or over the Internet. Live cattle prices are negotiated based on sex, age, weight, genetics, health, location, raising practices (certified humane, organic, natural, etc.) and estimated cost to finish. Truckload quantities of stock with similar traits are purchased by feedlot operators for delivery one to eight weeks in the future. At the feedlot, they are then finished on high grain rations for 120 to 140 days and slaughtered by packers at 1,200 to 1,400 pounds. Slaughter, distribution and processing activities conclude the supply chain.

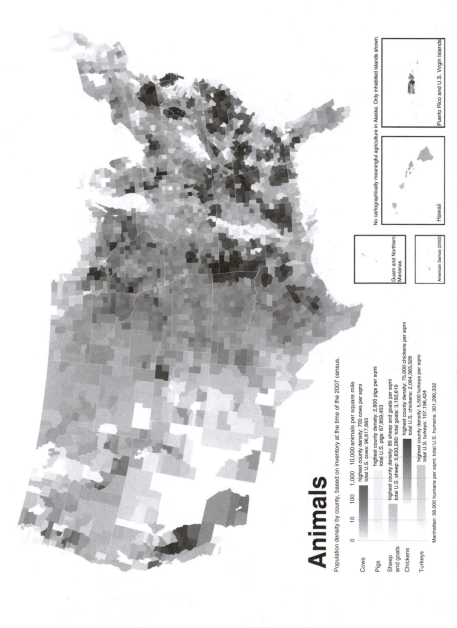

Animals

Population density by county, based on inventory at the time of the 2007 census.

| 0 | 10 | 100 | 1,000 | 10,000 animals per square mile |

Cows
highest county density: 700 cows per sqmi
total U.S. cows: 96,617,683

Pigs
highest county density: 2,800 pigs per sqmi
total U.S. pigs: 67,859,453

Sheep
and goats
highest county density: 85 sheep and goats per sqmi
total U.S. sheep: 5,833,280; total goats: 3,150,619

Chickens
highest county density: 75,000 chickens per sqmi
total U.S. chickens: 2,064,363,328

Turkeys
highest county density: 5,500 turkeys per sqmi
total U.S. turkeys: 107,196,424

Manhattan: 58,000 humans per sqmi; total U.S. humans: 301,290,332

Guam and Northern
Marianas

American Samoa (2003)

No cartographically meaningful agriculture in Alaska. Only inhabited islands shown.

Hawaii

Puerto Rico and U.S. Virgin Islands

Figure 3.3 **Locations of Meat Production in the USA, 2007** (Source: Map courtesy of Bill Rankin, 2009). Note: Animal population density by county, based on inventory at the time of the 2007 census.

Table 3.1 Animal Metrics/Supply Chain Attributes

	Beef	Dairy	Pork	Broiler Chickens	Layer Chickens
Main Regions of Production	Midwest and High Plains	New England, Midwest, California	North Carolina and Midwest	South, Midwest and Mid-Atlantic	South, Mid-Atlantic and Texas
Production Time	18–22 months	6–7 gallons daily	22–26 weeks	> 10 weeks	One egg daily
Cost per Serving	High	Low	Medium	Low	Low
Feeding to Maturity Concentration	Fragmented	Fragmented	Concentrated	Concentrated	Concentrated
Litter Size	One	One	6–13	One	One
Lifecycle of Animal	18–22 months	Several years	22–26 weeks	> 10 weeks	About two years
Gestation Period	Nine months	Nine months	114 days	24–26 hours	24–26 hours
Number of Animals Per Business Unit	> 500	120	5,000+	15,000+	500,000+
Average Age Prior to Feedlot	6–18 months	n/a	2 months	One day	n/a
Average Weight Prior to Feedlot	600–800 lbs.	n/a	40–100 lbs.	3–4 oz.	n/a
Average Time in Feedlot (days)	90–180	n/a	112–140	42–49	n/a
Average Weight at Slaughter (lbs.)	1,200–1,400	> 1,200*	240–270	2.5–8	> 3*

* Note that because these animals are bred to have high levels of milk and egg production, they weigh less when culled and are sold at a discount compared to their meat production counterparts.

Sources: USDA and National Chicken Council.

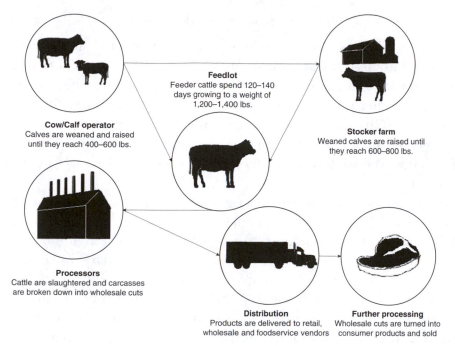

Figure 3.4 **US beef supply chain**

Finishing

Finishing is an important step in the beef supply chain. The primary purpose of finishing is to develop certain flavor, tenderness and marbling qualities within the final meat product, and to bulk up the animal. Thus, the dietary programs in feedlots typically have two goals: to achieve meat consistency across herds that were raised in varying climates and on varying diets, and to maximize weight gain. Diets vary, but may include forage (harvested or grazed herbaceous plants, such as hay and alfalfa) and/or grains such as corn, wheat and barley. Though not the industry standard, cattle may also be finished in open pastures or in large enclosed areas—sometimes called bunkers—that feature pens of varying sizes and provide more space per cow than the typical feedlot.

The forage quality of a given range or pasture varies according to soil, terrain, rainfall and climatic conditions, which in turn affects the carrying capacity of the land. Rancher costs rise with the need to supplement their own available forage with purchased grazing rights on land owned by others, and/or feed supplements. Because feed is their largest direct cost, operators are therefore concerned with feed efficiency—or the rate that feed translates into gained weight. Therefore, many have sought to optimize production by building increasingly large operations. Large-scale feedlots, with a capacity of 100,000 to 200,000 head, are known as concentrated animal feeding operations (CAFO). These operations attempt to leverage economies of scale by concentrating animals into small spaces, thereby reducing feed per unit and labor costs.

Concentration in the Supply Chain

The current US beef supply chain is highly fragmented at its outset and highly concentrated at the end. Approximately 750,000 ranchers command $500 billion in annual revenue, but only 5,000 ranchers own more than 500 head. In other words, the top fifty operators in the United States control less than 2% of the market. Feeders tend to be much more concentrated; the largest feedlots market about 80% to 90% of the feedlot finished cattle in the United States, whereas 95% of US feedlots have a one-time capacity of less than 1,000 head.

The meat processing industry—slaughterers, primary and secondary processors and distributors—is also very concentrated, particularly at the slaughterer level. Earnings in this segment are approximately $85 billion annually and the 50 largest slaughterers control 90% of the market. Secondary processing is less concentrated, with the top 50 companies managing 60% of the market. This spike in concentration in the supply chain can create issues for independent operators who wish to remain outside of the commodity system but require access to USDA-certified slaughterhouses and processing facilities to sell their beef. Without the volume required to access certified facilities, nontraditional operators typically have limited or no access to the entire retail market. Thus, the current supply chain structure of the beef industry compels commodity market participation.

Top firms in the beef industry include Tyson Foods, the largest slaughterer and beef products manufacturer; Cargill Meat Solutions, a diversified meat processor and distributor; and JBS-United States, a Brazilian corporation that owns two major processors—Swift & Company and Smithfield Beef Group—and the largest global feedlot operation.

Dairy

In the early 1600s, European immigrants brought dairy cattle with them to North America to supply their families with both dairy and meat products. Typically, families produced these products for their own or local use. As populations urbanized, dairies began to mass produce their product. Technologies such as commercial milk bottles, milking and bottling machines, health testing, pasteurization and refrigeration contributed to quality and safety assurance and thus the commercial viability of milk.

In addition to improving dairy product safety through research, testing and enforcement, the USDA launched numerous educational campaigns in the 1920s to increase milk consumption. Around this time, dairy farmers also began to breed cattle specifically for their dairy performance, a practice that continues today. Milk production is now the number one criterion for breed and individual cow performance; under-performing cattle are sent to slaughter for the lower quality meat or ground beef markets.

Historically, the US dairy industry was dominated by small family farms in the Northeast and South. Today, farms are growing in size and moving to the western United States. Between 1970 and 2006, the number of farms with dairy cows fell from 648,000 to 75,000; the total US combined herd also dropped in size, from 12 million to 9.1 million. Despite these drops, the average herd size has climbed from 19 to 120 cows per farm and overall milk production per cow has more than doubled, from 9,751 to 19,951 pounds per year.

The rise in average herd size is due to an overarching concentration in the market. Today, two basic dairy size classes exist: small family farms, which have fewer than 100 cows, and large dairy operations, which have more than 1,000 cows. Seventy-five percent of dairy operations today are small family farms; however, these operations contribute only 20% of annual US dairy production. Large dairy operators make up less than 2% of farms but contribute 38% of annual US dairy production. Small dairies tend to be located in the traditional dairy states of the Northeast and the Upper Midwest. Large dairies are predominately located in California and Colorado. Figure 3.5 illustrates the location of the milk cow inventory in the United States in 2007.

Small and large dairies have different supply chain characteristics. Large operators may have their heifers (un-bred females) raised off-site by a specialized farm while small operators typically raise their own heifers. Large operations purchase feed and grain while small farmers grow most of their own. Large operations usually confine their cows in barns or feedlots while small farmers often pasture their cows. Larger operators must also rely on hired labor while small operators usually depend on family work contributions or unpaid labor.

Dairy Supply Chain

The typical dairy supply chain is shown in Figure 3.6. Dairy cows must give birth to a calf about once a year in order to produce milk. Heifers and cows are carefully bred through artificial insemination to produce a calf with either optimal dairy or beef qualities. A cow's gestational period is nine months. Usually within 24 hours of being born, calves are taken from their mothers to be nursed in a sterile environment. These calves are weaned and then begin their lives in their respective supply chains.

During its lactation period a dairy cow produces about six to seven gallons of milk per day. A dairy cow's lactation period typically lasts about 300 days. Milk production peaks four to ten weeks after calving and then declines. Following lactation, a cow will have a 60-day dry period, after which she may be bred again to start the cycle over. Most dairy cows are culled, meaning they are taken out of the dairy supply chain if they experience reproduction problems or when

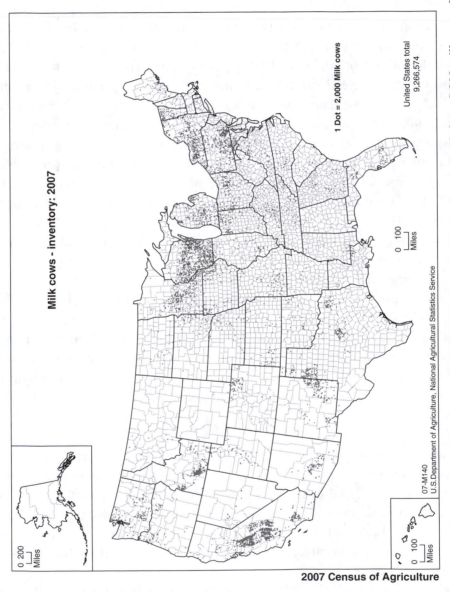

Figure 3.5 **Milk cow inventory in the USA, 2007** (Source: USDA: NASS, Census of Agriculture) *Key:* 1 dot = 2,000 milk cows. *Note:* United States total 9,266,574.

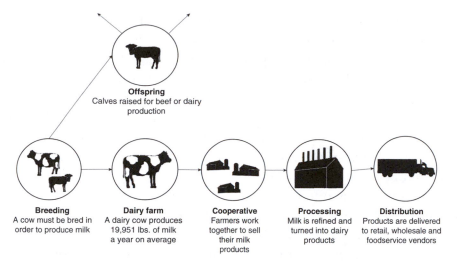

Offspring
Calves raised for beef or dairy
production

Breeding	**Dairy farm**	**Cooperative**	**Processing**	**Distribution**
A cow must be bred in order to produce milk	A dairy cow produces 19,951 lbs. of milk a year on average	Farmers work together to sell their milk products	Milk is refined and turned into dairy products	Products are delivered to retail, wholesale and foodservice vendors

Figure 3.6 **US dairy supply chain**

their milk production has permanently slowed. Cows may be culled for other reasons as well, such as injury. When dairy cows are culled they are sold to beef processors to be made into beef products.

Four distinct operational models exist with regard to dairy product manufacturing: farmstead dairies, dedicated patrons (or cooperatives), third-party purchasing and open market sourcing. Each model has a unique ownership structure, and input sourcing, processing, marketing and distribution practices also vary.

Farmstead dairies manufacture dairy products right on the farm, and in most cases, use milk exclusively from their own cows, although they may buy milk from neighbors. Farmstead dairies are decreasing in number; exemplars include Butterworks Farm in Vermont and Noris Dairy in Oregon, both of which focus on animal husbandry, sustainability and making high quality products. Both of these dairies enjoy passionate followings in their respective regions.

Dedicated patrons, or cooperatives, are models where "captive patrons" produce milk and deliver the raw fluid milk to a dairy plant on an exclusive basis. The dairy plants do further processing, such as pasteurization, homogenization, separation (into cream, non-fat, and percent fat blends) and other product creation (e.g., cheese, yogurt, ice cream). Under the cooperative structure, a group of farmers owns the brand and may own the processing facility as well, or will lease space in a processing facility if one is not owned.

The biggest US cooperative is the Dairy Farmers of America (DFA), which has roughly 17,000 members and 1.8 million cows, and produces and markets 62 billion pounds of milk per year. DFA also produces cheese, butter, dried whey, milk powder and many other dairy products for industrial, wholesale and retail consumers worldwide through its network of 30 manufacturing sites.

As the oldest and best-known cooperative brand, the Land O'Lakes cooperative consists of 4,600 farmer/members and approximately 980 smaller community cooperatives. These operations produce 3,000 dairy-based products at ten production sites and have over $12 billion in sales. On the organic side, Organic Valley Dairy has more than 1,400 organic farmers/owners in 33 states and three Canadian provinces, with more than $500 million in sales. The group is governed by two principles: to stay independent, keeping small and mid-size farmers in business; and to form and maintain long-term partnerships with quality manufacturers (co-packers).

With the third-party purchasing model, companies purchase 100% of their milk from third parties, such as cooperatives or brokers. In the open market sourcing model, milk is also purchased from third parties but no source information is available about the product. Both of these models are commonly used for private-label or store brand milk products, such as those produced by Safeway, Costco and others.

Finally, some very large companies blend these models, owning their own dairies but also purchasing milk produced by others. For example, Dean Foods buys from the DFA cooperative, but has also become the "king of milk" through its acquisition of dairies such as Horizon Organic, Berkeley Farms and Garelick Farms. Dean Foods' fifty dairy brands include Borden, Pet, Country Fresh and Meadow Gold; the brands mentioned above; and dairy substitutes, such as soy milk. Dean Foods' top customers include Wal-Mart, SuperValu, Sam's Club, Meijer and Ahold, helping the company generate $11 billion in sales annually.

Pork

As one of the oldest forms of domesticated livestock, pigs also came to the New World with Columbus. They quickly multiplied in the southeastern United States due to their omnivorous diet and nimble foraging ability, requiring little supportive feeding or care. Prior to the twentieth century, pigs were born in the spring and left to forage in the wild, then rounded up and slaughtered in the autumn. Pork was consumed as fresh meat, and preserved for use as winter food in the form of cured hams, bacon and sausage. Today, pork is one of the most popular meats, accounting for 38% of meat production worldwide.

In the United States, pork lost its dominance to beef in the early twentieth century due to strong beef industry organization and promotion, and negative associations of pork with diseases such as trichinosis. Pork also had marketability issues due to social status concerns and religious prohibition; pigs were associated with garbage-eating, poverty and pioneer survival food. Pig-keeping practices became increasingly efficient and productive starting in the 1930s, with the introduction of artificial insemination. The hog industry today is very industrialized, divided into four distinct specializations: sowing and farrowing,

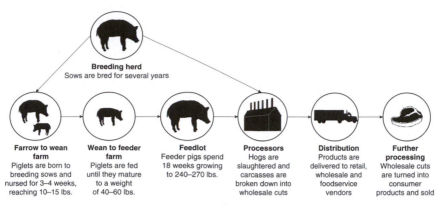

Breeding herd
Sows are bred for several years

Farrow to wean farm	**Wean to feeder farm**	**Feedlot**	**Processors**	**Distribution**	**Further processing**
Piglets are born to breeding sows and nursed for 3–4 weeks, reaching 10–15 lbs.	Piglets are fed until they mature to a weight of 40–60 lbs.	Feeder pigs spend 18 weeks growing to 240–270 lbs.	Hogs are slaughtered and carcasses are broken down into wholesale cuts	Products are delivered to retail, wholesale and foodservice vendors	Wholesale cuts are turned into consumer products and sold

Figure 3.7 **US pork supply chain**

nursing, finishing and packing/processing, as shown in Figure 3.7. With a relatively short gestational period of 114 days and litter sizes ranging from 6 to 13 piglets, pigs are highly productive animals with the ability to produce two litters per year. Piglets stay in farrowing facilities until after weaning (three to four weeks or 10 to 15 pounds) and are then either sold or moved to a nursery. The nursery maintains the young pigs until they reach 40 to 60 pounds. After eight weeks in the nursery, the feeder pigs go on to a finishing facility where they are fed until reaching 270 pounds (or 18 weeks), at which point they are sold to producer-owned marketing networks via livestock exchanges, or to large packers. Regardless of the ownership, the pigs are slaughtered and processed into wholesale cuts or boxed pork. Boxed pork is then purchased by purveyors who either butcher the animal into final cuts, such as chops and ribs, or carry out value-added activities such as smoking and curing for ham, bacon or sausage.

As feed makes up two-thirds of pork production costs, hog production has traditionally been centered in the Midwest, close to the feedstock. However, over the past 15 years, corporate hog farming has moved to eastern North Carolina, Oklahoma and Utah, driven by industry scale and specialization along with technological advances. These specific locations are popular due to their low population densities and lack of regulations concerning pig waste pollution.

Specialization and Concentration

While the total US hog inventory remains close to 60 million head, as seen in Figure 3.8, the number of farms dropped from 240,000 in 1992 to 70,000 in 2004. Thus, fewer, larger farms today are achieving the same output as the total once produced by small farms. Today, operations with more than 5,000 head account for 88% of the pig crop. Additionally, the industry is highly specialized, with only 18% of hogs coming from farrow-to-finish operations and 77% from

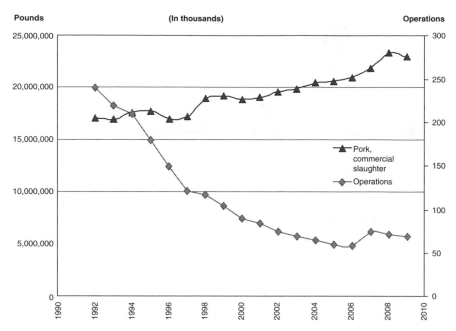

Figure 3.8 **Number of US hog operations and inventory, 1990–2010** (Source: USDA NASS).

specialized hog finishers. Consolidation in the industry and increasing vertical integration are threatening competitive pricing for hogs; long-term trends show live animal prices decreasing, impacting farmers.

The trend toward specialization is growing because efficiencies (faster weight gain per input of feed) seem to occur with age group segmentation for feeding; farms that cover hogs' whole life cycle, from farrow to finish, are not seeing the same levels of efficiency. Changes of scale and the trend toward specialization have been facilitated by the use of production contracts, which are contracts governing the relationship between hog growers and owners (also known as integrators or contractors). These contracts specify the inputs to be provided by each party and their respective compensation. Contracts also allow growers to specialize in specific parts of the animal's life: farrow to wean, wean to feeder pig, feeder pig to finish, etc. Ownership of the pig by the integrator usually occurs when it is purchased from farrow to feeder farms.

The top pork producers in the United States obtain hogs predominantly through contracts with growers, while also operating company-owned hog farms. Smithfield Farms is the largest pork producer in the United States and the world. Smithfield uses 480 company-owned farms and has contracts with an additional 2,155 growers to provide hogs for production in the United States.

Sixty-five percent of Tyson Foods' hogs are raised on a contract basis as well. Tyson buys pork from its contracted growers several days before it is needed for processing. Tyson negotiates directly with growers using several different methods, including spot market, formula and fixed price payments. Payment for hogs can be made on either a live weight basis or on a yield and grade basis.

Because so many hogs are supplied for production on a contract basis, contracts typically outline producers' standards of care and quality. Cargill, Hormel and Smithfield all have policies that require growers and their employees to be certified by the National Pork Board's Pork Quality Assurance Plus program. Additionally, Tyson specifies in its contracts that no herbicide can be used within 50 feet of a building housing its hogs.

Eggs and Poultry

Until the 1940s, most families in the United States kept a few chickens to supply their daily eggs and provide meat for the occasional chicken dinner. As urbanization occurred, small family farms, typically with fewer than 400 hens, began to meet these needs instead. By the 1960s, the industry began to segment—egg production versus meat or broiler production—and supply chain specializations began to develop: breeding companies; hatcheries (specialized incubator facilities designed to hatch fertile eggs); broiler, pullet or grow-out houses (facilities where chickens are fed to appropriate egg-laying or slaughter weights); facilities for egg collection, grading, and packing; and facilities for slaughtering and processing broilers.

Today, eggs and poultry are the most intensively produced and industrialized of all protein supply chains, with highly controlled environments, large scale flocks and few production facilities. This concentration and scale primarily resulted from consumer demand for cheap and uniform products; per capita consumption of eggs in the United States alone is estimated at about 246 eggs annually. Recent consumer concerns about animal welfare, chicken diseases and environmental impacts have also created a market for more animal- and environmentally friendly products such as cage free, free range, sustainable and organic eggs and chicken meat.

Egg Supply Chain

Figure 3.9 illustrates the US egg supply chain, which begins with a primary breeding company. Here, breeder hens lay eggs intended for hatching and use as layer hens. These eggs are sent to hatcheries. After hatching, the chicks go to pullet houses for 21 weeks to gain weight and are then moved to layer houses for their useable life—usually two seasons. The typical breeds in the egg supply chain are White Leghorns, which produce white eggs, and the Rhode Island Red, New Hampshire and Plymouth Rock breeds, which produce brown eggs.

Within the layer house, chickens in cages are set over conveyor belts that gently gather and transport the eggs to collection bins, i.e., flats with several dozen eggs apiece. The eggs are then washed, graded and packed by either the

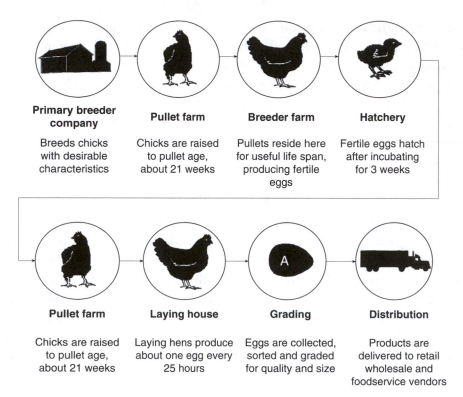

Primary breeder company	Pullet farm	Breeder farm	Hatchery
Breeds chicks with desirable characteristics	Chicks are raised to pullet age, about 21 weeks	Pullets reside here for useful life span, producing fertile eggs	Fertile eggs hatch after incubating for 3 weeks

Pullet farm	Laying house	Grading	Distribution
Chicks are raised to pullet age, about 21 weeks	Laying hens produce about one egg every 25 hours	Eggs are collected, sorted and graded for quality and size	Products are delivered to retail wholesale and foodservice vendors

Figure 3.9 **US egg supply chain**

layer facility or by other egg marketing companies. Typically, eggs are distributed to retailers the same day they are laid. After a layer finishes its productive life, it is sold for meat, but at a much-reduced price than that received for broiler chicken meat.

The technology used to gather, process and distribute eggs has allowed layer houses to develop immense capacity. Layer houses today often hold between 500,000 and 1 million hens. Because it takes 24 to 26 hours for a hen to produce an egg, a typical hen produces approximately 250 to 300 eggs per year. Thus, a layer house with 800,000 hens produces about 550,000 eggs each day. The US egg industry has over 280 million laying hens.

Market share in the egg industry is dominated by three main producers: Cal-Maine Foods in Jackson, Mississippi; Rose Acre Farms in Seymour, Indiana; and Rembrandt Enterprises in Rembrandt, Iowa. Cal-Maine Foods and Rose Acre Farms are members of the United Egg Producers (UEP) cooperative, which was established in 1968. UEP evaluates environmental, nutrition and animal welfare issues and engages in industry coalition building and government relations activities.

Despite UEP's efforts to maintain quality standards for egg production in the United States, the Humane Society of the United States found in 2010 significant animal abuse within Rose Acre Farms and Rembrandt Enterprises. The Humane Society's report states that hens were unable to reach food and water, were confined in cages smaller than a standard piece of paper and were sandwiched in their cages alongside dead hens, some of which were decomposing. Allegations such as these have been common in the egg industry, as caged hens are often treated as commodities rather than as animals. With major chains such as Subway and Wal-Mart switching to exclusively cage-free eggs, a shift in animal welfare could be on the horizon, with positive consequences for smaller-scale farmers. Cage-free eggs are primarily produced on smaller farms, thus more small farmers are now pursuing and obtaining national distribution.

Broiler Chain

The broiler supply chain is illustrated in Figure 3.10. Broiler chains tend to be vertically integrated, with most of the chain's functions performed by subsidiaries on behalf of a parent company (e.g., Tyson Foods). Similar to the egg chain, the broiler chain begins with a primary breeder; this company is responsible for formulating chickens that offer the characteristics a parent company is looking for in its meat. The fertile eggs from breeder hens are then sent to a hatchery. When the chicks are one day old, they move on to broiler farms. Here, a parent company typically contracts with an outside grower to raise the chicks until they are ready for slaughter. Full-sized chickens are usually slaughtered and butchered by the parent company. The meat may then be sent on for further processing into specific cuts, ready to eat meal components, and so forth. At the end of the chain, the chicken meat is distributed to wholesalers, retailers or foodservice vendors or exported abroad.

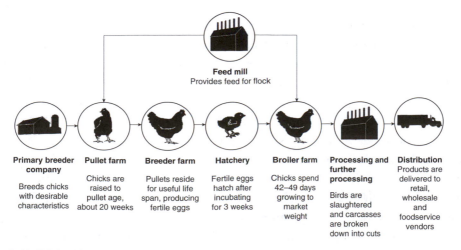

Figure 3.10 **US broiler supply chain**

Table 3.2 **Top US Broiler Producers**

	Market Share (%)	Average Weekly Production (million lbs., ready to cook weight basis)
Pilgrim's Pride	20.3	146
Tyson Foods	20.0	144
Perdue Farms	7.6	55

Source: National Chicken Council.

Within the broiler supply chain, parent companies often own the feed mills that supply the feed for their birds, and provide veterinarian services. The contracted growers provide housing, labor and litter. A contracted grower could have 300,000 or more birds. The size of these farms leaves them particularly susceptible to disease and the facilities must therefore be kept very clean. Few visitors are ever allowed into these farms due to bio-security issues, such as Avian influenza.

Today, more than 90% of all chickens raised for human consumption in the United States are produced by independent farmers working under contract with integrated chicken production and processing companies (parent companies). Table 3.2 lists the top broiler producers in the United States. Most of the remaining chickens are raised by company-owned farms.

Food Safety

As in many of the contemporary food chains, high input volumes being processed through increasingly long supply chains have increased food safety risks. Protein chains have an added risk because animal diseases can transfer between animals and people. Examples of communicable diseases include Avian Flu (H5N1) and Mad Cow Disease-BSE (*Bovine Spongiform Encephalopathy*). While not a communicable disease, *E. coli* (*Escherichia coli*) is a common bacteria that can transfer quite easily from animal products to humans.

Both Avian Flu and Mad Cow Disease-BSE have impacted domestic consumption and the international trade of animals considerably. For example, after the USDA's 2003 BSE announcement, most countries banned or restricted some or all of their imports of US beef and cattle products—including Japan, South Korea, Mexico and Canada, which together purchased almost 90% of US beef exports at the time. While the NAFTA partners resumed their beef imports the next year, Japan and Korea did not reopen their markets to the United States until 2006. Similarly, Avian Flu reduced poultry consumption significantly. For example, Italy reduced its consumption of poultry products by 70%. Millions of poultry animals died or were culled due to the disease.

On the processing and retail side, *E. coli* poses a tremendous problem for the beef industry. Healthy cattle may carry *E. coli* bacteria in their intestines and their meat can be contaminated with the germ during slaughter. Since multiple animals are grouped together for slaughter—their numbers reaching hundreds in some plants—bacteria can spread very quickly. If a human is contaminated, usually by not cooking meat at a high temperature, the germ can cause serious health problems, from nausea and vomiting to kidney failure and death. The germ can also pass from human to human. *E. coli* outbreaks related to ground beef have caused several massive, costly, lengthy recalls in recent years.

In response to consumer concerns with protein product safety, many countries have government agencies that establish and enforce safety control mechanisms, i.e., regulations. Regulations exist throughout the entire supply chain; in the United States, animal product rules are enforced by the USDA. In conjunction with regulatory controls, retailers frequently also have a code of practice to which meat suppliers must adhere. One practice is unique animal identification, which enhances traceability and accountability throughout the food supply chain.

Unique animal identification can be achieved through bar-coding or Radio Frequency Identification (RFID) tags on certain whole animals. The tags enable complete traceability from the animal's birth to its delivery as a bone-in carcass: parentage, breeding regime, feed programs, medical injection history, movement, butchering, audits, grading records, and so on. However, traceability is more challenging and difficult to implement when animal processing facilities cut or grind carcasses into small parts (e.g., ground beef) due to the immense blending that occurs when multiple animals are made into singular products. Thus, *E. coli* outbreaks with ground meat are likely to continue until a solution to this challenge has been developed.

Animal Welfare Issues

Because global demand for animal products continues to rise, animal growers and processors continue to seek out production methods that will maximize their efficiency, lower consumer price points and enable a profit. However, the industry actions required to achieve economies of scale—"factory farming," increasingly complex supply chains, etc.—have created concerns, for many, about animal welfare.

Consumers are increasingly concerned about the humane treatment of animals when choosing their meat. Retailers such as McDonald's and Whole Foods have taken the lead in addressing this issue. McDonald's hired the premier US authority on animal handling practices, Dr. Temple Grandin, to audit all of their protein supply chain partners (growers, feedlots and packing plants) and create animal handling guidelines. McDonald's effort revolutionized the industry since participants cannot sell to the company, a major meat purchaser, without going through the audit process. Today, more than 90% of the American Meat Institute's member packing plants administer these audits.

Similarly, Whole Foods invited animal welfare groups and scientists to join the grocer and their producers in identifying animal welfare issues for all of the species sold in Whole Foods stores. By spring 2008, the Global Animal Partnership (GAP) standard was created to improve the way farm animals are cared for from birth to slaughter. The standard has graduated levels of treatment and focuses on continuous improvement. The USDA's Food Safety and Inspection Service (FSIS) has approved Whole Foods' *5-Step Animal Welfare Rating System.* At the store level, the program features a labeling system to help shoppers identify the standard of animal treatment applied during production, and make choices that suit their preferences.

Case Study: Country Natural Beef at the Crossroads

Stacey Davies pulled his truck into the Roaring Springs Ranch. As the new Marketing Manager for the Country Natural Beef (CNB) cooperative, Stacey had a lot on his mind. The natural products industry had grown rapidly over the past decade, and CNB had become a major provider of naturally raised, value-added beef. However, the co-op's members were concerned about several issues: animal welfare, their carbon footprint, the economy and industry competition. The previous summer, several ranchers had suffered financially because their cows had fallen sick in a finishing feedlot and received treatment with antibiotics. Some cows died, and those that recovered had to be taken out of the natural beef program, impacting revenues. Stacey wondered what CNB could do to stay vital, with sales flat after many years of rapid growth.

Company Profile

CNB was launched in 1986, a precarious time for many family ranches. Wildly fluctuating commodity beef prices, high interest rates, mounting pressure from dieticians to eat less red meat and a perception that public lands were being over-grazed by cattle were decimating the industry financially, directly impacting the small family rancher. In response to these pressures, and with a critical need to survive, Doc and Connie Hatfield invited 14 other ranchers to their home in Brothers, Oregon.

After numerous long discussions, the idea of a marketing cooperative was born. The ranchers would deviate from the commodity beef model of production and instead produce a higher margin product—lean, natural beef—following high standards for ranching practices. The group would seek out alternative markets to sell their products; concerns about growth promotants and antibiotics in meat had been growing, and CNB discovered that some consumers were willing to pay a premium for natural meat products. Additionally, consumers were willing to pay more for beef production that practiced open land grazing, watershed management and habitat preservation. CNB recognized that its values and products aligned with consumers' new preferences. Over the next two decades, CNB grew from the original 14-family cooperative into a niche market leader, with about 120 family ranches in all the western states and Hawaii.

The CNB Business Model

CNB members were "consumer-centric" when developing their operational standards, knowing that these standards would differentiate their product. As shown in Table 3.3, ranchers owned the product from "birth to plate," or from mother cow to calf to steer, from ranch to feed yard. It was only at the retailer that ownership of the product transitioned; at this point, ownership became a partnership between the rancher and the retailer. (Note that

Table 3.3 **Traditional vs. CNB Supply Chain**

Supply Chain Member	Traditional Beef Characteristics	Traditional Ownership	CNB Beef Characteristics	CNB Ownership
Cow/Calf Operator	Cattle graze on ranch for 12 months	Rancher	Cattle graze on ranch for 12 to 18 months	Rancher
Stocker Operator	Cattle graze or feed for 12 to 20 months	Operator	N/A	Rancher
Feedlot	Cattle feed for 180 days on corn and grain (500 lb. average gain)	Feedlot	Cattle feed for 90 days on potato waste, small amounts of grain and corn (300 lb. average gain)	Rancher
Packer	Heavy cows and high fat marbling, unknown history	Packer	Lighter cows, lean meat, individual history recorded on ear tag	Rancher
Retailer	Different quality characteristics desired, depending on final retailer	Retailer	Healthy, natural beef with consistently lean characteristics	Rancher and Retailer Partnership

Source: CNB Case Study.

although the meat processing company AB Foods purchased animal carcasses from CNB, it sold the end product back to CNB, which then made its
payments to cooperative members). Figure 3.11 illustrates the key players in
CNB's supply chain. Other than ear tags and some office equipment, CNB
was a "brickless" organization, with no additional assets.

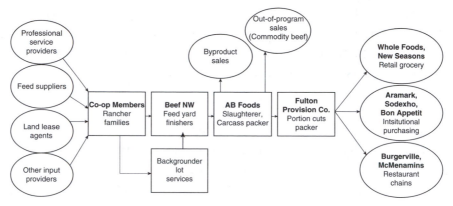

Figure 3.11 **Country Natural Beef supply chain**

Unique Practices

CNB steers were born from cows raised on member ranches, not purchased
from livestock auctions, a practice that made CNB livestock traceable to its
ranch origins. Cattle were free of antibiotics, growth hormone implants and
animal byproduct feed additives. Although eliminating hormones and antibiotics from the program was a big challenge for some ranchers early on,
because they had depended on these products for disease control, the
ranchers eventually mastered range management practices that naturally
improved the immunity of the herd. The founding ranchers adopted Holistic
Range Management, the basis of CNB's Grazewell Principles, to which each
rancher needed to subscribe. CNB also followed a 100% vegetarian diet for
cattle, even before mammalian protein was prohibited from ruminant feed
by the Food and Drug Administration in 1997.

Every CNB ranch was third-party certified for their animal, worker
and environmental practices by Food Alliance, a nonprofit organization
specializing in sustainable agriculture standards. Food Alliance assessed soil,
water and habitat conservation, pesticide reduction, labor practices and
animal welfare, and membership required the creation of a continual
improvement plan.

Third-party verification was central to the CNB brand promise of authenticity; few natural beef brands boasted the claim of outside agency audits for specific, measurable sustainability practices. Food Alliance membership was a lengthy process, taking over two years. The certification requirement discouraged some ranchers from joining, particularly those who did not welcome outside interference. However, the Food Alliance expectation raised the management standard in every stage of the CNB supply chain, from animal handling to feedlot operations.

Governance and Decision Making

Every ranching family in the cooperative was considered a member of the Board of Directors and as such exercised one vote and had veto power in decision making. In other words, decisions required consensus, meaning everyone would comment on a major issue and eventually give a "yes" vote, or an idea would not proceed. Members therefore would work tirelessly on solutions that everyone could live with.

The biannual board meetings opened in a "Full Circle," a ritual where members sat in a circle, introduced themselves and mentioned what issue concerned or pleased them the most. Agenda items were brought up at the beginning of the meeting, and then hashed out over smaller group meeting sessions. As members would argue and negotiate, those who chaired sessions would routinely remind attendees to "speak and listen with respect." Solutions from the breakout groups were proposed for a vote on the final day of the board meeting, in another round of Full Circle. Emotions often ran high in the group, which had a tradition of equanimity and transparency. Connie Hatfield also insisted, from the outset, that women take equal part in the organization, which gave the group broad perspective.

THE CNB SUPPLY CHAIN

Delivery Scheduling and Pricing

Every family ranch was a production unit and operated independently, acquiring and managing its own means of production, including land, labor, equipment and livestock. Families committed to "placing" calves at the feedlot at specific times during the year. These delivery slots were allocated based on a family's tenure in the co-op. Each year, the production team used demand forecasts to determine placement slots, which were announced at the biannual meeting, and ranchers promised to deliver based on their production schedule. Considerations in determining the slots included the time required to breed cows, wean calves, secure grazing capacity, and so forth.

The co-op used data from two dozen ranches of varying sizes to determine the costs of production each year, and used a cost plus method to determine their product's price. The entire carcass was pre-sold to committed buyers based on forecast numbers worked out with customers a year ahead. This price would not change over the course of the sales year. The fixed price eliminated the price fluctuations common to the industry and secured for the ranchers a steady and predictable cash flow. Note that although the price was fixed, CNB production office managers and customers constantly monitored meat sales data to adjust the sales price between meat cuts (e.g., ground beef versus New York steaks) in order to balance demand and supply.

CNB aimed to produce a leaner beef than premium commodity beef. Therefore, CNB did not adopt the USDA grading system, which grades most highly beef that has high amounts of marbling and fat, among other characteristics. The grades "Prime," "Choice," "Select" and "Standard" are the most commonly recognized of the eight USDA grades, with prices decreasing as the grade decreases ("Prime" being the best). Rather, CNB graded its beef against the "Bullseye" and "Target" goals that assessed lean characteristics (similar to the USDA's "Choice" and "Select" grades), and the size of the rib-eye steak cuts.

The ranchers were given three checks when paid: their basic poundage payment, which included a bonus if the "Target" meat specification was met; an additional bonus if the "Bullseye" requirements were met, as these had narrower specifications than the "Target" requirements; and an animal placement payment, which was higher in the winter months than in the summer months. The co-op members paid marketing fees, feedlot fees (feed cost per day plus veterinarian care) and insurance for the out-of-program cattle on a per-head basis.

Finally, the ranchers were required to spend two days a year doing in-store demonstrations—wearing their cowboy boots, hats and aprons—engaging shoppers with free meat samples, recipes and information. These in-store events helped CNB build a direct relationship with its customers; the ranchers also deepened relationships with meat managers during these events.

One rancher commented during a marketing tour, "marketing events represent a loss of time and money to members for whom ranching is a full time job. I drove 200 miles yesterday, spent six hours at one store, got up this morning to do it again here and I'll drive home tonight. But when it's all said and done, it's important each one of us get to know our customers, share stories, and let 'em know what goes into the product ... what their choice in selecting our beef means to ranchers and the land."

After each in-store event, the ranchers would submit a detailed report that captured changes in consumer attitudes, perceptions and preferences. This report was then published by the CNB production team in a newsletter.

External Partners

Three essential external partners comprised the rest of the CNB value chain: the feeder, the processor and the distributor.

FEEDER

When their calves were 14 to 16 months old, CNB members would send them to the Beef Northwest (BNW) feedlot in Boardman, Oregon. CNB cattle were pasture-fed longer than generic beef before going to the feed-lot, but shorter than beef sold as "grass-fed," which is purely pasture-fed. Because different grasses from different ranches created variations in the beef's flavor profile, BNW would aim to even out the beef with a standard-ized diet. CNB cattle therefore spent 90 days on a mixed ration of cooked potatoes (50%) and an alfalfa/corn mix (50%) before slaughter.

The short duration CNB cattle spent in the feedlot, as compared to com-modity cattle, was intended to reduce the amount of time the animals were subjected to the feedlot's stressful conditions. Careful record keeping, spe-cial care and separation from generic herds were important at this stage of the value chain to maintain the integrity of CNB's standards. Sick CNB cattle would be treated with vitamins and sulfa drugs and moved to antibiotics only as a last resort, and then sold as commodity beef. Prior to harvest, cattle would be watched to avoid the kind of weight gain that ameliorates tenderness and consistency attributes.

The cattle's average weight at the time of slaughter was 1,150 pounds, which was in line with the goal of producing smaller cuts of lean beef for customers. CNB aimed to have 90% of cattle meet "Target" specifications and 60% or more meet the tighter "Bullseye" specifications.

SLAUGHTER AND PROCESSING

AB Foods was CNB's processor. AB Foods would receive the cattle from BNW bearing identifying ear tags that traced the animals back to their rancher. Keeping the animals (and eventually the end product) separate from its commodity beef, AB Foods would slaughter the animals using the humane criteria set forth by CNB. Removal of non-edible parts, trimming waste and packaging the saleable meat into large sections followed.

AB Foods would then sell the beef sections and boxed meats to major pur-chasers. In addition, AB Foods would purchase for resale CNB's surplus boxed inventory and out-of-program cows, and sell them as commodity beef. It also sold CNB's animal byproducts (hides, hooves, innards, etc.) to the automotive, garment and sporting goods industries, and furnished car-cass analysis data (grade, yield, size and quality metrics) directly back to the ranchers.

DISTRIBUTION

CNB had several large retail customers who purchased a wide array of beef cuts and trimmings, sent directly to them from AB Foods. A regional fast food chain, Burgerville, became its primary restaurant customer, obtaining its meat from Fulton Provision Company, a secondary processor and spe-cialty meat distributor.

Whole Foods is the world's largest natural foods corporation, with 275 stores in the United States, Canada and the United Kingdom. Whole Foods was CNB's only national-scale retail partner and its biggest customer, accounting for roughly 70% of its total annual sales. Whole Foods' annual purchasing amounted to approximately 31,000 head, which directly sup-ported about 80 ranching families.

New Seasons Market, a privately held natural grocery chain of 11 stores in and around Portland, Oregon, bought approximately 570,000 pounds of CNB beef each year. CNB was the grocer's sole beef supplier. The product fit well with New Seasons' "Home Grown" labeling program, which identified products from northern California, Oregon and Washington. The grocery chain also tested a pilot program with CNB for "pasture finished" beef under the store's Pacific Village label. For this program, a CNB grass-fed group sup-plied around twelve head a week during the nine month grass growing season (non-winter). The pilot program found that customers were willing to pay about a $1 per pound premium over the cost of the regular natural prod-uct, but processing and transportation costs limited the store's margins.

Fulton Provision Company received boxed inventory from AB Foods. After receiving the boxed meat, Fulton would grind select parts into ground beef and distribute the product to grocery, restaurant and industrial buyers. Fulton was acquired by the foodservice giant Sysco in 2000, but retained independent operations in Portland, Oregon. Fulton supplied many high-end institutional meat buyers such as Sodexho and Bon Appétit Management Company (BAMCO), which provided foodservice to corporations and campuses, and boasted a commitment to good food and sustainability.

The regional fast food chain, Burgerville, purchased considerable amounts of CNB's ground beef. Since opening in 1961, Burgerville had concentrated on sourcing fresh, local agricultural products. Centralized direct purchasing for its 39 restaurants in Washington and Oregon was done from a long list of farmers and long-time suppliers. The chain's most popular sandwich, by far, was the hamburger, and Burgerville purchased all of its patties from CNB. Sales amounted to about 40,000 pounds of beef per week. The two companies had a symbiotic relationship: Burgerville relied on the strength of CNB's brand to sell its product, in part, and CNB relied on Burgerville to take a considerable amount of its ground beef. This in turn enabled CNB to sell high volumes of higher-end cuts to its retail customers, since all parts of the animal needed to be sold, and a cow has much more ground beef meat than it does high-end cuts. The cooperative became a major part of Burgerville's vision and the restaurant became CNB's primary restaurant customer.

COMPETITION

CNB faced several competitors. Regional grass-fed beef ranchers had started selling beef at near wholesale prices online, direct to consumers. The grass-fed beef product was marketed to environmental and health conscious consumers and chefs who preferred to avoid feedlot programs due to diet and animal handling issues. Estimates of domestic grass-fed beef production indicated that 65,000 head were sold in 2006 and 100,000 head were sold in 2007; demand was expected to reach 250,000 to 400,000 head by 2010.

Perhaps a more immediate threat, however, came from the proliferation of natural beef that began to be sold through traditional grocery stores, and the growing number of "artisanal" beef products that qualified as USDA "natural" beef. After purchasing Laura's Lean Beef in 2007 and Coleman Natural Beef in 2008, Meyer Natural Angus became a leading national producer and marketer of natural beef products. Its beef came from a 43,000-acre ranch in Montana and 200 contracted Red Angus cattle ranchers across the United States.

These ranchers produced approximately 10,000 head of cattle a month to sell as fresh and frozen product to foodservice outlets nationwide. They also sold direct-to-consumer and to grocery and restaurant chains including Whole Foods, Wegmans and Chipotle Mexican Grill. Between 2005 and 2008, the company grew from $10 million to $150 million in sales, and it announced plans to double its office space to grow

Internet sales. Meyer's corn-finished, USDA "Prime" product was sold using specific process claims, including humane certification by Farm Animal Care, and "verified origins" of the cattle to specific ranches.

Laura's Lean Beef recruited independent producers across the United States for its natural beef program: cow/calf operators, finishers and slaughterers. The company gave bonuses for increased weights and hitting lean targets, and also rewarded retained ownership. Incentives for finishers included free trucking, carcass data and ear tagging. Signed affidavits were required to ensure that no antibiotics or hormones were administered and that good animal husbandry practices were followed. Branded, portion-packed products (fresh beef, cooked entrées and frozen ground beef patties) were sold in 6,500 stores in 47 states, including Kroger, Albertsons and Lucky supermarkets.

Niman Ranch was another competitor. Niman Ranch's fresh and prepared beef, pork and lamb products were distributed through foodservice, specialty retailer and chain restaurant channels, such as Chipotle Mexican Grill and Big Bowl. Niman Ranch also sold product via the Internet, direct to consumer. The company sourced meat from about 650 contracted ranchers and processed about 400 cattle a week. Their website mentioned "third party verification" in reference to humane and sustainable practices and mentioned an affiliation with Dr. Temple Grandin, but did not cite the verifying agency or protocols.

Animal Welfare Concerns

Whole Foods commissioned a survey in 2006 that revealed that consumers were concerned with the safety and humane treatment of animals when choosing their meat, in addition to flavor. As noted in Chapter 3, Whole Foods in turn invited animal welfare groups and scientists to join them for a discussion about humane animal handling practices for all of the species sold in its stores. The Global Animal Partnership (GAP) standard was the result of this discussion. GAP laid out compassionate farm animal treatment standards. The USDA Food Safety and Inspection Service (FSIS) approved Whole Foods' *5-Step™ Animal Welfare Rating System*. At the store level, the program labeled select animal products to help shoppers better understand their choices. GAP standards, along with other animal handling standards, are summarized in Table 3.4.

At CNB's Spring 2009 board meeting, it became clear that Whole Foods was eager to have CNB onboard as its first GAP-certified supplier. Some ranchers voiced strong concerns about the practicality of applying the

Table 3.4 **Comparison of Animal Welfare Programs**

	Industry Guidelines (NCBA)	National Organic Program (USDA)	Certified Humane Program (HFAC)	American Humane Certified (AHA)	Animal Welfare Approved (AWA)	Global Animal Partnership Step 5 Plus
Antibiotics	Permitted	Prohibited	Permitted for treatment of disease only	Permitted for treatment of disease only	Permitted for treatment of disease only	Prohibited (all steps)
Growth Hormones	Permitted	Prohibited	Prohibited	Prohibited	Prohibited	Prohibited (all steps)
Access to Pasture	Not required; confinement to feedlots allowed	Required; temporary confinement allowed in some situations; feedlots prohibited	Not required; cattle may be maintained in feedlots	Not required; cattle may be maintained in feedlots	Access to pasture required throughout lifetime when weather climate permits	Cattle must live continuously on range or pasture
Identification	Hot branding and ear notching allowed; jaw brands not allowed	Not addressed	Hot branding and ear cutting prohibited; ear tagging permitted	Hot branding and ear cutting prohibited; ear tagging permitted	Hot branding and ear cutting prohibited; ear tagging permitted	Branding, wattling and ear notching prohibited; ear tagging permitted
Castration	Recommended be done before 4 months of age; no recommendation regarding anesthesia	Physical alterations must be performed to promote animal welfare, in a manner that minimizes pain and stress	Recommended be done as early age possible; anesthesia required for surgical removal after 2 months old	Recommended be done as early age possible; anesthesia required for surgical removal after 2 months old	Recommended be done before 2 months; use of anesthesia required	Prohibited

(Continued)

Table 3.4 **(Cont'd)**

	Industry Guidelines (NCBA)	National Organic Program (USDA)	Certified Humane Program (HFAC)	American Humane Certified (AHA)	Animal Welfare Approved (AWA)	Global Animal Partnership Step 5 Plus
Debudding/ Dehorning	Recommended be done before 4 months of age; no recommendation regarding anesthesia	Physical alterations must be performed to promote animal welfare, in a manner that minimizes pain and stress	Debudding in the first 4 months using hot iron; anesthesia not required	Debudding in the first 4 months using hot iron; anesthesia not required	Dehorning prohibited. Debudding only permitted on calves 2 months of age or younger	Dehorning prohibited (all steps); Debudding prohibited
Spraying of Heifers	Permitted	Not addressed	Prohibited	Prohibited	Prohibited	Prohibited (all steps)
Minimum Weaning Age	No limit; usually 7–8 months of age	Not addressed	Not addressed	Not addressed	6–9 months of age	Natural weaning is required

Source: Farm Sanctuary.

standard, and the potential impact that its adoption might have on the ability of CNB to specify its own production process. CNB considered drafting its own animal compassion standard with help from Grandin, whose work influenced GAP and other standards.

In addition, CNB's use of feedlots had become the focus of much attention. Challenges at BNW recently negatively impacted the bottom line for several ranch families. A surge of sick cows resulted in many going out-of-program, and this designation could cause tremendous financial losses for small ranches. Some ranchers also felt consumer pressure to move away from corn feed and confinement environments, thinking that CNB should instead prepare for the growing grass-fed beef market. In particular, consumers were growing concerned about animal treatment at feedlots. Two auditing agencies existed for feedlots; one reviewed standard operating procedures and the other reviewed animal handling practices. Although BNW was not "humane certified" they were "animal compassion tested."

The Next Steps for CNB

Stacey pondered the issues and choices that CNB's members were facing. He wondered if it made sense to add another feedlot just for Whole Foods' cattle, one that could be set up to meet its GAP specifications and perhaps be more centrally located. He remembered CNB's environmental program director telling him that "transportation to the feedlot for ranchers further out increases direct costs, and it's at odds with our aim to lower our carbon footprint wherever possible."

Stacey knew he needed to carefully decide on his next steps. If CNB forged ahead with an independent animal welfare standard, would it be accepted by Whole Foods and its customers? Also, commoditization of naturally raised beef was blurring the distinction between niche beef categories in the marketplace. What could CNB do to differentiate itself in various market segments? Would a move into grass-fed be feasible for CNB, given its relatively large scale? And, could such a move garner more business from Whole Foods and other potential customers in new markets?

Lastly, a group of CNB members had been working with local universities to assess the carbon footprint of feedlots. Stacey was curious to see if any progress had been made on the issue, since the in-store demonstration feedback to ranchers had indicated this topic was a major concern for consumers. He needed to determine how the co-op should respond to the increasing number of reports linking the meat supply chain to global warming.

Discussion Questions

1. What factors are increasing worldwide demand for meat, egg and dairy products, and why? Where is demand most increasing in the world? Where is demand flat?

2. Do you think increasing global consumption of meat, egg and dairy is a positive or negative trend, or both? Explain your reasoning, considering the health, trade and environmental impacts of consumption.

3. Research a recent food safety problem in the beef, dairy, pork, egg or chicken industry. Briefly describe the nature of the problem and identify where in the supply chain the issue is thought to have occurred. How did the problem impact producers, retailers and consumers?

4. Pick two of the animal proteins described in this chapter. For each, identify one major industry or supply chain change that has occurred in recent decades. Briefly describe the change and assess its impact on consumers, farmers and industry.

Additional Readings and Links

*   Dr. Temple Grandin's website provides a significant amount of information on animal behavior, humane animal handling practices and facility design, and provides links to additional articles on these topics: http://www.grandin.com/

*   Student-designed Adobe Flash presentation of the egg processing supply chain: http://library.thinkquest.org/05aug/00044/id35.htm

4

COMMODITY CROP SUPPLY CHAINS

In developing countries, small innovations can dramatically enhance the efficiency and effectiveness with which farmers use resources, and spur growth in farming-related businesses. For example, a recent innovation in pulverizer technology has spurred the growth of several hundred new businesses in the Kieni and Ol-Kalou districts of Kenya. These machines shred forage materials—such as grass and legume hays; maize, sorghum and millet leaves; rice straw; teff, wheat, barley and oat stalks; and bean stems—into pieces a few millimeters in length. The small pieces are easier to transport, store and feed to ruminant animals. They also enhance feed intake and nutrient availability for ruminants by 30% to 60% and reduce farm waste. Consequently, these machines increase the profitability of ruminant animal production for the farmers that use them. Not only has the technology contributed to farmer profitability and an increase in farm service businesses (i.e., the shredders); local producers have begun to fabricate the machines, which will make it easier and cheaper for farmers to access the innovation in the future, a win-win for all. The technology is now spreading to dairy farmer associations in the Kiboga and Masaka districts of Uganda and the Rwamagana, Gatsibo and Nyagatare districts of Rwanda.

Introduction

This chapter reviews commodity crop supply chains, focusing on the four basic commodity crops—corn, soybeans, wheat and rice—that make up the majority of the world's planted field acres and consumption. We assess the importance of these crops in the world economy, along with recent trends in supply and demand. We then examine the crops' supply chains—growing, harvesting, storage, processing and distribution—identifying issues and trends unique to each of the crops as we go. Finally, we explore policy and trade issues and assess sustainability concerns related to commodity crop growing practices and technologies.

Importance and Trends

The bulk of the world's diet—both humans' and domesticated animals'—is based on commodity crops. From 1960 to 2000, the world's population increased from three billion to six billion people and commodity crop production levels increased threefold, keeping up with demand. As a result, food prices remained relatively stable and, with abundant global food supplies, nations had little incentive to maintain food stockpiles or significantly fund research and development activities to increase crop yields. In recent years, however, this situation has changed. As Figure 4.1 illustrates, many factors are converging to create a demand that exceeds supply and, consequently, increases commodity food prices.

Demand Drivers and Shifters

Increasing global population—estimated at 75 million new people per year—changing weather conditions and decreasing food stockpiles are just some of the factors influencing demand for commodity crops. Additionally, as per capita incomes rise in developing countries such as China and India, consumption of meat, dairy and vegetable oils is increasing. This diversification into animal products is adding to the demand for commodity crops, which largely comprise animal feed.

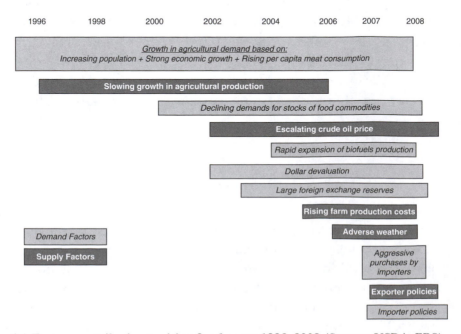

Figure 4.1 **Factors contributing to rising food costs, 1996–2008** (Source: USDA, ERS).

For example, in 2010, China made its first sizeable purchase of US corn in more than a decade: 1.2 million metric tons relative to imports of less than 100,000 tons from all countries in previous years. In the past, China was a major exporter of corn but its supplies have been strained due to a severe drought in its northern corn belt, along with dietary changes on the part of its growing middle class, which is consuming more corn-sweetened soft drinks and products from corn-fed animals like pork, milk and eggs.

Figures 4.2 and 4.3 illustrate the global production values and planted acres of the four basic commodities discussed herein. As can be seen from the figures, the planted area of a commodity crop typically shifts depending on prices.

Corn and soybeans have faced increasing demand in the world market over the past ten years as they are sources of both human and animal food. Demand has also increased for these commodities are they are used as replacements for petroleum-based products (e.g., fuel). Lately, wheat has been losing ground to corn and soybeans, quite literally, due to their higher prices; as corn and soybeans remain profitable, genetic improvements in wheat are also falling behind. However, wheat prices recently spiked due to world weather conditions and other demand drivers. Production of rice has remained relatively stable for the last twenty years. In the United States, rice is not considered a dietary staple and thus rice does not face the same demand as it does in other parts of the world, such as Asia, where rice is a dietary staple and where 90% of rice is grown.

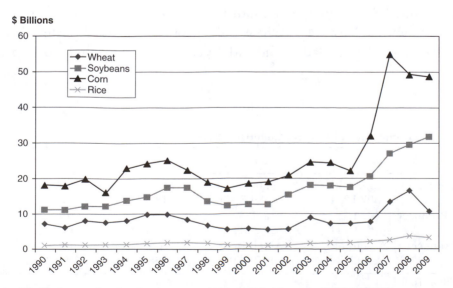

Figure 4.2 **Grain production in the USA, 1990–2009** (Source: USDA NASS).

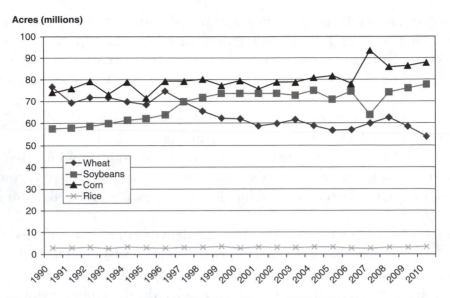

Acres (millions)

Figure 4.3 **Planted acres in the USA, 1990–2010** (Source: USDA NASS).

Global and US Production

Several countries contribute substantially to global production of commodity crops, namely China, Brazil, India, Argentina, Indonesia and the United States. The United States is the world's top producer of corn and soybeans. China is the world's leading producer of wheat and rice. The top three global producers of each commodity crop are listed in Table 4.1, along with their 2008 production volumes.

In the United States, most commodity crop production is centered in the Midwest, as shown in Figure 4.4. Wheat is also grown in the northwestern United States, as it can survive in relative cold and dry conditions. Although not depicted

Table 4.1 **Top Commodity-Producing Countries, 2008**

	Corn	*Soybeans*	*Wheat*	*Rice*
First Producer	United States 307.1 MT	United States 80.7 MT	China 112.5 MT	China 193.3 MT
Second Producer	China 166.0 MT	Brazil 59.2 MT	India 78.6 MT	India 148.3 MT
Third Producer	Argentina 22.0 MT	Argentina 46.2 MT	United States, 68.0 MT	Indonesia 60.3 MT

MT = Million Tons.
Source: Food and Agriculture Organization of the United Nations.

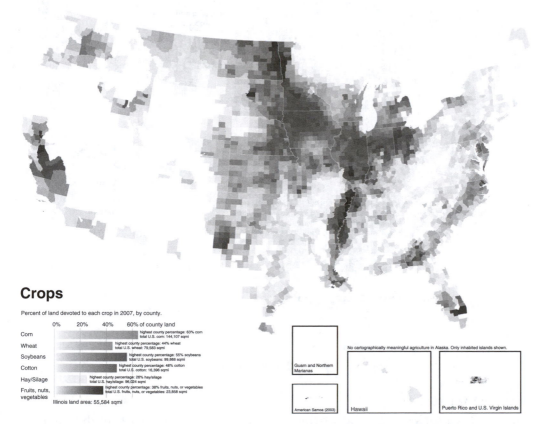

Crops

Percent of land devoted to each crop in 2007, by county.

0%   20%   40%   60% of county land

Corn — highest county percentage: 63% corn / total U.S. corn: 144,107 sqmi
Wheat — highest county percentage: 44% wheat / total U.S. wheat: 79,583 sqmi
Soybeans — highest county percentage: 55% soybeans / total U.S. soybeans: 99,868 sqmi
Cotton — highest county percentage: 48% cotton / total U.S. cotton: 16,396 sqmi
Hay/Silage — highest county percentage: 26% hay/silage / total U.S. hay/silage: 96,024 sqmi
Fruits, nuts, vegetables — highest county percentage: 38% fruits, nuts, or vegetables / total U.S. fruits, nuts, or vegetables: 23,858 sqmi

Illinois land area: 55,584 sqmi

Guam and Northern Marianas

No cartographically meaningful agriculture in Alaska. Only inhabited islands shown.

American Samoa (2003)   Hawaii   Puerto Rico and U.S. Virgin Islands

Figure 4.4 **Crop distribution in the USA** (Source: Map courtesy of Bill Rankin, 2009).
Note: Percentage of land devoted to each crop, by county, in 2007.

in the figure due to its low level of production, rice farming in the United States is concentrated in the South, in California and along the Mississippi River. The infrastructure required to process a given crop—storage, milling/extracting and transportation—is typically located near the farms that raise the crops. Animals that rely on crops for feed are also typically located close to the areas of feed production, although this is changing with the rise of concentrated animal feeding operations.

The Basic Supply Chain

All commodity crop supply chains share a basic structure: planting, harvest, storage, processing and distribution. The basic commodity crop supply chain is shown in Figure 4.5. The crop supply chains also share a unique issue related to traceability.

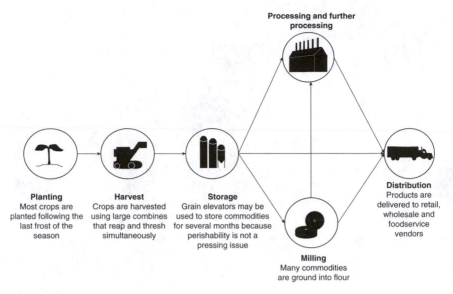

Figure 4.5 **The basic commodity crop supply chain**

Supply Chain Structure

PLANTING AND HARVESTING

Commodity crops are typically grown on large-scale farms with highly mechanized planting, tending and harvesting processes. For example, a typical Washington wheat farmer can manage 4,000 acres of wheat without supplemental labor. Corn and soybean farms can also have several hundred acres tended to by relatively few workers.

STORAGE

Commodity crops have long shelf lives when kept cool and dry. For example, if kept under 70 degrees Fahrenheit, dried grains and beans can last over ten years. Thus, once the bean or grain has reached a dried condition, minimal energy is needed to store the product, unlike most other raw foods. Grains and beans are therefore suitable for large-scale and commingled storage facilities. Notably, since grain and bean prices are typically dictated by the commodity market exchange, cooperative farm groups or individual farmers who have the ability to store their own dried product can benefit from the price fluctuations that happen throughout the year.

PROCESSING

Commodity crops are sold in their dried condition to companies that use the products directly, or are sold to different kinds of processors—such as mills,

Figure 4.6 **Grain storage on the Columbia River** (Photo: Timothy Brill, 2010)

extractors, meal grinders or packagers—depending on the crop. The refined products then end up in other processed foods and in animal products and non-food related industrial applications, such as plastics or ethanol.

DISTRIBUTION

Because perishability is not an issue, slower and hence cheaper transportation methods are commonly used to transport commodity crop products. In many cases, large storage facilities (e.g., silos) are located near barge or rail hubs for transportation to areas of demand.

Traceability

Traceability systems are recordkeeping systems that enhance food safety, helping companies quickly identify root causes and sources when a problem occurs in the supply chain. Traceability systems are also used for marketing, to keep foods with different attributes separate from one another. However, the design of the bulk commodity infrastructure challenges traceability efforts.

While the grain kernel itself is small, the scale of the typical commodity crop farm is large, and most finished grain is commingled in storage facilities along the supply chain. This complicates efforts to segregate products—for instance, organic from non-organic corn. Furthermore, it makes the use of identity preservation (IP) systems, which are much stricter than segregation systems and require documentation to guarantee that certain traits are maintained throughout the chain, very costly. As such, the cost of separating or using IP systems can often outweigh the benefits.

This issue has become particularly salient for international trade as the European Union has proposed regulations for mandatory traceability and labeling of genetically modified foods and feeds. As much of the US commodity food chain includes genetically modified organisms (GMOs), the ability to segregate non-GMO crops is an increasing concern.

Corn

Corn is the most important commodity crop in the United States. Approximately 400,000 US farms produce corn on more than 86 million acres, which accounts for more than one-quarter of the harvested crop acres in the country. The United States is also the largest corn producer in the world; national production accounts for more than 40% of the world's supply. The United States is, finally, the world's leading corn exporter, shipping out about 20% of its production, or 60% of the world's total corn exports.

The majority of the corn grown and consumed in the world is not what the average consumer enjoys as "corn on the cob," which is sweet corn. Of the vast acreage planted in corn, only 254,000 acres (less than 0.2%) are sweet corn. The remaining acres grow field or dent corn, which is suitable for animal feed, ethanol and corn products (corn syrup, corn starch, etc.). Countries that import US corn—Japan, Mexico, South Korea, Taiwan and Egypt, among others—do so primarily to feed domestic animals. Overall, about 80% of all corn grown in the United States is consumed by domestic and overseas

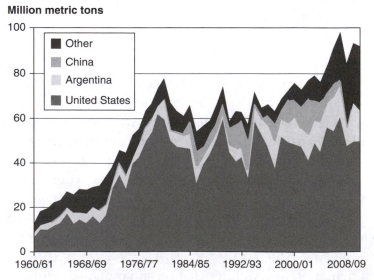

Figure 4.7 **Leading world exporters of corn, 1960–2009** (Source: USDA: FAS, Production, Supply and Distribution Database (PS&D)).
Note: Updated 2010.

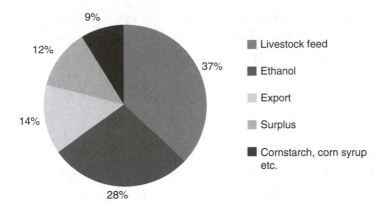

Figure 4.8 **Breakdown of uses for US corn** (Source: USDA and National Corn Growers' Association).

livestock, poultry and fish in the form of ground grain, silage and high-moisture and high-oil corn.

As part of the Poaceae family, corn—or *Zea mays*—is thought to have been domesticated in the Tehuacan Valley of Mexico. Maize production appears to have taken precedence over all other activities for early indigenous North and South American groups, and cobs over 5,000 years old have been found in caves in New Mexico. Maize was brought to Europe for cultivation by Columbus after his 1492 expedition.

Settlers in the United States planted corn throughout the Midwest, now known as the "Corn Belt." Peak planted acreage occurred in 1917 in the United States, with 111 million acres. Although fewer acres are planted today, yields have increased dramatically thanks to research and technological advances in production. For example, in 1906, farmers typically produced 31.7 bushels per acre; by the 1980s, the yields were at 109.5 bushels per acre. Corn is the most-studied plant in genetics, physiology, soil fertility and biochemistry. Today there are over 500 uses for corn in addition to its use for food: plastics, packing material, insulation, adhesives, chemicals, explosives, paint, insecticides, pharmaceuticals, organic acids, soaps and many more.

Corn Supply Chain

Corn seed (a kernel off the cob) is typically planted in the early spring, after the last frost, and takes between 70 and 90 days to mature, depending on the variety and average temperatures. When the corn kernels reach a desired moisture content, the corn is harvested by either special combine, which removes the corn but not the stalk, or the entire plant is harvested for silage or animal feed. Additionally, corn can be threshed (kernels removed from the cobs) with a threshing attachment.

For field corn, it is advantageous for farmers to let the corn dry on the stalk before harvesting since that is more economical than using other supplemental drying methods after harvesting. However, field drying depends on weather conditions and can be a risky proposition. After harvesting, the corn can be stored on the farm in silos for improved market flexibility, reduction of aflatoxin and for use as the farm's own animal feed. If not stored on the farm, the corn must be shipped to a grain storage facility for sale and distribution. Corn that hasn't been dried is highly perishable and faces the same supply chain issues as fresh produce. Therefore, fresh corn must be shipped immediately.

Field corn that goes on for further processing is typically sent to a corn refining plant. Corn refiners use shelled corn, stripped from the cob during harvesting. Refiners separate the corn into its component parts—starch, oil, protein and fiber—and convert them into higher-value products. According to the Corn Refiners Association, the United States has 27 corn refining plants located in twelve states, supplied by 41,000 suppliers. These refineries make a number of products, including sweeteners (23 billion pounds of glucose, dextrose, high fructose and crystalline corn syrup), co-products (26 billion pounds of oils, feed, meal, steep water and fiber foods), starches (6.6 billion pounds of modified and unmodified corn starch for food and industrial use) and ethanol (1.2 billion gallons of fuel and beverage alcohol) each year. The most significant players in the corn business are Cargill ($108 billion in sales) and Archer Daniels Midland (ADM) ($70 billion in sales).

Soybeans

The United States is the largest producer and exporter of soybeans in the world. In 2009, there were close to 77.5 million planted acres in the United States, which produced a record high of more than 3.25 billion bushels. The top five producing states—Iowa, Illinois, Minnesota, Indiana and Nebraska—account for over half of US production annually. Just under half of the US harvest is exported each year to China, Mexico, Japan, Taiwan and the European Union.

Soybeans are part of the Fabaceae or bean family; the particular species is the *Glycine max*. It is an annual plant used for food and oils, and to add nitrogen to the soil as part of crop rotation, typically alternating with corn. Soybeans can produce at least twice as much protein per acre as any other major vegetable or grain crop, five to ten times more protein per acre than land set aside for grazing animals to make milk and up to fifteen times more protein per acre than land set aside for meat production.

From ancient times until the early 1900s, China was the world's largest soybean producer, growing over 70% of all soybeans. In the early 1900s, the USDA classified soy as an industrial product rather than a food. Soybeans remained a minor crop in the United States until the 1930s, at which point interest increased in importing soy for various uses, including food. The United States doubled its soybean production in 1942 to meet its wartime need for more domestic food products, including proteins, fats and meals. Since then, the United States has surpassed Japan and China in soybean production.

In non-Asian countries, soybeans are used to create many kinds of products but it is typically sought for its oil, meal and hulls. Thirty million tons of soybean meal and hulls are consumed by livestock as feed each year, and soybean oil makes up almost 80% of all edible oil consumed in the United States. The oil is also used in non-consumables such as anti-corrosion agents, soy diesel fuel and waterproof cement. Soy is also used in building materials, cosmetics, clothing items, inks and soaps. Soy food products have also gained in popularity in recent years as researchers have discovered their health benefits. For example, isoflavones are said to promote healthy tissue. Soy today can be found in baby formula, chips, smoothies, ice cream, meat alternatives, coffee, cheese, energy bars, tempeh and tofu. The retail value of soy food sales in the United States has increased from $394 million in 1980 to more than $4 billion today.

Asian cultures have long used soybeans as a food source, and most soybeans purchased in Asia are for whole bean applications. Both fermented and non-fermented soy are consumed in Asia. Fermented soy foods include tempeh, soy sauce and miso; non-fermented soy foods include tofu, soymilk and soy sprouts. About 10% to 15% of all US soybeans go to Japan, Korea and Taiwan.

Soybean Supply Chain

Soybeans are planted in the field between early and late spring, depending on the latitude, geographic region and variety. Farmers may plant up to ten soybean varieties each season to enable extended growing. The most common soy plants end up with two to three beans per pod. When the soybeans are mature and dry (the beans' moisture is less than 14% in the field), the plants are harvested. In the United States, this typically occurs in October or November. Like other commodity crops, soybeans are harvested by a combine that pulls off the pods, threshes the beans out of the pods and moves the beans into a transport truck. Beans that did not reach the appropriate moisture level in the field typically require additional drying.

The beans are moved by truck to regional transport facilities, such as railroad or river terminals, which then ship the beans to the customer's grain-buying station, processing plant or harbor facility for shipment overseas. Along the supply chain, the beans are stored in silos or other storage bins until being moved to their next destination.

Once the beans are sold to processors, they are made into various products. They are either processed directly into products made from whole soybeans, such as soymilk, flours and tofu, or refined further. In the latter case, processors will grade, clean, dry and crack the hull from the soybean. The hulls go on to be made into animal feed or fiber products. The remaining portion goes on to be converted into animal food flakes or full-fat soy flour. The flakes can be further soaked in a solvent to extract soybean oil and lecithin, a product used for baked goods, dairy products and instant foods. The residual defatted soy flakes are ground into animal food or other soy flours for baked goods.

As with corn, Archer Daniels Midland (ADM) and Cargill are two of the world's largest soy processors. Ag Processing, Inc. is the largest farmer-owned processor in the world.

Wheat

From a global perspective, wheat is the most-produced and most-consumed grain, and its production takes up more arable land than any other crop. China is the world's leading wheat producer, followed by India. While wheat trails corn and soybeans in terms of US production—60 million planted acres and 2.2 billion bushels harvested—the United States produces and exports 10% and 30% of the world's wheat, respectively. Worldwide demand for wheat has increased in recent years. The USDA therefore projects a 22% increase in US wheat exports by 2016. The primary recipients of US exports are Sub-Saharan Africa, Japan, Egypt and Mexico. The US exports over 2 million metric tons of wheat each year to each country. The total impact of the wheat industry on the US economy was $20.6 billion in 2009.

Wheat adapts well to harsh environments and can be grown in several climatic zones. Wheat production is a perennial process and in many locations, it can be harvested year-round. Wheat's durability and longevity as a crop make it a foundational food in many regions; the crop represents about 20% of the world's food source overall.

Not all varieties of wheat grow well in the regions in which they are needed, thus requiring trade. For example, US imports of certain wheat varieties are increasing as a result of increased consumption of bread, pasta and biscuit products, for which appropriate wheat is not available in the United States. Other countries, such as Nigeria, Iraq, Mexico, Japan and Algeria are not well-suited for wheat production—consuming far more wheat than they could ever produce, or falling victim to severe droughts—thus requiring imports.

Like corn, wheat is a member of the Poaceae family, which includes barley, rye and other wild grasses. Wheat's many varietals are classified under the *Triticum* genus. The wheat plant appears to have originated in the Fertile Crescent of western Asia and northern Africa over 75,000 years ago. Wheat has been cultivated for over 10,000 years, and its production, historically, appeared

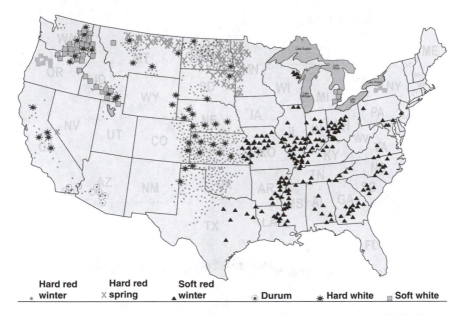

| Hard red winter | Hard red spring | Soft red winter | Durum | Hard white | Soft white |

Figure 4.9 **Wheat production by class in the US** (Source: Map courtesy of US Wheat Associates, Inc.).

to mark the beginning of city-based societies, requiring farming, processing, storing and trading skills on the part of its cultivators.

Three major advancements expanded and refined the wheat industry as we know it today. The first came in the early 1800s, with soil chemistry analysis. Farmers gained knowledge about how to replenish essential minerals in their soil after harvesting, improving crop performance. The second advancement— improvements to milling technology—also came about in the 1800s. In 1834, the first steam-driven steel roller mill was introduced, using steam engine technology to create an automated milling process. The third advancement was the overall mechanization of agriculture that occurred in the 1800s, particularly mechanical harvesting. Technological advances continue to enhance wheat production today. Figure 4.10 displays worldwide production levels over the past fifty years.

A wheat kernel or seed is comprised of three main parts: the endosperm, the bran and the germ, as shown in Figure 4.11. The endosperm makes up about 83% of the grain and is the part of the wheat that is typically used in refined bread flour. It contains very little nutritional value compared to the bran and the germ. The bran makes up about 14% of the grain and is rich in fiber, vitamins and minerals, including magnesium, riboflavin, thiamin, phosphorus, niacin, iron and zinc. The germ makes up the remainder of the kernel and contains vitamin E, magnesium, riboflavin, thiamin, phosphorus, niacin, iron, zinc, fat and protein.

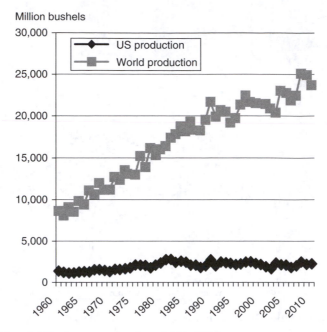

Million bushels

Figure 4.10 **World and US wheat production, 1960–2010**

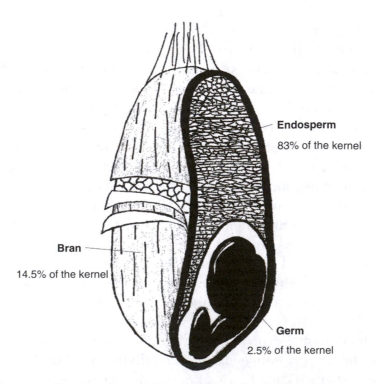

Endosperm
83% of the kernel

Bran
14.5% of the kernel

Germ
2.5% of the kernel

Figure 4.11 **Anatomy of a wheat kernel** (Source: Wheat Foods Council).

Table 4.2 **Types of Wheat**

Hard Red Winter	This class of wheat is used for common bread and all-purpose flour, making it most available for bakers. It has a medium to high protein content and comprises more than 40% of the U.S. wheat crop.
Hard Red Spring	Hard red spring wheat has the highest amount of protein content of the six classes. Its high protein characteristic makes it good wheat to use in designer breads.
Soft Red Winter	The soft red winter wheat has a low-to-medium protein content and a soft endosperm. This class is a top choice for confectionery products.
Hard White	The hard white wheat class is the newest class of wheat that is closely related to the red wheat, except for its color, flavor, and fiber content. This class of wheat is a premium for pasta products. This wheat is mainly transported in the United States, and only limited amounts are exported.
Soft White	Soft white wheat has a low protein content and is similar in characteristics to the soft red wheat. This class of white wheat is used in many first-rate products.
Durum	Durum wheat is the hardest of all wheat and has high protein content. This class of wheat is very versatile and used for a variety of pastries and flatbreads.

Source: Jim Beuerlein.

There are thousands of varieties of wheat divided into six classes, as summarized in Table 4.2. Hard wheat classes have high protein content and are suitable for bread, buns, pasta, pizza crusts and other bread products. Soft wheat classes have low protein content, and are optimal for cookies, cakes, pastries, crackers, Asian noodles and steam breads. White wheat classes are ideal for most bakers because white wheat does not need bleaching and does not have a bitter flavor like other classes of wheat. Wheat byproducts are typically used to feed livestock and poultry. Wheat straw is used for livestock bedding or hay, newsprint, paperboard and other products. Wheat grain is also used as a starch for paste, alcohol, oil and gluten. Thus, the entire plant has some useful function.

Wheat Supply Chain

The wheat production process begins on the farm with planting, tending and harvesting. The planting time for different classes of wheat varies. Spring wheat classes are generally planted in the spring and harvested in the summer. Winter wheat classes are planted in the fall, and then grow in the spring and are harvested in the summer. Wheat takes about ninety days to grow and sunny weather is optimal for wheat maturation.

Wheat must go through an extended drying period before harvesting, which is highly weather-dependent. Warmer weather results in an early harvest, while cool, damp weather can delay the harvesting process for weeks. Once wheat reaches maturity, it needs to be harvested quickly, as wheat moisture content is an important factor in quality and test weight. The highest quality of wheat can be achieved by harvesting wheat early, while it still has some moisture, and then drying it through artificial procedures. High-quality wheat is typically harvested first to ensure crops are not damaged by over-drying, weather-related issues, diseases or pests. Other advantages of early harvesting include reduced crop damage from high winds or hail and preventing drying and rewetting of mature wheat by rain. Early harvesting also makes best use of the growing season, potentially enabling a soybean crop to grow after the wheat harvest.

Harvesting involves several steps. First, a combine cuts and feeds the wheat. Next, the cut and fed wheat is threshed, a process that separates the wheat grain from the straw. The separated grains are collected in a special pan in the thresher. After threshing and separating, the wheat grains are cleansed with a fan and blower. After cleaning, the grains are transferred to a storage area, such as a silo, where they are dried for farm use or for distribution to mills or consolidation points. The wheat is then transported in bulk by truck, boat or rail. Transport costs are primarily responsible for the discrepancy in prices between surplus and deficit areas.

Flour Milling

Wheat is the most common grain ground into flour and wheat flour accounts for 75% of the grain product market. Generally, 100 pounds of wheat yields 72 pounds of white flour using standard milling procedures.

The first step in the milling process is wheat grading; the manufacturer receives the wheat and inspects it to ensure that it contains its specified protein content. After inspection, the grains are sorted and cleaned. They are then soaked in water for one to three days, spun dry and sent to the grinder and miller. At the grinding, the grains are blended with different grade grains and grains with different moisture content to get the desired flour quality. The flour is then processed with bleaching and oxidizing agents, and vitamins and minerals are added as required by law for enriched flours. After completion, the flour is packed into brown sack bags and sent to distributors. Distributors often then pack the flour into smaller bags—frequently 2, 5 or 25 pound bags—label the product and send it to retailers and wholesalers.

Each year, US mills grind around 750 million bushels of wheat. Flour demand is driven by consumers' demand on commercial bakers for specific final products, such as bread, whole grains and other commodities. The bread and cake industry consumes approximately 75% of the flour milled in the United States. The total domestic demand for the industry in 2009 was $11.1 billion. From 2007 to 2009, the milling industry has shown a strong growth in exports, with approximately 16% constant annual growth. However, millers are currently being challenged by private label brands associated with US grocery chains. Millers are trying to regain their advantage by improving technology and enhancing sustainability practices to reduce ozone emissions and meet green environmental standards.

The grain milling industry in the United States is composed of about 250 companies with combined annual revenues of about $13 billion. The milling industry is highly concentrated and mature; continued consolidation has resulted in the top 50 companies accounting for about 90% of industry revenue. Milling is a capital-intensive industry due to high grain and labor costs. Other common capital inputs include electricity, packaging materials and equipment repair. The profitability of a milling company depends on the effective management of these inputs, and on minimizing rodents, insects and molds in facilities. Large companies have the advantage of advanced milling technology and diversified product lines. Small operations compete by specializing in organic, non-GMO or heirloom grains. Major millers include ADM, Cargill, ConAgra and General Mills.

Rice

Like wheat and corn, rice—or *Oryza sativa*—is part of the Poaceae family and has a long history. Traces of the wild plant have been found in the Yangtze River Valley in China dating back 14,000 years, with domestication occurring an estimated 12,000 years ago. Rice spread rapidly throughout Southeast Asia, India and Pakistan in the second millennium and then to Africa, the Middle East and Europe. It arrived in colonial South Carolina in approximately 1694 and, as a labor-intensive crop, utilized slave labor. The rice mill was invented in 1787, which increased the crop's profitability; after the Civil War and the loss of slave labor, the rice culture in South Carolina and Georgia virtually disappeared.

Rice has also been grown in other parts of the United States since the mid-1800s, primarily in areas with natural marshes and low-lying prairies. Arkansas, Louisiana and east Texas have been centers of production since the nineteenth century. Rice is also grown in Mississippi. The other major rice producing area in the United States is California, which benefited from Chinese immigration and labor to produce rice as early as the 1850s. California is now the second-largest rice producer in the United States, after Arkansas, with much of its production concentrated near Sacramento. More than 100 varieties of rice are commercially produced in the United States today.

Although rice is a minor commodity in the United States, it is the second most-produced crop worldwide, after corn. Rice is also the most important grain produced in the world in terms of human consumption, since much of the corn crop goes to animals; rice makes up more than one-fifth of the calories

Table 4.3 **Top Rice-Producing Countries, 2008**

Rank	Country	Production Level (in million tons)
1	China	193.4
2	India	148.3
3	Indonesia	60.3
4	Bangladesh	46.9
5	Viet Nam	38.7
6	Thailand	31.7
7	Myanmar	30.5
8	Philippines	16.8
9	Brazil	12.1
10	Japan	11.0
12	United States	9.2

Source: Food and Agriculture Organization of the United Nations.

consumed by humans worldwide. Rice is commonly used in food aid programs sponsored by governments and non-governmental organizations (NGOs). The United States alone supplies around 500,000 metric tons of rice each year to humanitarian and other aid programs worldwide.

Nearly 700 million tons of rice is produced every year on 155 million hectares of land; more than 90% of this rice is grown in Asia. The dominant rice producing countries are China and India, accounting for 29% and 22% of global production in 2008, respectively. Other major rice producing countries are listed in Table 4.3. Rice farms are, on average, almost double the size of other commodity farms in the world, at 400 acres.

Thailand is the world's leading rice exporter, shipping out more than 9 million tons annually, while the Philippines is the leading rice importer, with annual imports of approximately 2.4 million tons in 2008. The United States ranks eleventh in rice production in the world, generating less than 1.5% of rice each year, but ranks fourth in annual rice exports, at 3.3 million tons. In the United States, high production levels are important due to the large capital investment required for irrigation equipment, automated equipment and land.

Rice is typically consumed in its kernel form, but the separate components of the rice grain have different uses. The outside rice hull is inedible but can be used for fuel or mulch. The outer layer of brown rice, the bran, can be removed to make white rice; food grade bran can then be used in cereals, baking mixes and vitamin concentrates. Non-food grade bran is used in livestock feeds. Rice bran oil can also be extracted and used as cooking oil. In the United States, just over half of rice used for food is used in its kernel form. Its next major use is in processed foods, such as cereals, baby food, frozen foods, mixes, snack foods, candy, energy bars and canned food products. Another major use for rice is as a starch source in beer; rice has in some cases replaced traditional malted barley because of its high sugar yield and color, flavor, stability and performance qualities. The remaining rice is used for pet food.

Rice is one of the most protected global agricultural commodities, and some markets have high subsidies, tariffs and other border protections intended to hamper the import of certain types and forms of rice. In the United States, almost all rice producers receive government payments, including flexibility contract payments and emergency assistance. In recent years, these subsidies have added as much as 50% to the price farmers receive from the market. Payments are based on each farm's history of rice production and farmers do not necessarily have to produce a crop to receive the payment.

Rice Supply Chain

The traditional method of growing rice is quite different from that for wheat and corn. For lowland rice, seeds are planted in small seedbeds, and the young seedlings are transplanted into flooded and plowed fields in the early spring. Floodwater must have adequate nutritional content and the plowed fields are dammed, channeled and formed into paddies with about five inches of water. The entire effort is labor-intensive. Thus, lowland rice is appropriate for areas with high rainfall (or ample water) and low labor costs, which fits the profile of most rice-producing Asian countries. In areas without adequate moisture, upland rice is used. This type of rice is planted directly into the soil, from which it extracts nutrients.

With either method, the rice is harvested in about 120 days. Harvesting is done manually in the developing world. Farmers cut rice plants with a knife and tie them into bundles to dry, then people or animals thresh the rice. Harvesting is done mechanically in the developed world. A combine harvests, removes and cleans the grain, which is later dried at high temperatures in storage bins or columnar dryers. After the harvest, the grain is milled to remove debris and the grain's outer hull, which exposes the bran, creating brown or paddy rice. Further milling removes the bran, resulting in white rice. This can be further polished for an even more refined product. During milling, the rice kernel often breaks, creating something called "broken rice." This product is not as valuable as unbroken rice but it can be sold to various processors, cereal makers and dog food manufacturers.

In Asia, small mills are located close to the points of harvest and hulled rice is stored until it is ready for further processing. These small finishing mills typically have a capacity of less than 100 metric tons per day. In Japan, brown rice is often milled as it is purchased due to high quality standards.

Thus, this rice can be five times the price of other rice products. In the United States, rice is transported by truck, rail or barge to large mills, which typically process around 1,000 metric tons of rice per day. Because freight is relatively inexpensive in the United States, transportation of unhulled rice is not an issue. Rice mills in the United States operate year-round.

The US rice industry has two distinct producer regions: the South and California. Producers in the South tend to work as part of a cooperative or farm independently. For instance, Arkansas, which has the most acres in rice production in the United States, is dominated by producer cooperatives. The Riceland cooperative has 9,000 farmer-members, who grow 32 million cwts of paddy rice each year generating $870 million in sales.[1] Producers Rice Mill, also based in Arkansas, sells approximately 16 million cwts of paddy rice per year. Mississippi and Missouri are home to large privately-owned companies, including AC Humco in Mississippi (7 million cwts) and Louis Dreyfus in Missouri (6 million cwts). And Louisiana is still dominated by family-owned rice mills, having not yet experienced the consolidation occurring in the rest of the South. Outside of the cooperative structure, rice farmers in the South do not commit their product at planting time, rather selling it to the highest bidder when the time is right.

California was, at one point, dominated by two large rice cooperatives, but today the cooperative structure is fragmented. Eighty percent of California rice is sold through contractual arrangements called paddy pools, in which rice is committed to one mill (typically owned by the association). The rice's price isn't known until the crop is sold. The remaining 20% of rice is sold by independent pools, without a mill association. The biggest paddy pool is the Farmer's Rice Cooperative, which sells 10 million cwts of rice annually. Pirmi (Anheuser-Busch) is the second largest producer, handling about 8 million cwts of rice. California Pacific Growers is third, with 4 .5 million cwts.

Budweiser is the biggest rice customer in the United States, as rice is one of the five ingredients in its beer. Japan is California's biggest rice export customer and it takes all of its requirements during the first six months of the crop year (about one-third of California's rice production). This forces all mills selling to Japan to produce and ship two-thirds of their rice during a six-month period. Thus, California rice millers must build up capacity just for this period. Influenced by the Japanese model, California is also seeing a resurgence of small, high quality milling facilities that handle high value, niche rice products.

---

1 Rice is typically measured in short hundredweights, or cwts, with 1 pound equaling about 0.01 cwts.

Policy Issues

In the United States and in many other countries, government incentives and trade programs have significantly impacted the structure of the commodity crop industry. Incentive programs use government subsidies to maintain prices during difficult times and promote the export of food. While the original intent of these programs was to create long-term stability for farmers, in fact, over the last 70 years, farmers and farm families in the United States have continued to exit the profession. Consequently, rural communities have declined in population and economic condition, and the farm landscape has been one of continuing consolidation of acreage into large-scale corporate farms and the creation of economy-of-scale supply chains.

Together, the 2007 Energy Bill and the 2008 Farm Bill increased the subsidy program, which enables payouts of close to $1 trillion to US farmers today. The Direct Payment Program gives money to farmers and landowners regardless of crop prices or farm profits; payouts are based on the farm's history of sales. The Counter-Cyclical Payment Program provides additional payments when crop prices fall below a certain price floor set by Congress. These payments recently declined by almost $3 billion because crop prices rose. The Market Loss Assistance Payment Program operates in a similar manner, providing a subsidy when market prices drop below perceived costs. Finally, the Federal Crop Insurance Program subsidizes insurance companies that pay out for crop losses. As the value of a crop increases, the payout increases and thus the overall US subsidy increases.

Corn, soybeans, wheat, rice and cotton account for 70% of the subsidies received by farmers in the United States. Corn is the most subsidized crop with the government giving almost $74 billion in subsidies to 1.64 million farmers between 1995 and 2009. Wheat, soybeans and rice follow: $31 billion to 1.37 million farmers; $23 billion to 1.04 million farmers; and $12.5 billion to 70,000 farmers, respectively. Sixty-two percent of farmers in the United States do not collect any subsidies at all; 10% of farmers collect 74% of all the subsidy money.

Global Impact of US Policy

The policies of the US government can strongly impact global food prices. One example is wheat. Recent policies have essentially dictated a reduction of wheat in favor of other grains. For example, funding for biofuels like ethanol has incentivized the production of corn, an essential ingredient in ethanol production. Consequently, US farmland is being diverted from wheat to corn. Since wheat is a staple crop worldwide and the United States is the world's top wheat exporter, US policy is contributing to skyrocketing food prices worldwide.

Likewise, during the global recession, the United States crafted stimulus packages that, compared to other currencies, greatly increased the speed of inflation, weakening the dollar's value. This has global implications. On the commodity market, for instance, these packages have created a long-term condition in which it will be harder to purchase US commodities domestically. Thus, more crops are being and will be shipped overseas.

Agricultural policy can also take the form of trade agreements, which both positively and negatively impact the world. The North American Free Trade Agreement (NAFTA) is one example of this. NAFTA is a large, regional cooperative trade policy between the United States, Canada and Mexico, adopted in 1994. NAFTA eliminated quotas on imported grains, particularly corn, going into Mexico. Before NAFTA, Mexico only imported corn when its farmers' production fell short of the country's needs. With US corn subsidy programs in place, encouraging high growth and enabling a sales price of about 30% below the true cost of production, US corn can now essentially be "dumped" into Mexico. Dumping is encouraged by the favorable loan rates made available to Mexican corn buyers through US export agencies, which can reach as low as 3%, compared to the unfavorable interest rates offered by Mexican lenders, which are closer to 25% to 30%.

Not surprisingly, since NAFTA came into effect, US corn exports to Mexico have soared: 9 million metric tons compared to about 1 million metric tons before NAFTA. This is good business for US corn growers. However, these policies have also contributed to greater inequalities for US and Mexican small and family farmers because large, corporate farms have been better positioned to take advantage of the loans.

Social and Environmental Issues

Today, the most critical social issues related to commodity crop production are price increases and food shortages, which particularly impact developing countries and poorer populations. The environmental impact of commodity crop production is also increasing, largely due to trends noted earlier: population growth and increasing global consumption of animal products. These issues, and others, are discussed below.

Price Increases/Food Shortages

A primary concern with any increase in commodity food prices is the impact this has on lower income, food-deficient countries. Families in such countries depend on staples such as corn, wheat, rice and vegetable oil for much of their nutrition, and a sizeable percentage of their income goes to pay for these necessities. Thus, a rise in food prices will disproportionately impact poor countries, as compared to wealthier nations. This trend tends to hold true for poor families in wealthy countries, as well.

One example of this is the recent increase in the cost of wheat. With the United States incentivizing corn production over wheat production, the demand for wheat has skyrocketed, and the increasing price has put wheat out of range for many non-US citizens who depend on it for daily nutrition. Weather problems have also created shortages. Wheat in particular is susceptible to drought and floods, and with climate change, many growers are now getting either too much or too little rain. Most recently, the global recession has raised food prices, contributing to shortages and increased food prices. Food riots have occurred in recent years in Egypt, Indonesia and Mexico due to the high cost of basic commodities.

An additional issue, impacting developed nations more so than others, is the decline in consumption of whole grains. Nutritionists and health advocates agree that consuming whole grains—grains in which the bran, germ and endosperm remain in the final product—is far superior to consuming refined grains, in which the grain has been milled to remove most of the bran and some of the germ. However, consumption patterns for whole grains are very low, particularly in the United States, and certain ethnic groups and low-income people consume many fewer whole grains than the population as a whole. These disparities can be attributed to issues with food access, traditional diets and food costs, among others.

Natural Resources and the Environment

Compared to raising animals, grain farming has relatively low greenhouse gas emissions and requires little water. However, the sheer acreage of land devoted to crop production worldwide results in high cumulative levels of emissions and water use, which significantly impact the environment.

Rice in particular has high water requirements and high methane emissions. Because rice cannot hold carbon under anaerobic conditions (i.e., under water), the microbes in the soil convert carbon to methane, which is released through the plant and the water. Climate change models are predicting higher sea levels, which may worsen the problem. A rise in the sea level of 10 to 85 centimeters would cause fields to remain flooded for longer periods of time. This would in turn cause more fermentation of the soil's organic material; i.e., more methane. A 2010 study of 227 farms in six major rice-producing countries found that rice yields in many parts of Asia are already falling, perhaps due to climate change. Yields in some locations had fallen 10% to 20%.

Soybeans are also significantly impacting the environment. In the last 60 years, the world's soybean harvest has increased from 17 million tons to 250 million tons. This is due in part to the way soybeans grow. The soybean plant uses the majority of its energy to fix nitrogen into the soil, as opposed to producing seed. Therefore, the plant is not as responsive to fertilizer as other crops, and farmers must plant more acres if they wish to increase yields.

Soybeans have particularly impacted Brazil's agricultural landscape and environment. Since 1970, almost 20% of the Amazon rainforest has been cleared to make way for agriculture in Brazil, and there are predictions that another 20% of its trees will be cut down in the next twenty years. Since the Amazon produces over half of its rainfall via the moisture it releases into the atmosphere, cutting its trees reduces rainfall, which in turn dries out the remaining trees. The desiccation has already created severe droughts, including one in 2005 that reduced river levels by 12 meters and left many communities without sufficient water. The rainforest also recycles rainfall from coastal and inner regions and ensures an adequate water supply for Brazil's agricultural trade, so a reduction in rainfall will necessitate the use of other sources of water. Finally, the rainforest stores large amounts of carbon. When deforestation occurs, large amounts of carbon are emitted into the atmosphere, further driving climate change.

Genetically Modified Organisms

The general idea behind genetic modification is that plants and animals can be imbued with qualities and characteristics not native to their species via DNA alteration. Such technology, perfected in the 1980s and 1990s, has the potential for positive impact. For example, the creation of a drought-resistant wheat could help prevent food shortages by increasing supply. However, GMO technology has many unknown implications for human health and the environment, and raises serious concerns about the balance of power in an increasingly concentrated agricultural landscape. For these reasons, GMO producers have been (and continue to be) at the center of deeply significant legal battles in the United States. Some countries have banned the cultivation and sale of GMO products outright.

Monsanto released the first GMO in 1996: Roundup Ready seeds for soybeans, cotton, canola and corn. The idea behind Roundup Ready was that farmers could use the herbicide, Roundup, during the growing season to eliminate weeds without the fear of killing their crops. The stated benefits were that crop yields would increase and farmers could use fewer pesticides overall, saving them money and allowing them to be gentler on the environment.

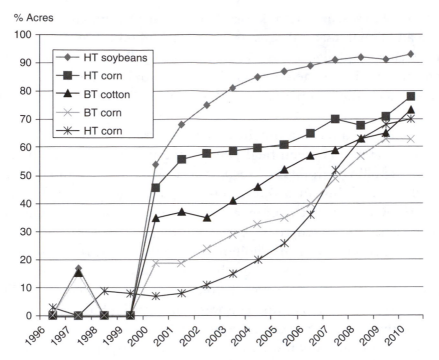

Figure 4.12 **Acres planted with GMO seed, 1996–2010** (Source: USDA ERS).

The use of GMOs spread rapidly, and since the release of Roundup Ready more companies have entered the market and new varieties of GMO seeds have been invented, with desirable traits like insect resistance. By 1999, GMO seeds were planted on 100 million acres globally. By 2007, 59% of the soybean crop in nine countries used genetically modified beans. In the United States and Argentina, 85% and 98% of soybeans, respectively, were genetically modified by 2008. Figure 4.12 shows GMO crop use in the United States, Argentina and Brazil.

Controversy over the safety of genetically modified crops began in 1998, soon after the release of Roundup Ready. The public's response to GMOs was particularly intense in the United Kingdom. People were concerned about the health effects of GMOs on humans; Mad Cow Disease had shaken people's confidence in the safety of modern farming technology. Increased allergens in food were also an issue of debate, as was the spread of antibiotic resistance.

Additionally, debate ensued about a particular GMO technology: the terminator gene. Traditionally, farmers have allowed part of their crop to go to seed each year in order to collect seeds to sow the next year. The terminator gene, when present, is a sterilizer; the genetically modified plant cannot reproduce. For farmers, the use of a plant with this characteristic would require the purchase of new seeds the next year from the seed company. This, in turn, would put additional financial pressure on small and mid-sized farmers. Public pressure elicited a pledge from Monsanto's CEO, Robert Shapiro, "not to commercialize sterile seeds technologies" in 1999. However, Monsanto acquired Delta and Pine Land Company, the patent holder for the terminator gene, in 2007.

Cross-pollination and containment are also issues of serious concern. While roads serve as barriers between fields, decreasing the chance that a non-GMO crop will cross-pollinate with GMO seed, cross-pollination can and does occur. In the United States, this effectively results in a patent violation, and Monsanto has aggressively prosecuted a number of farmers and soybean cleaners for "growing" Monsanto's patented soybeans, although this was not their intent. Fighting prosecution creates an additional, potentially insurmountable financial burden for small and mid-sized producers. In 2001, United States Supreme Court Justice Clarence Thomas wrote the majority opinion in a case that helped Monsanto enforce its seed patents. This was controversial for many, as Thomas worked for Monsanto as a lawyer in the late 1970s.

Cross-pollination and containment issues raise non-political concerns as well. With regard to containment, a study by Cynthia L. Sagers of the University of Arkansas found that genetically modified canola plants have taken root in the wild in North Dakota: 80% of the canola sampled on 3,000 miles of highway was genetically modified. Since these plants are resistant to Roundup, they are essentially hard-to-eliminate weeds. Cross-pollination of non-genetically modified plants with plants that have the terminator gene could damage plant diversity.

Currently, almost half of all genetically modified commodities are grown in the United States, where labeling is not required. Other large producers include Argentina, Brazil, India and Canada. In Europe, GMO labeling is mandatory, creating issues for US commodity crops, as noted earlier. Imports of corn from the United States to Japan failed Japanese inspections for being GMO-free in June 2005. The presence of BT10 corn in shipments to Japan illustrates the difficulty US producers face with regard to commingled storage and supply chains.

Finally, the promise of certain GMO traits, namely reducing the need for chemical pesticides and herbicides, has yet to be realized. Between 1996 and 2008, it is estimated that GMO crops were responsible for an increase of 383 million pounds of herbicide in the United States alone. The main reason is the emergence of herbicide-resistant weeds that are difficult to control. Currently the GMO industry is creating new and more powerful herbicides to try and combat its herbicide-resistant weeds. However, this solution may only breed weeds with resistance to more chemical families, thereby compounding the problem in the future. Many organizations are calling on the government to conduct periodic surveys to assess the true benefits, costs and risks associated with GMOs.

Company Profile: Shepherd's Grain

Karl Kupers and Fred Fleming both ran Washington wheat farms that had been in their family for generations, and they wanted to keep these farms in the family. However, the men were running into some problems. Current farming practices were taking a toll on the land, wheat prices were being determined by the commodity market and family farms throughout the United States were starting to disappear because they could not turn a profit.

In 1999, Kupers and Fleming heard about Food Alliance, a nonprofit organization that certifies farms, processors and distributors for their sustainability practices, and decided to start Shepherd's Grain. They wanted Shepherd's Grain to operate in a way that would allow the land to remain productive, would offer a fair price to consumers and would help save family farms. Since then, Shepherd's Grain has used their sustainability and fair pricing model to differentiate themselves from their competition. Its three primary goals are environmental health, social and economic equity and economic profitability.

Shepard's Grain promotes environmental health by taking care of the land, soil and animals. In particular, its 33 farmers employ a direct-seeding method and work to eliminate pesticides. With direct seeding, farmers no longer till or invert the soil with the plow but plant their seed directly into the ground and into the residue of the previous crop. Direct seeding's advantages include the reduction of soil erosion, which reduces runoff into local rivers and streams, and less fuel burned because of the lack of tilling. Additionally, when a farmer tills the land, carbon dioxide in the soil is released into the atmosphere. By direct seeding and not tilling the land, the carbon stays in the soil, producing better crops and healthier soil. To ensure diseases and pests do not build up in the soil, the company's farmers also rotate their crops. Other crops farmed include barley, mustard, canola, peas, corn, oats and sunflowers. Pesticide use is therefore minimal.

Because Shepherd's Grain produces a high-quality flour using practices that align with their customer's values, they are able to sell their product outside of the commodity market, and thus charge a fair price. Its prices are set by calculating the cost of production for the wheat, adding a modest profit and dividing the total by the yield. The fair prices enable reasonable profitability for the farmer; the transparent pricing builds trust with the consumer.

Shepherd's Grain flour was first used by regional artisan bakeries and restaurants in the Pacific Northwest. Recently, Shepherd's Grain joined with Stone-Buhr to produce flour for the mainstream consumer. Stone-Buhr and Shepherd's Grain's supply chain is extremely transparent. They created a website called FindtheFarmer.com which allows the customer to enter the lot code from their bag of flour and find out exactly what farm produced the wheat for that flour. It also gives biographical information about the farmer, and provides an area to ask the farmer direct questions about the flour. In addition to their bulk products and retail products— which are distributed by thirteen companies, including Food Services of America, Sysco, DPI, Merlino Foods and US Foodservice—Shepherd's Grain is now sold online through cheftools.com.

Shepherd's Grain stands out as a company that focuses on consumer values—sustainability, fair prices and a high-quality, locally produced product—and is reaping the rewards of that choice.

Discussion Questions

1. What natural resource does commodity crop production most affect and what are the repercussions?
2. What government incentives exist in the United States to encourage food production? Who benefits from the current incentive structure? Who loses out? Are these incentives appropriate, in your opinion?
3. How has the United States impacted non-US consumers with its agricultural policies and incentives? In your opinion, what, if any, are the United States' international obligations when drafting agricultural policies and incentives?
4. Many argue that sustainable and organic food production techniques do not have the capacity to feed the world. What are the assumptions likely used to support this argument? How might it be refuted?

Additional Readings and Links

- NAFTA: http://www.ers.usda.gov/publications/wrs0201/wrs0201f.pdf
- United Nations Food Policies: http://www.fao.org/corp/publications/en/
- US Agricultural Policy: http://usain.org/governmentrelations briefingdocs.html

- Fun, interactive link that shows the wheat supply chain: www.howwheat-works.com
- Clemmitt M. 2008. "Global food crisis: What's causing the rising prices?" *CQ Researcher*, v. 18, no. 24.
- Hatfield, J.L. 2008. "The Effects of Climate Change on Agriculture, Land Resources, Water Resources, and Biodiversity." *Report by the U.S. Climate Change Science Program and the Subcommittee on Global Change Research*, Chapter 2.
- Pearce, Fred. 2008. "Water Scarcity: The Real Food Crisis." *Yale Environment 360* article. http://e360.yale.edu/content/feature.msp?id=1825

5

FRUIT AND VEGETABLE SUPPLY CHAINS

Stahlbush Island Farms is a family-owned farm in Oregon's Willamette Valley, founded in 1985. The owners, Bill and Karla Chambers, adopted sustainable farming practices in the belief that "farming practices should leave the soil, air, water, plant life, animals and people healthier." The company launched its retail brand of sustainably grown frozen fruits and vegetables in 1998. Today, Stahlbush is a vertically integrated operation, cultivating, harvesting and processing its own and others' fruit and vegetable crops. In 2009, Stahlbush completed construction of a $10 million biogas plant. The anaerobic digester, which runs on food processing waste, provides almost double their current gas needs. Other sustainable practices at Stahlbush include conservation tillage to reduce erosion and increase organic soil content; drip tube irrigation systems to reduce evaporation; habitat buffer zones to prevent runoff and maintain wildlife; employee training; and employee reimbursement for general education, computer, agricultural safety and occupational safety classes. Stahlbush was the first farm certified as "sustainable" by Food Alliance, in 1997. Today, Stahlbush farms consist of nearly 5,000 acres, with almost a third of their production certified organic.

Introduction

This chapter evaluates fruit and vegetable supply chains. We begin with an industry overview, assessing demand factors and production and distribution patterns in the industry. We then present the basic produce supply chain. Finally, growing, processing and marketing variations in the chain are explored, specifically value-added processing and organic and direct sales activities. The latter activities pertain to sustainability trends in the industry.

Industry Overview

Fruits and vegetables are essential to the human diet. Adequate intake of these foods is necessary for proper growth and development in children, and can reduce the risk of heart disease, stroke, cancer, and vision loss in adults. However, average daily consumption of fruits and vegetables is far lower world-wide than the level recommended by public health organizations. While most recommendations suggest that children and adults consume a minimum of five servings of fruits and vegetables daily, more than three-quarters of adults in 52 countries consume less than this amount.

Worldwide, fruit and vegetable consumption is strongly impacted by geography, climate and price. For example, people living in urban areas may have limited access to fresh produce if they are distant from farms and gardens. Likewise, individuals living in rural areas that are poorly suited for fruit and vegetable production may have to purchase fresh produce from stores. If the fruits and vegetables available to these consumers are out of their price range, their consumption may decrease, or their reliance on canned and jarred produce may increase. For these reasons, higher income countries and people typically have greater access to a healthier, more diverse diet than do poorer countries and people.

Access to fruit and vegetables, however, does not necessarily lead to consumption. Personal taste significantly impacts diet, particularly in industrialized countries where processed foods are widely available. Data show that Americans in particular resist eating green vegetables, some of the most nutrient-dense foods, consuming them at rates that are low relative to other industrialized countries. The most popular vegetable in the United States is the potato, but it is often consumed in its fried form, contributing more fats and carbohydrates than essential micronutrients. Another popular vegetable in the United States is corn, which, as a starch, also fails to provide the nutritional benefits of leafy greens and other vitamin-rich vegetables. The trend of eating out has further decreased green vegetable consumption relative to meat and starch consumption in the industrialized world.

While global consumption of fruits and vegetables is generally inadequate, the demand for a steady, year-round supply of fresh fruits and vegetables—particularly out-of-season fruit and exotic crops—is increasing. China is strongly contributing to this trend: Asia now leads the world in fruit and vegetable consumption, as shown in Table 5.1, with its per capita vegetable supply more than doubling over a twenty-year period. Europe, Oceania and North and Central America follow Asia in per capita supply, respectively, while Africa and South America trail behind.

Table 5.1 **Supply of Vegetables Per Capita, 1979 and 2000**

Region	1979	2000
Africa	45.4	52.1
North and Central America	88.7	98.3
South America	43.2	47.8
Asia	56.6	116.2
Europe	110.9	112.5
Oceania	71.8	98.7
Developed countries	107.4	112.8
Developing countries	51.1	98.8
World	66.1	101.9

Note: In kilograms per capita per year. Source: Fresco and Boudoin.

Production and Consumption Trends

Prior to the 1800s, fruits and vegetables could only be stored or preserved (canned, pickled, salted, dried, etc.) if they were to be consumed out of season. As rail networks were completed throughout the United States, agricultural producers were increasingly able to transport fresh fruits and vegetables long distances. In 1867, the first patented refrigerated rail car was built. Ice could be harvested from frozen winter ponds and stored in insulated ice houses for use in warmer months. Blocks of ice would then be placed at both ends of a railcar and air would be forced over the ice, cooling the car's perishable contents. These improvements vastly increased the distance that fresh produce—and other perishable commodities, such as meat and dairy—could travel.

Mechanical refrigeration suitable for transportation use was developed in the late 1940s. Many ships and railcars were fitted with small cooling units, allowing perishable products to be moved even greater distances, including globally. This expanded the scope and scale of the produce trade, and in turn, expanded the variety of fresh fruits and vegetables available to consumers. By the 1970s, sizeable amounts of perishable food were also being moved by refrigerated truck. Today, produce sold in the United States can travel up to 2,500 miles from farm to table, and even farther if sourced globally. Thus, consumers today have a variety of fresh fruits and vegetables available to them year-round, often defying the climatic reality of their particular geography.

While year-round access to fresh produce has benefited consumers nutritionally and gastronomically, concerns about the environmental and social impact of global production and trade are shifting demand patterns yet again. Consumers are beginning to question the production methods used to grow and ship their food. More consumers are purchasing organic fruits and vegetables and "buying local" from natural food stores, food cooperatives, farmers' markets and community supported agriculture arrangements (CSAs). Big merchandisers like Wal-Mart and Costco are noticing these trends, and have recently made significant moves into the organic and locally branded produce markets to avoid losing share.

Global Trade

Today, approximately 700 million tons of fruit and 800 million tons of vegetables are grown and sold around the world, totaling 1.5 billion tons of perishable product. Five crops—bananas, grapes, apples, melons and oranges—account for approximately 60% of global fruit production, by weight. Three vegetables—potatoes, sweet potatoes and tomatoes (scientifically a fruit but considered a vegetable for food purposes)—account for 63% of global vegetable production, by weight.

The leading producers of the three primary fruit and vegetable crops are shown in Tables 5.2 and 5.3, respectively. Clearly, China is the global leader in fruit and vegetable production, supplying 34% of the major produce categories grown in the world. Production in China has surged in the last three decades; the country's aggressive economic reforms enabled it to increase its output by almost 250% between 1980 and today. India and the United States are also major producers, accounting for 8% and 5% of major crop production, respectively. Countries in Latin America, the Caribbean, Africa and the European Union (EU) also produce sizeable amounts of certain crops that are well-suited to their given climates.

Climatic variation is, in fact, a fundamental reason for international trade. As noted, demand for out-of-season and exotic fruits and vegetables has increased substantially in the past century. Therefore, trade is often counter-seasonal. For instance, grapes and avocados are imported from the Southern Hemisphere to the United States and EU during their winter months (generally January through April). During the US summer, US apples, grapes and stone fruits are

Table 5.2 **Leading Producers of Primary Fruit Crops, 2008**

Bananas	Weight	Apples	Weight	Grapes	Weight
India	26.21	**China**	27.5	**Italy**	8.52
China	8.04	**US**	4.24	**China**	6.79
Philippines	8.68	**Iran**	2.66	**US**	6.38
Brazil	7.00	**Turkey**	2.26	**France**	6.04
Ecuador	6.70	**Russia**	2.21	**Spain**	6.00
TOTAL	93.39	**TOTAL**	64.25	**TOTAL**	67.22

In million cwt.
Source: United States Department of Agriculture, Economic Research Service.

Table 5.3 **Leading Producers of Primary Vegetable Crops, 2008**

Potatoes	Weight	Tomatoes	Weight	Sweet potatoes	Weight
China	1,257.9	China	741.7	China	2,254.0
India	759.8	US	253.5	Uganda	76.9
Russia	636.6	Turkey	218.7	Nigeria	57.4
Ukraine	430.9	India	189.3	Indonesia	40.3
US	412.7	Egypt	166.4	Vietnam	32.0
TOTAL	6,925.6	TOTAL	2,783.3	TOTAL	2,784.4

In million cwt.
Source: United States Department of Agriculture, Economic Research Service.

exported to Central and South America. Most countries engage in some amount of international produce trade during the year in order to meet consumer demand.

The United States imports more fruits and vegetables than any other country, followed by the EU and Japan. In particular, the United States imports tropical fruits that it cannot grow easily, such as bananas and pineapples. It also imports seasonal produce for which there is strong year-round demand, like grapes. The United States exports significant amounts of apples, oranges and orange juice. It imports apple juice, however.

Figure 5.1 illustrates the overall value of US fruit and vegetable imports and exports between 1990 and 2007. Notably, the nation's imports are not keeping up with its exports, thus the US is seeing a significant trade deficit in this area. Table 5.4 details the United States' major fruit trade partners in 2009.

Trade in fruits and vegetables is not solely global in scope; domestic trade also enables countries to match seasonal production with demand. In the United States, five states account for 80% of the country's fruit and vegetable production value, much of which is shipped domestically. California is the leading US fruit and vegetable grower, supplying 50% of US produce. The state secured its leading position by building vast irrigation systems in its agricultural valleys, which are well-suited for vegetable crops. For instance, California produces 75% of the spinach, 75% of the fresh tomatoes and 95% of the processing tomatoes grown in the United States. California is also the leading producer of strawberries, grapes, oranges and peaches in America. Florida, Arizona, Georgia and New York are the other leading fruit and vegetable producers in the United States, accounting for 15%, 7%, 4% and 4% of the nation's production values, respectively.

Concentration in the industry is increasing. Although 1,300 companies have a combined annual revenue of about $60 billion, the 50 largest companies

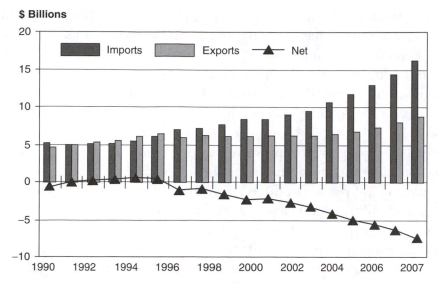

Figure 5.1 **US fruit and vegetable trade, 1990–2007** (Source: Congressional Research Service). *Note:* Includes fresh and processed products; excludes nuts.

Table 5.4 **US Fruit Trade Partners, 2009**

Partner	Imported	Partner	Exported
Mexico	4,433,496	Canada	2,584,140
Costa	2,863,886	Mexico	884,026
Guatemala	3,360,455	Japan	686,469
Ecuador	2,592,912	Hong Kong	390,591
Chile	1,908,582	China	294,150
Honduras	1,326,784	Taiwan	282,976
Colombia	1,123,024	South Korea	261,873
Others	2,060,769	United Kingdom	195,905
World	19,669,907	Indonesia	7,605,380

In 1,000 lbs; excludes juices.
Source: United States Department of Agriculture, Economic Research Service.

generate approximately 70% of that revenue. Major companies include Del Monte, Heinz and JR Simplot; grower cooperatives such as Diamond Foods and Ocean Spray; and divisions of larger food companies such as ConAgra and General Mills. Many companies are vertically integrated with farming, processing and distribution all owned and held by one parent company.

The Basic Produce Supply Chain

Managing fruit and vegetable supply chains is a challenging task—actually many tasks—crossing state and international borders, involving dozens of intermediaries between the farmer and the consumer. The basic supply chain for fresh produce is shown in Figure 5.2. Because fruits and vegetables are perishable, the salability of the product is contingent on the supply chain's ability to transport fresh goods to consumers quickly, once harvested. Therefore, maximizing quality and value in the supply chain requires close coordination and collaboration between all supply chain partners. Primary partners include harvesting crews, dock and warehouse workers, brokers, freight and shipping agents and buyers.

The major aspects of the produce supply chain are growing, harvesting, cooling, packing and distribution/storage. The dynamics of this chain vary, however, with individual products' growing environments, picking requirements, perishability, fragility and intended point of sale (e.g., grocery, restaurant, processor, export, etc.). Throughout the entire supply chain—from the point of harvest to the final point of sale—fresh fruits and vegetables need to be stored at cool temperatures to prevent spoilage. Therefore, supply chain management for produce is often referred to as cold chain management. The cold chain for the most basic produce crops—field, orchard and berry crops—is described in detail below.

Planting and Growing

Many fruits and vegetables are field crops, typically grown from seed. Field crops may or may not need to be replanted each year, depending on the plant type. For instance, asparagus is a perennial crop, meaning the individual plants are productive year after year, but cucumbers are an annual crop, meaning the plants are only productive for one year and must be replanted the next

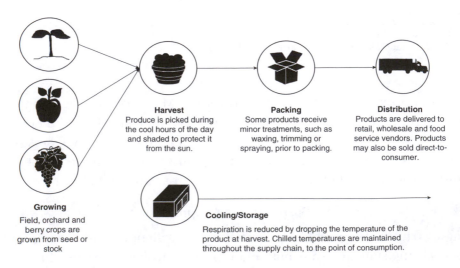

Harvest
Produce is picked during the cool hours of the day and shaded to protect it from the sun.

Packing
Some products receive minor treatments, such as waxing, trimming or spraying, prior to packing.

Distribution
Products are delivered to retail, wholesale and food service vendors. Products may also be sold direct-to-consumer.

Growing
Field, orchard and berry crops are grown from seed or stock

Cooling/Storage
Respiration is reduced by dropping the temperature of the product at harvest. Chilled temperatures are maintained throughout the supply chain, to the point of consumption.

Figure 5.2 **Fresh produce supply chain**

year to yield a crop. Field crops can be planted by hand or by mechanical means.

Fruit is also grown in orchards. Orchards consist of perennial trees that last many years and are typically propagated by grafting, budding or cuttings versus grown from seed, as these methods enable faster tree maturation and more consistent development of desirable characteristics. The layout of an orchard impacts everything from plant health to harvesting efficiency. Because orchards are relatively permanent, their design is therefore important.

Finally, berries are perennial crops that are also typically propagated by hand. Berries vary widely in physical type. For instance, raspberries, blueberries, and cranberries grow on shrubs while grapes grow on vines. Berry plants also vary considerably in their maintenance requirements. For example, blackberries tend to grow rapidly and thus hinder easy management, while grape vines are carefully managed by vineyard operators, particularly wine grapes. Berries can be labor-intensive to harvest. Therefore, many berry crops command a high value. Note that some plants are scientifically berries but are not discussed as berry crops for food purposes, e.g., pumpkins.

Harvest

The innate quality of a fruit or vegetable product is substantially impacted by the seed or plant stock used to grow a crop, and its growing conditions. However, harvest, processing and distribution activities also significantly impact a product's end value. Fresh produce must be picked at the right time, and the cold chain properly managed between harvest and sale, in order to maximize a product's worth. Growers receive the highest prices for good quality fresh produce; the price drops as the condition of the product deteriorates. At this point, it must be sold in lower-priced markets for frozen, canned, juiced or pulped goods.

Field, orchard and berry crops are typically picked when ripe or when sugar conditions are optimal. All of these crop types can be harvested manually but some can be picked with machines, depending on the crop's layout and the fragility of the fruit or vegetable. Typically, the more manual the harvest, the higher priced the final product. Grading and sorting activities may occur at the time of picking, or may be done after harvest. Ideally, produce is picked in the cool hours of the day and shaded to protect it from the sun.

As an example, melons are picked by multiple teams of workers (10–20 people) who progress through a field with a moving tractor pulling a trailer of cartons. The melons are manually picked, tossed up to the trailer, sorted by size, stacked on a pallet and transferred to a waiting truck. The truck drives to a cooling shed every few hours, where the melons are rapidly cooled in preparation for distribution.

Cooling

In most fruits and vegetables, deterioration begins as soon as the product is harvested. Deterioration occurs through respiration, but respiration can be reduced to an acceptable level by dropping the temperature of the crop. For products that will be sold fresh to consumers, cooling is therefore important as it enables a longer retail shelf and refrigerator life. For products destined for processing, cold chain management is also important to ensure food safety.

As an example, strawberries picked ripe in the field have 72 hours to get into the hands of consumers. A strawberry may spend more than 72 hours in its supply chain, however, due to the need for careful handling and packing, and due to long transportation distances to some markets. Moving a strawberry quickly from its field to a chilled environment can extend its freshness and thus enable more flexibility in its supply chain. However, because strawberries deteriorate so quickly, most are actually picked before they are ripe and therefore never achieve optimal flavor for end consumers.

Several methods exist to remove field heat from products, the first step in cold chain management. The five most common methods—forced-air cooling, hydrocooling, room cooling, vacuum cooling and icing—are detailed below. Table 5.5 compares different cooling methods in terms of cost and impact on product quality.

FORCED-AIR COOLING
Forced-air cooling is the most widely used cooling method for just-picked produce, as it is faster than other methods and thus preferred for crops that have high rates of respiration (i.e., they deteriorate quickly) and crops that warrant optimal preservation (i.e., high value crops). In forced-air cooling, high

Table 5.5 **Cost and Quality Impacts of Cooling Methods**

	Forced-Air	*Hydro*	*Room*	*Vacuum*	*Icing*
Capital Cost	Low	Low	Low	Medium	High
Product Moisture Loss (%)	0.1 to 2.0	0.0 to 0.5	0.1 to 2.0	2.0 to 4.0	No data
Potential for Contamination	Low	High	Low	None	Low
Water Contact With Product?	No	Yes	No	No	Yes
Water-Resistant Packaging Needed?	No	Yes	No	No	Yes
Energy Efficiency	Low	High	Low	High	Low

Source: Thompson.

velocity cold air is pushed through produce containers, creating extensive contact between cold air and the product.

HYDROCOOLING

Hydrocooling is similar to forced air but cold water moves continuously through a product via showers or submerged batches. This cooling method can be more efficient than air cooling, but the water must be clean to avoid contamination. Additionally, some packed products are sensitive to or intolerant of moisture, therefore requiring the use of water-resistant packaging. Hydrocooling is most commonly used for root, stem and flower-type vegetables, and for melons and tree fruits.

ROOM COOLING

Room cooling uses a refrigerated room and cold air, pulled from the ceiling by a fan and circulated around a product. An advantage of room cooling is that produce can be cooled and stored in the same place, reducing handling. A disadvantage is that room cooling is very slow relative to other methods and may not be suitable for produce with high respiration rates. Room cooling is often used for commodity fruits and vegetables, such as citrus and apples.

VACUUM COOLING

Vacuum cooling is achieved by putting a product in a vacuum. The reduced water vapor pressure allows water to evaporate quickly and the surface temperature of the product to drop. Typically, vacuum cooling is used for produce that has high surface-to-volume ratios, such as leafy greens.

ICING

Icing uses crushed ice to cool and maintain product temperature. In this case, the produce is covered or embedded in slush ice. Icing is used infrequently in modern processing. Typically, icing is limited to commodities like broccoli, which were traditionally packaged in this manner.

After field heat is removed, a product's cool temperature is maintained until it reaches the end of its supply chain. A fruit or vegetable's ideal temperature will vary based on its physical makeup; generally, however, temperatures need to be cool enough to slow metabolic processes and arrest pathogens, but high enough to avoid frost and freezer damage. As an example, orchard fruits are kept at around 32 degrees Fahrenheit, citrus fruits are kept at 37 to 45 degrees Fahrenheit, and tropical fruits, like bananas and pineapples, are kept at about 54 degrees Fahrenheit.

Grading and Packing

Many fruit and vegetable growers pick their crops into large bins and then transport the bins to packhouses, which are either commercially or cooperatively owned. In the packhouse, products are graded and packed according to use and destination—e.g., processing, retail sales, export market, etc. Some products also receive minor treatments before packing, such as waxing (apples), trimming (broccoli and other greens) and anti-germination spraying (potatoes). After packing, the products are moved to distribution warehouses for later shipment to retailers and restaurants, to ports or airports for international shipping, or to manufacturing facilities for processing. Produce may also be placed in cold storage at the packhouse.

The packing material selected for produce is very important. Good packaging works hand in hand with temperature maintenance to extend produce shelf life. When fruits and vegetables consume oxygen they expel heat, water and carbon dioxide, which contribute to produce aging. Fruits and vegetables also expel ethylene, a gas that accelerates ripening. Carbohydrates and other substances important to the product's taste and nutritional quality break down in these conditions. Thus, good packaging slows respiration and reduces the accumulation of decomposition liquids (moisture). Good packaging also protects produce during storage and transit and conveys supply chain and marketing information to end users.

Many packaging types are available to producers today. Corrugated cardboard boxes, foam boxes, plastic tubs, mesh bags, clamshells, films and pallets are well-known examples. Demand for packaging in the United States is expected to reach $4.7 billion by 2012 as overall demand for perishable products increases. The most significant packaging materials and methods today are described below.

BULK PACKAGING

The goal of bulk packaging is to improve product movement and storage. Most fruits and vegetables are bulk-packed in corrugated cardboard boxes with or without wax coatings. Waxed corrugated boxes are best for wet produce like lettuce or broccoli, while dry items like apples, potatoes and onions use normal corrugated boxes. The box's shape and strength prevent produce from being crushed and bruised and enable rapid loading and unloading of produce in the distribution system. While corrugated boxes remain the leading produce packaging type, environmental concerns are affecting the use of waxed corrugated boxes as they are difficult to recycle.

Instead, moisture-resistant recyclable boxes and reusable plastic containers (RPCs, or "totes") are seeing growth in the industry. While RPCs have a significantly higher upfront cost than corrugated boxes, they are durable and, in many instances, have a significantly lower carbon footprint than their cardboard counterparts. The produce industry is also slowly shifting to the use of plastic pallets over wood pallets for environmental and food safety reasons. Wal-Mart and several other supermarket chains have been recognized for their increasing use of RPCs. While RPCs are becoming more common in shipping, many retailers are also increasing their use of value-added packaging (e.g., clamshells, discussed below) to display produce. Examples of RPCs and plastic pallets are shown in Figure 5.3.

CLEAR, HARD-SHELL PLASTIC PACKAGING (CLAMSHELLS)

Clear packaging presents produce well, promoting freshness to consumers. The hard shell also protects produce during transport and integrates products easily into ready-to-eat and fresh-cut fruit and vegetable displays. However, many companies use virgin or nonrenewable natural resources to make these kinds of containers. Post-consumer recycled polyethylene terephthalate (PCR PET) packaging is now available, which is made from recycled soda and water bottles. PCR PET requires much less energy and water to produce than virgin plastic and results in lower greenhouse gas emissions. However, low recycling rates in the United States and the lack of recycling infrastructure for PCR PET often mean that both virgin and PCR PET containers end up in landfills. According to the Environmental Protection Agency, nearly six billion pounds of clamshell packaging waste was generated in 2007, and only 23% of that was recycled.

MODIFIED ATMOSPHERE PACKAGING (MAP)

MAP substitutes the oxygen inside an airtight package with a protective mix of gasses that lower pH and inhibit bacterial growth. MAP has allowed the lettuce

Returnable plastic totes   Plastic pallets

Figure 5.3 **Advances in bulk produce packaging**

and greens market to expand significantly by extending the overall shelf life of fresh cut greens from 4 days (for lettuce) or 6 days (for spinach) to about 14 days. MAP packaging is also used for products like red meat, seafood, fresh cut fruit and salads.

Distribution and Storage

Over 95% of the produce transported in the United States, including produce imported from Mexico and Canada, is moved by truck, amounting to more than 5 million truckloads of produce each day. Small volumes of produce are shipped in refrigerated railcars or piggyback trailers (cargo trailers that can ride on flat railcars or be attached to a truck's tractor unit). An almost insignificant amount of produce is shipped by air.

With the current highway and railroad freight infrastructure at or near capacity, it is estimated that the existing US transportation system will not be able to handle the 100% increase in freight traffic projected in the next 25 years. Significant investments will need to be made to increase freight capacity to appropriate levels; investment estimates for railway infrastructure alone total $148 billion. The trucking industry is facing additional issues that will negatively impact capacity, including driver shortages, new labor regulations dictating the length of the allowable driving day and more aggressive emissions standards for refrigerated trucks.

As perishable items, fruits and vegetables are susceptible to disruptions in the cold chain; i.e., transportation and storage disruptions. Thus, addressing capacity issues in the transportation infrastructure will be necessary to facilitate growth in the industry. Increasing efficiency in the transportation system will also be necessary. For example, more flexible loading and unloading procedures at receiving docks could allow drivers to reduce their waiting time, minimizing transportation disruptions. Today, however, many large retailers instead have rigid schedules of anticipated truck arrivals and unclear or inefficient loading and unloading procedures, which leads to idling, additional fuel costs and increased emissions.

Because global trade in fruits and vegetables has increased, ports have also become critical links in the produce supply chain. West Coast ports are handling much of the fruit and vegetable export business today. With fruit and vegetable imports projected to vastly increase in the next few years, all ports and container ships in the United States will likely see higher volumes. Ports can be a particularly weak link in the supply chain when union contracts expire. For instance, in 2002 the Los Angeles/Long Beach Port Lockout, involving the International Longshore and Warehouse Union, backlogged port shipments from October through December. The lockout caused US farmers to lose revenue due to spoilage, decreased product quality and increased storage costs. Losses were estimated at approximately $500 million each week.

Information Exchange in the Supply Chain

The true potential of a supply chain can only be realized if information exchange occurs between partners. Information sharing between growers, logistics providers and retailers is critical to the timely movement of perishable inventory. Good information management also eases food safety investigations when problems occur. Conveying information to consumers about food sources and production methods can enhance the marketing activities of growers and sellers. These aspects of information exchange are discussed below.

INVENTORY MANAGEMENT

Sharing information between supply chain partners—particularly demand forecasts—ensures appropriate timing for crop picking, processing and delivery, which in turn reduces pipeline inventory, spoilage and energy consumption. Continuous monitoring enables fast product movement and reduces the bullwhip effect of inventory fluctuation across the supply chain. All of these outcomes enhance revenues for supply chain partners.

FOOD SAFETY

Because produce is often consumed raw or with only minimal processing—i.e., without cooking or other interventions that can eliminate pathogens—most food-borne illnesses in America can be traced to produce consumption. In fact, leafy greens, tomatoes, sprouts and berries are among the ten riskiest foods consumed by Americans. Table 5.6 summarizes outbreak data on the ten highest-risk foods regulated by the Food and Drug Administration, which is responsible for produce, egg and dairy safety (the USDA regulates and inspects meat products).

Contamination can occur at any stage of the supply chain, so risks must be managed from farm to table. Common pre-harvest and harvest sources of contamination are irrigation water, pesticides, manure and wild and domestic animal waste, including farm runoff. Post-harvest contamination sources include workers, equipment and improper storage temperature at any point in the cold chain. At the retail stage, storage conditions and employee and consumer handling present additional contamination risks. Consolidation in the industry is complicating food safety management. For instance, the 2006 E. coli contamination of pre-cut California spinach was limited in scope, but the high volume of spinach processed by a single producer and the limited information available about the product's supply chain caused a major industry disruption.

Table 5.6 **Ten Riskiest Foods Regulated by the FDA**

Food Type	Reported Outbreaks
Leafy greens	363 outbreaks involving 13,568 reported cases of illness
Eggs	352 outbreaks involving 11,163 reported cases of illness
Tuna	268 outbreaks involving 2,341 reported cases of illness
Oysters	132 outbreaks involving 3,409 reported cases of illness
Potatoes	108 outbreaks involving 3,659 reported cases of illness
Cheese	83 outbreaks involving 2,761 reported cases of illness
Ice Cream	74 outbreaks involving 2,594 reported cases of illness
Tomatoes	31 outbreaks involving 3,292 reported cases of illness
Sprouts	31 outbreaks involving 2,022 reported cases of illness
Berries	25 outbreaks involving 3,397 reported cases of illness

Source: Center for Science in the Public Interest.

When contamination occurs, identifying its source is often difficult and time-consuming. The suspect item (along with any packaging or labels) is usually no longer available for testing by the time an illness is reported. Moreover, fresh fruits and vegetables are often taken out of their bulk packaging and sold loose, without information about their source. Finally, practices such as packing and repacking add complexity to trace-back investigations.

Scanner labels and radio frequency identification tags (RFID) have improved traceability in the produce supply chain. Bar codes and RFID tags can contain product descriptions, lot numbers identifying growers, a product's harvest and pack dates and a comprehensive record of handlers, handling activities and handling dates. US and Canadian produce marketing groups recently launched the Produce Traceability Initiative (PTI) calling for GS1-128 bar coding on every case of produce by 2012. Some growers are already going farther than this, adding individual labels to each fruit or vegetable shipped. For instance, Sun Valley Packing Company of Reedley, California manually applies sticker labels on each individual piece of fruit it sends out. To identify case contents, the packer prints its coding directly on the company's shipping cases.

MARKETING

Many producers today are using traceability technologies to enhance their marketing efforts. For example, Coosaw Farms labels every watermelon it grows with a unique code. When consumers enter this code online, they can learn exactly when and where the melon was harvested and read about Coosaw Farms. The company's story helps the consumer connect with the product and builds brand loyalty.

Value-Added Supply Chains

Food products become value-added in one of two ways: they are processed in a way that gives the raw product an incremental value above its original market worth, or they are grown and processed in a way that differentiates them from similar products in the market. In the produce industry, common value-added processing activities include washing, cutting, canning, freezing, drying and juicing. Common attribute differentiations include organic or sustainable growing practices and geographic demarcation, e.g., "Home Grown" labeling or Europe's Appellation d'Origine Contrôlée seal for wine.

Value-Added Processing

In the United States, commercial freezing and wine-making activities, relative to all non-citrus processing activities, are on the increase while canning activities are decreasing. Other processing trends, such as juicing and drying, are relatively flat. Figure 5.4 shows the breakdown of processing trends for non-citrus fruit between 1980 and 2009. Besides these basic value-added activities, produce can be made into jams and jellies, be incorporated into blended or baked goods, turned into extracts and flavorings or undergo other types of processing. Many of these activities are discussed in more detail in Chapter 8.

A typical supply chain for a large fruit processing company is illustrated in Figure 5.5. In this example, multiple farms feed raw product into the company's packhouse and juice facility. The packhouse receives the highest quality product (e.g., minimal blemishes). The juice plant gets less attractive produce from

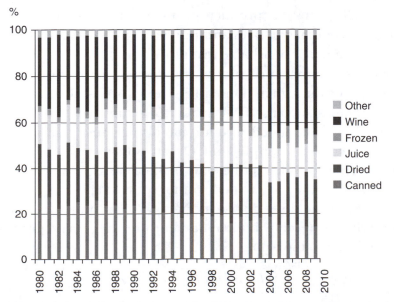

Figure 5.4 **Value-added processing trends, 1980–2010 (for non-citrus fruits)** (Source: USDA ERS).

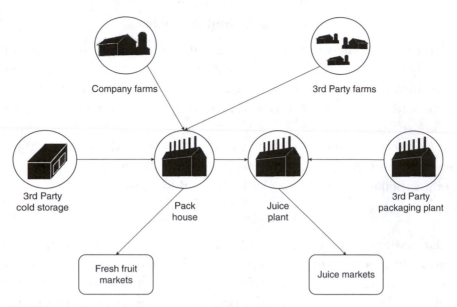

Figure 5.5 **Value-added production supply chain (juice)**

company-owned or third party farms. It also receives surplus product from its own or others' packhouses and cold storage facilities. The company's packing plant ships its fresh fruit product to retail and other fresh fruit markets while the juice plant ships its product to the juice market.

As is evident from the illustration, selling to multiple markets can help fruit and vegetable companies deal with variations in produce quality and supply. Additionally, all forms of production management—vertical integration, contracting and spot market sales and purchasing—are useful in helping fruit companies manage their perishable inventory.

As demand for convenience products increases, many growers are adding processing capacity through in-house investments or co-packing arrangements. For example, Sunkist, a major fruit grower, recently expanded into fruit processing. Pursuit of value-added revenue has also created markets where none previously existed. For example, the Ocean Spray Cranberries cooperative expanded the cranberry market beyond niche Thanksgiving sauces and fresh and frozen berries when it created cranberry cocktail and juice blends in the early 1960s. At the time, cranberry juice was not on the consumer radar. POM Wonderful has recently built a market for pomegranate juice, a hitherto unappreciated fruit in the United States.

Value-Added Differentiation

As with value-added processing, attribute differentiation extends to all food categories on the market—meat, dairy, crops, produce, etc. Additionally, all of these food categories have benefited from recent trends in differentiation; organic sales are up across the board, for instance. However, value-added attribute differentiation made its first and strongest inroads in the produce industry. Therefore, organic and geographic value-adds are discussed in detail below.

ORGANICS

Anxieties about fertilizer and pesticide residues in food, concerns about the environmental consequences of large-scale farming and a renaissance of consumer interest in whole and natural foods have prompted consumers to seek out organic products. Benefits of organic agriculture include healthier soil composition and thus healthier plants; enhanced drought resistance in crops; lessened levels of soil erosion; and lessened ecosystem and bodily contamination from synthetic fertilizers, pesticides, fungicides and herbicides.

However, organic farming is more time- and skill-intensive than conventional farming. Organic farmers must learn how to manage pests and weeds without synthetic chemicals, which requires getting to know their environment and crops. Organic farming can also require more manual labor than conventional farming, as basic tasks like weeding may not be able to be done through chemical means. Labor costs for organic farmers can therefore be 30% or higher than those of conventional farmers; because base costs are higher, workers' compensation and payroll taxes also tend to be higher. The more intensive nature of organic farming often curbs these farmers' ability to earn off-farm supplemental income. Sixty percent of organic farmers list farming as their primary occupation, compared to 45% of farmers overall. Organic production's higher costs and lower short-term yields typically result in higher consumer prices. They also, however, result in higher revenues for the farmer.

Despite the price premium, organic products today account for 3.5% of food sold for home consumption in the United States. Fruits and vegetables are the largest sector of the US organic market, accounting for 38% of organic food sales, and 7% and 6% of overall fruit and vegetable sales, respectively. These sales comprise a $9.5 billion market in the United States, which is expected to continue to grow. Berries, apples, bananas, grapes and citrus are the most-purchased organic fruits in American supermarkets. Packaged salad mixes, carrots, lettuce, tomatoes and onions are the most-purchased organic vegetables in US supermarkets. The overall demand for organic products is illustrated in Figure 5.6.

The rapidity with which consumers are transitioning to organic has encouraged many of the world's largest corporations to include organics in their core business strategy. In turn, incentives now exist for organic farmers to expand production and for conventional farmers to convert to organic methods.

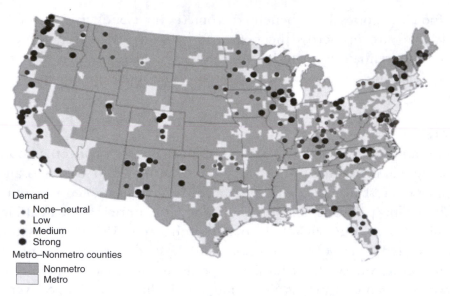

Demand
• None–neutral
• Low
• Medium
● Strong
Metro–Nonmetro counties
▨ Nonmetro
☐ Metro

Figure 5.6 **Demand for organic products in US farmers' markets** (Source: USDA ERS).

For example, Earthbound Farms, which started as a two-and-a-half-acre raspberry and baby greens farm near Carmel, California has become the largest grower of organic produce in the United States, selling more than 70% of all organic lettuce marketed in America. The company's products today are grown in six different California counties, two Arizona counties, Colorado and Mexico, comprising 33,000 acres of farmland.

Conventional farmers who want to go organic face high transition costs. Their soils must be pesticide-free for at least three years before they can market their product in America as "organic." During this time they incur the higher costs of organic farming methods without the benefit of organic's price premiums. A direct loan program exists to help new organic farmers establish production, but this program does not support existing farmers seeking to switch to organic, or farmers who inherit their land.

Because organic growers are often small in scale and because organic production is strongly influenced by the weather and seasonality, organic fruits and vegetables have a more variable supply pattern than conventional produce and produce grown by large farm operations. Hence, one market challenge is to smooth out seasonal variation for some organic commodities, which in turn requires better coordination of planting and harvesting across production regions, and closer collaboration between growers and buyers in planning and marketing. In recent years, contracting has been used to help stabilize the industry; forward buying allows growers to guarantee a market for their crop and ensures buyers a steady supply of product. Growth and diversification in the organic farming industry is also enabling these kinds of supply chain improvements to occur.

Other issues facing organic producers include implementing expensive food safety measures; obtaining organic certification; quality assurance; maintaining and managing cold chains without support from commodity market infrastructure; and using technology to keep up with wholesaler and retailer information demands. Organic producers are also under pressure to consolidate. As other countries (particularly Mexico and Central American countries) earmark more agricultural production for the US market, it will become increasingly difficult for organic farmers to compete with organic imports produced with lower labor costs. The resilience of the organic philosophy, in the face of conventional business pressures, remains an open question.

GEOGRAPHIC DIFFERENTIATION

In recent years, consumers have become increasingly interested in supporting local businesses. This interest extends to food and agriculture; i.e., supporting rural communities and helping maintain family farms by buying local. While "local" is often broadly defined, the idea implies purchasing food that is grown and processed in a geographic region close to the consumer. Thus, consumers establish their own purchasing parameters, commonly limiting their buying to a certain geographic radius—e.g., within 50 miles of New York City—or to certain counties, states or regions, e.g., New England or the Upper Midwest.

While the local purchasing trend originated with niche consumers, the movement is beginning to influence public policy. For instance, some state governments are encouraging large institutional purchasers, such as hospitals, schools and prisons, to "buy local," which could help sustain farmers and rural economies in states with a "buy local" initiative. The USDA also recently added a local production component to its Value-Added Producer Grant program, which makes substantial competitive funding available to producers to assist with business planning and marketing activities. The "buy local" movement is also influencing the purchasing policies of large grocery chains, such as Wal-Mart. Wal-Mart US recently established a goal of sourcing 9% of its produce locally by 2015 (defining local as within a given store's state). Wal-Mart Canada expects to source 30% its produce locally by 2013, with 100% of its produce purchased from local farmers, when possible.

Proponents of the "buy local" concept feel that it is a boon to small farmers. Margins can be comparatively high as farmers are not subject to the whims of the commodity market. In turn, farmers gain independence and enhanced control over their farming methods and operation. For some farmers, building relationships with consumers and getting positive feedback about their product is also a rewarding experience.

However, operating outside of the commodity market—and thus without the support of its substantial marketing and supply chain infrastructure—creates its own set of challenges for farmers and purchasers alike. Farmers selling outside of the commodity market often must develop new marketing skills to convince buyers, particularly commercial buyers, to purchase their product. Farmers must also take on new responsibilities that typically are not required for commodity market sales, such as forecasting and product distribution. Farmers may also need to enhance crop diversity and obtain cold storage capacity to extend their growing season, reduce risk and stabilize cash flow.

While some of these activities require skills that are atypical in conventional farming, the biggest hurdle to operating outside of the commodity market is often a basic lack of time. Simply put, any time a farmer spends devising a marketing concept for his or her product, or driving to town to distribute product, maintain vendor relationships and grow the vendor pool, is time not spent growing a crop or maintaining the farm. While simplistic conceptually, these are very real challenges for many farmers operating outside of commodity markets.

Local purchasing can be a challenge for certain types of buyers, as well—particularly retailers, restaurants and food service companies. Individual farmers may have insufficient volume, inconsistent supply quantities or inconsistent product quality to reliably service these buyer groups. Unforeseen problems, like transportation disruptions or severe weather, can delay supplies, creating significant issues for institutions that depend on highly predictable product supplies to meet their production demands. Likewise, some institutional purchasers, such as public schools, no longer have the equipment or staff expertise required to clean and safely prepare raw, unprocessed foods. In addition, since the current produce supply chain primarily moves product between California and Florida and the rest of the United States, the infrastructure may no longer exist to support regional processing. Thus, while philosophically and nutritionally appealing, the "buy local" concept can be complicated to execute.

For farmers, a good alternative to trying to sell locally to major food purchasers is to sell directly to consumers via farmers' markets, CSA arrangements or even over the Internet. Often, the consumers purchasing from these venues value high quality food and are motivated to purchase products that have clear social and/or environmental benefits, justifying their price premium. A bonus to the farmer of selling direct is that consumers in these markets anticipate, and in fact may appreciate, the variation in supply that farms naturally experience. For instance, carrots may not be available in a given week, but when they are ready for harvest and brought to market, their quality is likely to be extremely good and consumers are delighted. Selling at farmers' markets and through CSA arrangements can reduce some of the transportation burdens associated with retail, restaurant or food service sales, as well, although farmers' capacity can still be strained by the weekly need to go to market.

Direct sales channels are rapidly growing in the United States. As Figure 5.7 illustrates, the number of farmers' markets in the United States has more than tripled in the last fifteen years, enabling more Americans to "buy local." Several CSA models also exist. In a subscription CSA, consumers purchase and receive a share of a farm's crop during its growing season. The farmer is the manager, and decides what to plant, how frequent deliveries will be and the price per share. Typically subscribers are not required to work on the farm or assist in the delivery process. In a shareholder CSA, consumers organize themselves and hire a farmer to grow their desired crops. Land for farming may be purchased, leased or rented. Food sorting and delivery are done by the consumers. The consumer group may be formally organized as a non-profit. The CSA concept is beginning to spread to non-produce items; meat CSAs, for instance, are beginning to take shape in some urban areas.

Large-scale food purchasers in the United States are beginning to show interest in direct buying models such as those embraced by individual consumers. Institutional CSA programs are cropping up, in which purchasers commit to buying large volumes of product directly from farmers, thereby helping farmers plan their crops and reducing unit prices for institutions. Wholesale farmers' markets are also appearing in the United States, which work well for retailers and restaurants.

Wholesale farmers' markets have existed internationally for years. Two examples are the Marché International de Rungis, outside of Paris, and the Ontario

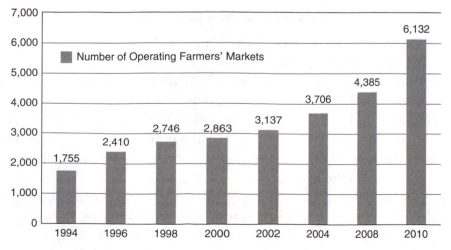

Figure 5.7 **Growth of farmers' markets in the US, 1994–2010** (Source: USDA).

Food Terminal near Toronto, Canada. Rungis has been operating at its current location since 1969, but this market is an extension of the famous wholesale market in Les Halles, which operated in central Paris for almost eleven centuries. Rungis is a large, functional and comfortable indoor facility that accommodates 82 Paris-area farmers. Rungis generally caters to buyers who fill large orders from multiple farmers, typically paying a premium for the Ile de France brand, which guarantees freshness, flavor and quality. The Ontario Food Terminal rents space to farmer tenants but also sources products from afar. About 475 tenants on average sell products at Ontario, which has 80,000 square feet of cold storage capacity and an average throughput of almost 1 million tons of product per year. Buyers must be registered with the Ontario Food Terminal Board, proving they are not end consumers, and pay $150 biannually to get an access card.

The complexity of the "buy local" movement, in practice, has led some to advocate for regional food purchasing as opposed to local-only buying initiatives—e.g., in-state or 100-mile purchasing policies. A move to source and sell products regionally, instead of in very tight geographical networks, may enhance food options in locations that have extremely limited growing seasons, and may enable farmers and consumers to better balance the natural crop surpluses and shortages that often occur due to variations in weather, etc. In other words, regional sourcing could provide a more adequate and secure food supply than the local-only movement, while still protecting natural resources, enabling economic development in rural areas and countering the foreign food import trend.

Company Profile: Red Jacket Orchards

Red Jacket Orchards, located in the Finger Lakes region of upstate New York, has been owned and operated by the Nicholson family since 1958. While the initial operation was limited to fruit farming and a small roadside stand, the company has slowly added processing, distribution and sales capacity in the decades since, in response to industry trends. Today, the company has a unique, high-quality line of fresh fruit and value-added products that are sold throughout the eastern United States, primarily in New England and the Mid-Atlantic.

RJO's commitment to quality and product differentiation have given the company a strong regional brand and reinforced its viability as an independent, family-owned operation. In the last decade, RJO has also moved toward sustainable crop management, which is helping enhance the long-term health of the farm and assisting with marketing. Thus, RJO is a strong example of how vertical integration and differentiation in the marketplace can enable a producer to thrive in the fruit industry.

Farm Overview

The land farmed by RJO has been in fruit production since the late nineteenth century. By the time Joe and Emily Nicholson bought the property in 1958, orchards and non-tree fruits were growing on the site; apples, pears, grapes, strawberries and raspberries were the primary historical crops. The Nicholsons' farm was originally 90 acres in size. The acquisition of additional land over the past fifty years has resulted in a 600-acre farm operation. Today, seven farms in an eight mile radius produce numerous fruit crops and a small number of vegetables.

Apples are the primary crop and are grown on 350 acres. The use of dwarfing rootstocks enables a tree density of 1,100 trees per acre, which in turn generates a high yield of high quality fruit. Orchards with larger trees have a much lower capacity, and because sunlight is restricted, may produce lesser-quality fruit. Dwarfing rootstocks also encourage plant health. Trees have good access to sunlight, which leads to more colorful and flavorful apples. The orchard also has good airflow, which improves drying conditions, reduces the need for fungicides and pesticides, and reduces favorable habitat for insects.

RJO's other 250 acres grow summer fruits, including European prune plums, Japanese plums, apricots, peaches, nectarines, Chinese pears, sweet cherries, sour cherries, blueberries, strawberries, raspberries, gooseberries and red currants. RJO's vegetable crops include rhubarb, hot peppers and tomatillos. Some land also houses RJO's production and administration facilities. The company employs 60 to 70 people, depending on the season.

Supply Chain Integration

Fruits and vegetables are harvested with their respective supply chains in mind. Products that will be sent to market quickly are picked when ripe. Products that will be stored or sent to distant markets are harvested when mature but before they are fully ripe, as they will continue to ripen off the tree or vine. Ripeness is determined by assessing the sugar content, firmness, starch seed and skin color of a given crop.

The company has cold storage on site to facilitate quick cooling. Most fruits are chilled and stored in a cold storage room that is kept as close as possible to 32 degrees Fahrenheit and 21% oxygen—conditions in which apples respire and mature normally. Fruits that need to be chilled very quickly, like strawberries and raspberries, are also chilled with forced air before they are placed in cold storage. RJO is able to store several thousand bushels on site, enough to accommodate all of its summer fruit and early apples.

RJO is also a part-owner in a cooperative cold storage facility, which allows for Controlled Atmosphere (CA) storage. CA rooms are sealed to maintain a low level of oxygen—1% to 2%. The lower oxygen level reduces fruit's respiration rate and slows ripening. This in turn allows fruit to be stored for a longer period of time than it could in room storage, and thus allows for near-perfect fruit when the room is opened and the fruit finally packed.

RJO's primary value-added products are cider and juice. Straight apple juice and cider, blended products, fruit nectars and seasonal juice comprise the product line. Blemished fruit that are unsuitable for fresh consumption are sent from RJO's packhouse to the juicer for value-added production. The company also sells a limited quantity of dried fruit and fruit jams, butters and sauces, which it manufactures through a co-packing arrangement.

The company's products are sold at its on-site store and at regional farmers' markets, including through New York City's Greenmarket system. Greenmarket is a year-round, weekly network of 21 markets in Manhattan, Brooklyn and Queens. An additional 32 markets are open seasonally, giving RJO substantial opportunity for direct brand building with consumers. As Mark Nicholson, Executive Vice President, noted, "There aren't many farmers that have their own retail outlets in New York City. But through the farmers' markets we are on the street in New York selling retail product five to seven days a week in multiple locations."

RJO's year-round presence in the city is encouraging it to consider a CSA for its urban clientele. If launched, the CSA could provide subscribers with seasonally appropriate fruit and value-added products. Fresh fruit and value-added products are also sold in retail locations in the area. Nine major retailers carry RJO's products, as do numerous gourmet retailers. Recently, RJO contracted with Whole Foods to sell its juice. The Whole Foods arrangement has vastly increased the company's reach; RJO's name is now on store shelves from Boston to Austin, Texas. Finally, RJO sells a limited quantity of fresh fruit and value-added products direct to consumers online.

With the exception of the juice sold through Whole Foods and its online sales, RJO carries out its own distribution activities. A company-owned distribution center in Brooklyn helps RJO maintain a consistent presence in the New York City area. Ownership of the distribution component of its supply chain allows RJO to maintain product freshness, and thus, its brand.

For example, RJO is known for the incredible quality of its fresh apricots, which typically go from farm to market very quickly. As Nicholson explained, this is atypical in the region: "It is very difficult to get a good, fresh apricot on the East Coast because apricots are a delicate crop. The varieties planted and the shipping methods used mean that most apricots sold in this region are like cardboard. But we produce a superior apricot and get it to market quickly." The strategy has paid off; RJO's produce is often critically acclaimed by food reviewers in the region.

Integrating across the supply chain has allowed RJO to capture value that would otherwise be lost. Its processing activities push annual revenues over $5 million, which is substantial for a 600-acre fruit farm on the East Coast. Vertical integration has also allowed RJO to maintain product quality and deepen the brand's value. These, in turn, have enabled the farm to maintain its independence from the commodity fruit market.

Differentiation in the Marketplace

To distinguish its products in the market, RJO has, for decades, carefully selected its fruit and vegetable varieties. As Nicholson explains, "Having been retailers and wholesalers [before starting the farm], we had a lot of experience with direct consumer purchasing and recognized that we wanted to have products that other people didn't have. That led to the prunes, the plums, the apricots—niche markets that can't be filled by other large commercial producers." Mike Biltonen, Vice President of Farm Operations, reiterates the point: "Diversity is an important part of what makes RJO unique. We are always innovating."

The fruits and vegetables grown by RJO therefore tend to be optimal for production in the Finger Lakes region. Collaboration with nearby Cornell University, which has a strong plant breeding and genetics program, helped RJO establish unique apple varieties, for instance. Supply chain requirements, including perishability and product fragility, also factor into the decision-making process when orchards or crops are replanted.

Because it focuses on niche, high-quality products, RJO only sells through retail partners that share the company's values, particularly a desire to decommodify well-known products. Nicholson relays the origins of this practice: "In the 1960s, my dad was running the sales desk, the farm and the packing house. He was really busy but the plus-side of him doing that is that he didn't really want to deal with all these buyers coming to him, looking for the lowest and cheapest price. So we decided then that we were not looking to be the major supplier for one large supermarket. Rather, we shop the niche markets."

Nicholson further notes that the "buy local" movement has made this practice both easier and more difficult. "Right now, all these local grocers want to buy local – everyone wants it, because that's what consumers want. But no one knows exactly how to make it happen, logistically. The companies that are doing it best are those that have committed themselves, their dollars and their structure to doing it right, from marketing to sourcing, figuring out that you need more than one supplier, but then figuring out how to manage ten suppliers."

Sustainability

Over the past decade, the Nicholsons have also made a move to operate their farm in a more sustainable manner. Their motivations are twofold: they wish to preserve their land's long-term health and value, and they believe that a move toward sustainability can facilitate distinction in the marketplace. RJO's sustainability focus has three primary components: Integrated Pest Management (IPM), certified organic production and Food Alliance certification.

RJO has utilized IPM as a crop management strategy for years. IPM relies on cultural and biological controls to manage a farm's ecosystem, as opposed to strictly chemical means. Proper plant selection, proper soil preparation, pest population monitoring and threshold development—i.e., determining the actual point at which pesticides should be applied to protect a crop's economic value from pest damage—are fundamental to IPM. While chemical controls may be used, they are selectively applied to minimize damage to the ecosystem. RJO currently uses basic IPM on all of its apple acreage. Within five years, RJO plans to have 100% of its acreage managed using advanced IPM techniques.

While advanced IPM is acknowledged among scientific and industry communities as a low-impact, more "natural" method of crop management, RJO plans to go further along the sustainability continuum to certified organic production. This is planned, in part, in response to market demand for organic products. As Biltonen explained, consumers "know biodynamic and they know organic. Trying to identify with IPM, as a standalone concept, is pretty much a lost cause. It needs to be marketed in conjunction with other sustainability efforts." While advanced IPM is not itself highly marketable, its use will reap a benefit for RJO, as it will make certified organic production both easier and more cost-effective to implement.

RJO's apricots, prunes and plums are also Food Alliance certified. The certification, which assesses the sustainability of an entire operation—environmental factors as well as social justice factors, such as worker pay—was important to RJO to help consumers understand their intentions as a company. As Biltonen explained, "What people want to know more than anything else is that you are at least trying to do things right on the farm. Certification can assist with that." Nicholson adds, "We shared the Food Alliance values and it had a solid reputation. And, as 'local' becomes more ubiquitous, we need to find ways to continually differentiate ourselves in the marketplace. Food Alliance is helping us achieve that." Over the next few years, RJO plans to seek Food Alliance certification for other products that it markets.

RJO's commitment to sustainability will, eventually, influence its choice of packing materials and fleet vehicles. Today, however, the company is focusing on improving its farming practices, as this alone will take significant effort and time. As Biltonen explained, "Becoming green and becoming more sustainable isn't something we can do with a flip of a switch. It's an evolutionary process, one that we are committed to throughout our company."

RJO is a unique company that has managed to maintain its independence and thrive as a family-owned business in spite of a decades-long trend toward consolidation in the fruit industry. The company's integrated farming, supply chain, marketing and sales efforts have allowed it to consistently bring high-quality, unique products to market. Its commitment to product diversity and sustainability also make it an exemplar in the industry.

Discussion Questions

1. How has consumer preference impacted the produce supply chain in the last century? How might increasing demand for organic or local products influence the produce industry today?
2. What is the cold chain? What are the environmental impacts of cold chain management and how might these impacts be reduced?

3. Define spot market purchasing, contracting and vertical integration. How are these concepts employed in the industry?
4. Describe the benefits and drawbacks of the "buy local" movement from the farmer's perspective. Describe the benefits and drawbacks of the "buy local" movement from a purchaser's perspective.
5. Research a recent food safety problem in the produce industry. Briefly describe the nature of the problem and identify where in the supply chain the issue is thought to have occurred. How did the problem impact producers, retailers and consumers?

Additional Readings and Links

- *Edible Communities*, a national network of quarterly publications featuring news about local producers and agricultural issues. To see if an *Edible* publication is written for your area, go to http://www.ediblecommunities.com/content/edible-publications/
- A one-hour documentary on sustainable agriculture, written from the perspective of the Washington apple industry: *Broken Limbs: Apples, Agriculture and the New American Farmer;* available for purchase at http://www.broken-limbs.org/
- The *Iowa Local Food & Farm Plan*, an interesting example of how government is moving to support "local": http://www.leopold.iastate.edu/foodandfarm/ilffp.pdf
- Pirog, R., T. Van Pelt, K. Enshayan and E. Cook. 2001. "Food, Fuel, and Freeways: An Iowa Perspective On How Far Food Travels, Fuel Usage, And Greenhouse Gas Emissions." Leopold Center for Sustainable Agriculture, Ames, Iowa.

6
FOOD REGULATIONS AND VERIFICATION MECHANISMS

The first national grocery chain to embrace a program to measure the environmental impact of its wild-caught seafood is Whole Foods Market, which recently teamed with the Monterey Bay Aquarium and the Blue Ocean Institute to create a color-coded seafood rating system. All seafood in Whole Foods stores is rated on the primary environmental factors affecting it: fishing methods and concerns about over-fishing of the species. Ratings include green, yellow and red, with green-rated seafood considered sustainable, a yellow rating indicating concerns exist about the species' status or catch methods, and red being given to fish that are caught in a way that is harmful to other wildlife or that are overfished. Whole Foods is using this color-coded, first party endorsement system in conjunction with its third party Marine Stewardship Council certification program, which certifies wild-caught seafood as sustainable.

Introduction

Consumer interest in ecological and social issues is at an all-time high, with more than 50% of consumers considering at least one sustainability factor when choosing a consumer good. Books and films revealing problems with the food chain have become extremely popular, including Michael Pollan's best-selling book, *The Omnivore's Dilemma*, and the films *Food, Inc.* and *King Corn*. Consistent media coverage of food safety issues and revelations about animal handling practices, food contamination, employee treatment and many other processing and supply chain problems are also encouraging consumers to strengthen their food purchasing criteria. Formerly, consumers chose products on the basis of value, convenience and price. Now, in addition to those criteria, they consider factors like healthiness, food miles, environmental stewardship, farmer justice and brand authenticity.

Not only have consumers added to their list of criteria; their priorities are shifting. Social issues such as where and how a product is made are gaining in priority while attributes like convenience are slipping. As Chris Pomfret, a Unilever marketing executive explained: "People want to know what lies behind a brand and the extent to which its values are aligned with their own ... Today, the issue is what a brand says about someone, as a badge indicative of the individual's values and view of the world."

However, while values like convenience and price are easy for a customer to discern, most of the newer consumer values cannot be readily discerned during the purchasing encounter. For example, consumers can easily detect color, size and price from observation. These types of things are referred to as readily apparent attributes. But, most content and process attributes are imperceptible. For example, the difference between genetically modified corn and conventional corn, or organic produce and conventional produce, or the animal handling practices used to create a product are difficult if not impossible to identify on the surface.

Distinguishing characteristics that cannot easily be identified by consumers are called credence attributes. These attributes can refer to the content or physical properties of a product (e.g., calcium in milk or Omega 3 in juice) or production process characteristics (e.g., country-of-origin, shade-grown, organic, humane treatment). Producers of these foods need to communicate these attributes to consumers for the attributes to be known. Thus, the consumer typically relies on information conveyed by the producer through some kind of marketing claim, transmitted by a label, website or other information source.

In this chapter, we look at how credence attribute claims are conveyed to consumers, and how these claims are regulated by the government and verified by industry and non-profit organizations. We first look at government's role—specifically the USDA's role—in regulating food quality and information claims. We then examine the types of claims that can be made around food credence attributes. Finally, we explore the food certifications that have gained a significant market presence worldwide.

Food Regulation and Verification

The USDA plays a dominant role in food product regulation and verification. USDA was created on May 15, 1862 when Abraham Lincoln signed the Agricultural Act. Today the USDA is headed by the Secretary of Agriculture. The department's main functions are to promote farmer welfare, protect food safety, research agricultural practices and study American and international production and consumption patterns. Over time different agencies have formed within the USDA to address each of these responsibilities, as summarized in Table 6.1.

Table 6.1 **USDA Food Agencies**

Mission Area	Agencies of the USDA	Purpose
Farm and Foreign Agricultural Service	Foreign Agricultural Service Risk Management Agency Farm Service Agency	These agencies help protect farmers from the uncertainties of farming by offering assistance to farmers through the use of commodity, credit and emergency assistance programs.
Food, Nutrition and Consumer Service	Food and Nutrition Service Center for Nutrition Policy and Promotion	These agencies use nutritional science to improve health within the US through nutrition education and policy.
Food Safety	Food Safety and Inspection Service	The FSIS strives to ensure that the county's proteins are safe to eat and properly labeled.
Marketing and Regulatory Programs	Agricultural Marketing Service Animal and Plant Health Inspection Service Grain Inspection, Packers and Stockyards Administration	These agencies work nationally and internationally to market US food products.
Natural Resources and Environment	Forest Service Natural Resources Conservation Service Office of Environmental Markets	These agencies fight to protect and restore the natural environment through the use of good land management practices.
Research, Education and Economics	Research, Education and Economics National Institute ofFood and Agriculture Agricultural Research Service Economic Research Service Natural Agricultural Library National Agricultural Statistics Service	These agencies conduct research and development activities to create a competitive US food system.
Rural Development	Rural Development	This agency works to improve the nation's rural communities.

Source: USDA.

With regard to claims verification, the USDA allows certain terms to be used on food, such as organic, natural, naturally raised, cage free, free range, free roaming, pasture raised and grass fed. Some of these terms have vague working definitions. In many cases, compliance is not verified through on-site audits. Rather, producers simply supply documentation if requested. Certified organic and cage free claims do require verification, however.

To ensure the safety of America's foods, the USDA's Food Safety and Inspection Service (FSIS) holds mandatory inspections of many food products. The Federal Meat Inspection Act of 1906, in conjunction with the Poultry Products Inspection Act of 1957, mandates inspection of all meat and poultry products sold across state lines. FSIS also monitors state programs that inspect meat, for example, the Iowa Department of Agriculture's Meat and Inspection Bureau. State meat inspection programs exist to facilitate the inspection of meats that will be sold intrastate only. Meat grading is also conducted by the FSIS, but quality grading is a voluntary program that must be paid for by the producer. In addition, the FSIS inspects all pasteurized egg products for safety. All other food products are regulated by the Food and Drug Administration (FDA).

Marketing Claims Verification

As the demand for values-based products increases, producers are seeing new opportunities for increased revenue, and thus both authentic and "green-washed" product claims have exploded in number. Consequently, consumers are increasingly in the position of needing to determine for themselves the validity of credence attribute claims. To understand their product choices, consumers must therefore consider what is expressed or implied, what is needed to substantiate the claim and how the claim is qualified. Claims are therefore separated into three different groups: first-, second- and third-party claims.

FIRST-PARTY CLAIMS

In a first-party claim, producers state that they have produced their products a certain way. No outside verification applies. Rather, buyers need to simply trust the producer, or invest their time to assess the claim. Examples of first-party claims are statements like "produced in location X" or "eco-friendly." In the first case, the food product could indeed be grown in location X. It could also just be packaged or assembled in location X and not actually grown there. In the second case, eco-friendly means nothing in particular and this claim, while common, is not regulated or verified by any agency or organization. Therefore, although certain attributes are implied, "eco-friendly" actually has no clear meaning or significance. In a third example, a farmer at a farmers' market could verbally state that he or she uses organic methods. While consumers typically trust farmers selling at these venues, no outside verification has occurred to support this claim.

First party claims can also be issued by industry groups. For example, there are numerous industry groups claiming to handle animals in a humane manner. For beef, the National Cattlemen's Beef Association (NCBA) states that its herds are humanely raised, based on its guidelines for the care and handling of beef cattle. However, NCBA's guidelines specify that access to pasture is not required; that confinement to feedlots is acceptable; and that hot iron branding, castration without anesthesia and the use of electric cattle prods are allowed. Additionally, NCBA does not audit to its guidelines and the NCBA has declared publicly that it doesn't believe auditing of animal care is necessary. NCBA also has no quality assurance program.

SECOND-PARTY CLAIMS

In a second-party claim, a purchasing entity certifies that a producer has met a certain set of guidelines. The producer's assessment is performed by a person or organization that has a user interest in the product (e.g., traders, retailers or consumers and their organizations). For instance, retail grocery organizations may develop purchasing guidelines for food products, have their sellers verify that their products meet these guidelines, and then make claims to their customers that their products have a certain set of attributes. One of the challenges with this certification type is that collusion can occur between producers and sellers, at the expense of the consumer. Namely, both the producer and the seller may benefit from making certain claims; thus, the depth and significance of the claim may be less than what is implied.

THIRD-PARTY CLAIMS

In a third-party claim, an independent party with no vested interest in the outcome conducts an audit to determine if a producer has met certain standards. Third-party certifications are considered the most credible since the evaluating party is independent of the supplier, the retailer and the consumer. Certifiers are public or private organizations responsible for accessing, evaluating and verifying safety, quality, process and other claims based on a set of standards and compliance methods. Examples of systems, processes and products include Good Agricultural Practices, Good Manufacturing Practices, and/or Good Management Practices (e.g., ISO 9000); labor practices (e.g., Fairtrade); environmental standards (e.g., ISO 14000, Rainforest Alliance); organic, biodynamic or sustainability standards (e.g. Oregon Tilth, USDA Organic, Demeter Biodynamic® Farm Standard, Food Alliance). Some private retailers also have standards that are audited by independent third parties. McDonald's animal handling standards are an example of this.

Because third-party certifications are the most popular and legitimate of all food certification mechanisms, the remainder of this chapter will cover the significant third-party certifications in the marketplace.

Government Certifications

USDA Organic

The Organic Trade Association considers organic production to be "the most heavily regulated and closely monitored production system in the Unites States." Organic food came under regulation when the Organic Food Production Act (OFPA) of 1990 established the National Organic Program (NOP) to create and enforce standards for organic production. NOP describes organic production systems as responsive to "site specific conditions…integrating cultural, biological and mechanical practices that foster cycling of resources, promote ecological balance and conserve biodiversity."

NOP requires that an Accredited Certifying Agent (ACA) inspect a producer's facilities and ensure compliance with OFPA standards before it marks its product with one of the three allowed organic labels. In order to be labeled "100% organic," a product must be made entirely from organic ingredients. A simple "organic" label may used on products with at least 95% organic ingredients, and products with more than 70% organic ingredients may be labeled "made with organic." To maintain their certification, producers are obligated to participate in annual and random inspections. Farms with less than $5,000 in gross annual agricultural income from production are exempt from the certification process.

While NOP spells out many of the details of organic production, certain restrictions are key to the program. Organic food products must be produced without the use of synthetic substances, except those named on the National List of Allowed and Prohibited Substances. Examples of allowed substances are shown in Table 6.2. Also, land used for farming must not have had any prohibited substances applied for a minimum of three years before certification. Fertilization, pest control and soil quality are to be managed using sustainable methods like crop rotation, cover crops and permanent vegetation. Additionally, all seeds must be sourced from a certified organic seed company and the use of genetically modified organisms is prohibited.

Animals certified as organic must be fed an organic diet and live under conditions that simulate the animal's natural environment, such as access to pasture and natural sunlight. The use of growth hormones and antibiotics are prohibited. Livestock must also spend a majority of their life living according to organic standards. For instance, organic management must start by the second day of life for poultry and one year prior to giving milk for dairy animals.

Table 6.2 **List of NOP-Approved and Prohibited Substances**

	Non-agricultural substances allowed	Synthetic substances allowed (crops)	Non-synthetic substances prohibited (crop)	Synthetic substances allowed (livestock)	Non-synthetic substances prohibited (livestock)
Example	Acids (citric, lactic, ascorbic)	Alcohols	Ash from manure burning	Alcohols	
	Yeast (nonsynthetic)	Ethanol	Arsenic	Aspirin approved for health care	
	Microorganisms	Isopropanol	Lead salts	Glucose	
	Dairy cultures	Soap based herbicides	Tobacco dust	Electrolytes (without antibiotics)	Strychnine
	Calcium carbonate	Soap-based algaecide	Sodium fluoaluminate	Chlorine dioxide	
	Silicon dioxide	Elemental sulfur	Sodium nitrate (restricted	Butorphanol vaccine	
	Xanthan gum	Vitamin D3	to no more than 20% of crop's nitrogen requirement)	(with written consent of licensed veterinarian)	

Source: GPO Access.

All other livestock must live under organic management from the last third of gestation or hatching.

Manufacturers of organic processed goods must also be certified organic by an ACA. A finished product must be made from at least 95% organic ingredients to carry an organic label. The last 5% of the product may be made with non-organic ingredients. This leaves room for certain ingredients that do not exist widely in organic form. For example, because supplies of organic hops are very small, the USDA decided to allow the use of non-organic hops in certified organic beer. Other allowed ingredients include non-agricultural substances like lactic acid and citric acid, and non-organically grown agricultural products like cornstarch and gum arabic. Packaging materials must also meet organic standards and not include any prohibited substances.

USDA organic standards also address commingling issues. Farmers and food processors are expected to take preventive measures to keep organic foods from coming in contact with non-organic foods. Producers must maintain documentation proving that they took all steps necessary to prevent commingling in order to maintain their certification. Identity preservation is critical to organic foods because the product must be able to be traced back to the farm to ensure its integrity. Falsely portraying a product as organic constitutes an $11,000 fine for each offense.

The US organic market has displayed steady, long-term growth since its official inception in 1990. In this year, sales of organic food products were $1 billion. In 2009, 3.7% of all food and beverage products sold were certified organic, comprising a $24.8 billion market. In line with these numbers, organic product availability has vastly increased. Today, organic products are available in 20,000 natural food stores and 75% of conventional grocery stores. Farmers are also benefiting from these trends. In 2007, the average organic farm had $217,675 in sales, while traditional farms reported an average of only $134,807 in sales. The growth in organic food product sectors between 2000 and 2010 is illustrated in Figure 6.1.

Because the organic sector has had steady growth since the mid-1990s, many large food processing firms have entered the market. Many of the largest food processors in North America, like Kraft, ConAgra, and Dean Foods are now involved in organics. While many companies have launched organic lines of their existing brands, horizontal integration is also a widely used method to enter the market; i.e., large companies acquire existing organic brands. These relationships are often kept quiet so that the integrity of the organic brand does not come into question. Today, popular organic brands like Kashi,

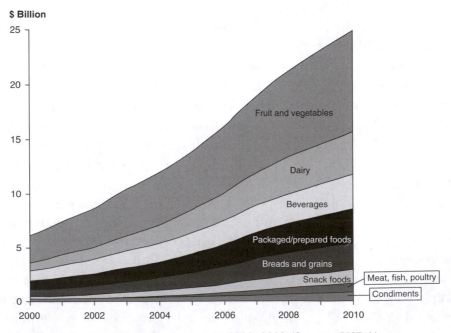

Figure 6.1 **Growth in the organic food sectors, 2000–2010** (Source: USDA).

Odwalla and Boca Foods are owned by Kellogg, Coca Cola and Kraft, respectively. Many consumers are unaware of these relationships, however. Ownership of many well-known organic brands is illustrated in Figure 6.2.

International Organic Standards

The European Union (EU), Canada and Japan each have their own organic standards. Governments in these countries use ACAs as third-party certifiers, similar to the way organic claims are verified in the United States. The EU implemented organic production regulations in 1991. Certification is executed at the national level, so many different national certification logos exist within the EU. To reduce confusion, an international EU certification logo was launched in 2010 to phase out and replace the individual national logos. Many of the EU regulations are similar to those in the US, the main difference being that land only has to undergo a two-year conversion period to become organic, rather than the US standard of three years.

Canada implemented Canadian Organic Standards (COS) with the creation of its Organic Products Regulations in 2009. Products are required to be certified if they carry the organic label, or if they are traded over provincial or international borders. Because the United States and Canada are such large trading partners they have formed an equivalency agreement honoring one another's organic certifications, with a few exceptions. This means that US farmers will only need to be certified under NOP and not also COS when products are exported to Canada, and vice versa. However, because the two regulatory systems have some fundamental differences, exceptions apply. The use of antibiotics is allowed in dairy cows under COS, so these may not be sold as organic within the United States. Similarly, COS does not consider produce from soil-less systems as organic, so US farmers may not label hydroponic and aeroponic produce as organic in Canada.

In 2000, Japanese Agricultural Standards (JAS) for all agricultural production—including organic production—were established. These were reviewed in 2005 and standards for organic livestock production were added. Farmers and processors who are certified with a Japanese ACA are allowed to use the Japanese certified organic label on their products. Japan began honoring NOP standards in 2002 when an equivalency agreement was reached with the United States. Some exceptions exist to this agreement, primarily foods produced with certain chemicals that are not allowed under JAS.

Non-Government Food Certifications

While the USDA Organic standard covers a wide variety of food types, the program is primarily concerned with the environmental aspects of food

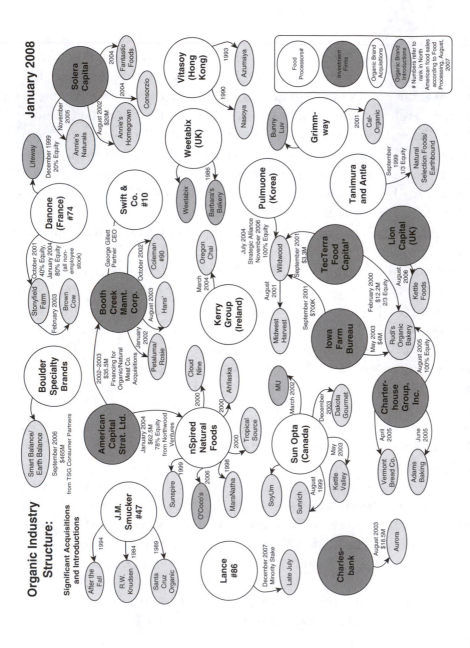

Figure 6.2 **Organic industry structure: significant acquisitions and introductions** (Source: Phil Howard, Assistant Professor, Dept of Community, Agriculture, Recreation and Resource Studies, Michigan State University. www.certifiedorganic.bc.ca/rcbtoa/). *Notes:* *Investors include the State of Iowa, Pioneer, DuPont and ADM. Numbers refer to rank in North American food sales according to Food Processing, August, 2007.

production. Thus, substantial room exists in the market for certification programs aimed at other consumer concerns. Non-governmental and nonprofit organizations fill this niche. Their certification standards and labels vary primarily by the scope of the social and environmental criteria they assess and the food types they examine, as shown in Figure 6.3. The Ecolabel Index, a global directory of various certification programs, has documented 125 food-related certification programs worldwide. Of these, 40 labels are operating in North America. The remainder of this section will discuss the most recognizable non-governmental certifications in the United States and abroad.

FAIRTRADE

The concept of fair trade emerged more than 60 years ago through alternative trade organizations that offered consumers in developed countries products purchased directly from small producers in developing countries. The first fair trade certification initiative began in 1988, triggered by a sharp drop in world coffee prices when the International Coffee Association failed to renegotiate price quotas. This initiative culminated in the first fair trade certified coffee and label, "Max Havelaar," named after a fictional Dutch character that opposed the exploitation of coffee pickers in Dutch colonies.

In 1997 the Fairtrade Labelling Organizations International (FLO) united Max Havelaar with fair trade movements that had developed in other countries. Thus, FLO became the international umbrella organization for 17 fair trade

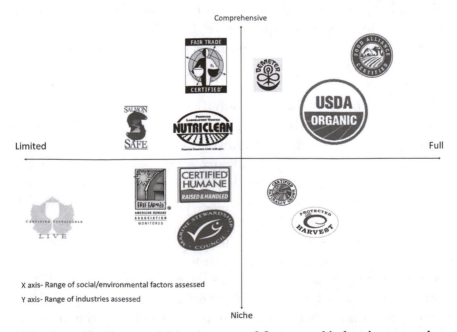

X axis- Range of social/environmental factors assessed
Y axis- Range of industries assessed

Figure 6.3 **Food certifications: social/environmental factors and industries assessed**

labeling organizations worldwide. FLO's focus is to enhance economic and environmental sustainability for farmers and their communities, guaranteeing a minimum purchase price to fully cover production costs and social premiums to enable investment in producer communities. With coffee, for example, the base price paid for Fairtrade coffee in 2009 was USD $1.26 per raw pound, with an additional $0.15 added for organic coffee.

Importers purchase from Fairtrade producer groups as directly as possible, aiming to eliminate the middle man and help farmers compete in the global market. The Fairtrade standards ensure that employees who work for Fairtrade farms have safe working conditions and fair wages, and that they have "freedom of association," or the right to unionize if desired. Fairtrade farmers and farm workers decide how to invest Fairtrade revenues, typically investing premiums in social and business development projects such as scholarship programs and healthcare services. Fairtrade standards also encourage, although they do not require, that certified organizations implement an integrated crop management system to minimize environmental impact.

FLO has two sets of standards, one for small farmer cooperatives and one for organizations with hired labor, and focuses its certification activities solely in developing countries. A related, but independent, organization performs the certifications for FLO. Today, Fairtrade certifies bananas, cocoa, coffee, flowers, fruit, honey, juices, rice, herbs, sugar, tea and wine (along with non-food products like cotton, sports balls and composite products). In 2008, Fairtrade certified sales amounted to approximately $4.5 billion worldwide, with 827 certified producer organizations representing over 1.2 million farmers and workers in 58 countries. Approximately $57 million was distributed to communities in 2008 for use in community development initiatives.

FOOD ALLIANCE

Food Alliance is a non-profit organization that develops sustainable agriculture and food handling standards. The group launched in 1993 in the Pacific Northwest, creating a market incentive for the adoption of sustainable agricultural practices. Today, Food Alliance is the most comprehensive of the food standards. Through independent third-party verification (International Certifiers Association), farms, ranches, food packers, processors and distributors can be certified; standards exist for many different types of produce, animals and commodities.

Food Alliance certification is a lengthy process. Participants pay an initial fee for a comprehensive onsite audit assessing soil, water and wildlife habitat conservation; labor practices; pesticide reduction; and animal welfare, after which a continual improvement plan is drafted. Participants obtain a trial membership and have two years to make the operational changes necessary to retain certification. Food Alliance certification requires a signed affidavit and audit renewal every three years. After gaining certification, producers pay either a flat minimum yearly fee or a fee based on percentage of sales (whichever is more) to use the Food Alliance label on their products and marketing materials.

To date, Food Alliance has certified 275 farms and ranches in the United States and Canada—spanning 5.1 million acres—and 18 processing and distribution facilities in the United States. Food Alliance certified product sales are estimated at $100 million. Food Alliance's certification criteria are detailed in Table 6.3.

MARINE STEWARDSHIP COUNCIL

Like Food Alliance, the Marine Stewardship Council (MSC) develops standards and ensures certification to those standards, although MSC's standards specifically focus on sustainable fishing and traceability in the seafood supply chain. MSC was founded in 1997 by the World Wide Fund for Nature, an NGO, and Unilever. The organization became fully independent in 1999. As of 2010, there are 7,220 seafood products with the MSC eco-label sold in 74 countries worldwide, and 97 fisheries have been certified as meeting MSC's environmental standard for sustainable fishing. An additional 132 fisheries are currently undergoing assessment. Over 1,500 companies have met MSC's Chain of Custody standard for seafood traceability.

Public awareness of the MSC eco-label has more than doubled since 2008, according to market research. Close to one in four adults in the United States, Canada, Germany, the United Kingdom, France and Japan are aware of the MSC sustainability certification label. Germany boasts the highest level of awareness at 36%, up from 11% in 2008. Companies such as Whole Foods and Wal-Mart are buoying this trend, supporting the MSC certification and using the standard to buy their wild-caught seafood. Despite its increasing popularity, the organization has been criticized by some because it refuses to certify aquaculture programs and has created an exclusive sustainability label that has dramatically inflated the price of sustainably sourced fish.

FOOD CARBON FOOTPRINT AND LIFE CYCLE ASSESSMENT

One of the newest areas of food certification and labeling involves assessment of carbon dioxide (CO_2) emissions. An estimated 25% of the emissions produced by industrialized nations comes from their food production systems. Numerous causes exist: an intense reliance on pesticides and fertilizers, large livestock industries, fossil-fuel intensive food transportation methods, factory processing, packaging and large-scale distribution systems.

The carbon footprint—or the total set of greenhouse gases emitted by a food product—is a sub-category of the Life Cycle Assessment standard.

Table 6.3 **Food Alliance Certification Audit Criteria**

Criteria

Fixed Standards*

- No GMO seeds (or breeds) used
- No Food Alliance-prohibited pesticides used
- No hormones used
- No sub-therapeutic (feed additive) antibiotics used
- Continuous improvement

Soil and Water Conservation Evaluation Criteria

- Continuing education for soil and water conservation
- Buffer strips around waterways
- Soil erosion prevention
- Tillage selection practices and soil compaction prevention
- Irrigation systems
- Irrigation water conservation
- Nutrient management
- Soil organic matter management

Reducing Pesticide Usage Evaluation Criteria

- Continuing education for reducing pesticide usage
- Integrated pest management planning
- Weather monitoring
- Crop monitoring/field scouting
- Lowest effective application rates/reducing application rates
- Pesticide selection, justification and resistance management
- Pesticide record keeping
- Application equipment calibration and pesticide drift management
- Hazardous material storage

Safe and Fair Working Conditions Evaluation Criteria

- Minors, children and family members in the workplace
- Grievance procedures and policies
- Recognizing and supporting employee input for workplace improvement
- Farm worker support services
- Discipline process
- Nondiscrimination policy
- Hiring practices and communicating expectations and policies
- Work force development and new skills training
- Compensation practices
- Employee benefits
- Worker housing and family support services
- Pesticide handler/applicator safety
- Hazardous materials emergency management
- Sanitation and general safety

Wildlife Habitat Conservation Evaluation Criteria

- Continuing education for wildlife habitat conservation
- Habitat conservation improvements
- Invasive species prevention and management
- Threatened and endangered species protection
- Wildlife food, cover, and water
- Linking individual wildlife habitat conservation activities together

* Note that companies being audited must comply entirely with Fixed Standards, and must attain an average score of at least 3.0 in each of other four areas assessed.
Source: Food Alliance.

FOOD REGULATIONS AND VERIFICATION MECHANISMS

137

Carbon emissions from agriculture, processing, packaging and distribution/
transportation comprise a food product's carbon footprint. The complete Life
Cycle Assessment of a product also considers the use of natural resources and
chemical inputs in the production process or raw extraction stage, and the
emissions or pollution outputs that occur during the production, distribution
and use of the product. The complete Life Cycle Assessment process also
considers product waste and waste disposal transportation activities. The results
of carbon analysis are reported in kilograms of carbon dioxide per kilogram of
product.

European countries and retailers are making an effort to develop labels that
effectively communicate carbon emissions data to consumers. Great Britain and
Sweden have particularly ambitious carbon labeling programs.

In 2001, the British government created an independent company, the
Carbon Trust, to help move the country to a low-carbon economy. Carbon Trust
developed a measuring standard (PAS 2050), which is now an industry norm.
Carbon Trust has helped retailers use and communicate carbon emissions
data to their consumers through their "Carbon Reduction Label," shown in
Figure 6.4. For example, Tesco started working with Carbon Trust in 2007 to
assess the footprint of 20 of its products, including orange juice and potatoes.
After assessment, these products were labeled to help consumers understand
the impact of these products and their purchasing choices. Tesco plans to
label 70,000 of its grocery products with carbon emissions data about their
manufacturing and distribution processes.

The Nutrition Department of the Swedish National Food Administration has
also implemented a carbon footprint labeling program for selected grocery and
fast food products. Several Swedish companies are also putting emissions
calculations on their food items. For instance, the burger restaurant Max posts
emissions information on its menu board, and Lantmannen, a farmer group,
labels its chicken, oatmeal, barley, and pasta products.

One of the challenges of emissions labeling is that research and discussion
about the carbon assessment process is ongoing. Agreements have not yet been
made about which inputs to include (e.g., fertilizers, fuel for tractors,
packaging, product transportation) and which to exclude (e.g., tractor
manufacturing, retailing energy costs). Additionally, variations in nature and
agricultural practices create variability in the food supply chain. Debates
therefore exist over whether products should have permanent scores or have
their scores updated according to season and location. Likewise, debates exist
over whether individual product streams should be measured, or if product
stream averages should instead be scored. Sweden's system uses average scores,
but an organizing body is needed to address questions like these and develop
unified standards.

reducing with
the Carbon Trust

Figure 6.4 **Carbon Trust label**

Conclusion

As consumers look to buy food products that match their social and environmental values, governments, nonprofits and industry leaders are responding with certification schemes, regulations and eco-labels. In many cases, these labels have helped create and support a sustainable food system. But, improvements could be made to avoid "greenwashing" in the food industry. For example, a government eco-labeling program that considers the environmental aspects of all phases of food production, processing and distribution could help consumer decision making. However, existing regulatory agency perspectives would need to shift, and numerous parties would need to agree on measurement approaches. With the ongoing proliferation of eco-labels, especially in the food arena, it is in the best interest of consumers and society to consider a consolidated and objective approach to eco-labeling, since the overuse of independent certifications and labels could reduce the effectiveness of the concept.

Case Study: **Portland Roasting Coffee Company**

As Mark Stell waited to board the plane to Bujumbura, the capital city of Burundi in Africa, he contemplated an exciting market opportunity for his coffee roasting company. Within a few short weeks, Portland Roasting Coffee Company (PRC) was pitching Fred Meyer, a major regional grocery retailer, and landing this account could help grow revenues by as much as 25%. Last year, Stell had made significant investments in new roasting and packaging equipment and he knew he had the capacity and infrastructure to supply a large account.

PRC would also promote the virtues of the Farm Friendly Direct (FFD) program. From the beginning, PRC had developed trade relationships with individual coffee growers, paid premium prices and invested additional funds in local projects that directly benefited the lives of coffee farmers and their communities. The FFD program was featured on the company's website, in marketing materials and on product packaging. PRC would have to convince Fred Meyer that FFD coffee was superior to conventional third-party certifications such as Fairtrade, USDA Organic and Rainforest Alliance certified coffees offered by competitors.

Stell also realized that the FFD program alone would not be sufficient to secure the account. Grocery retailers were also concerned about price, order fulfillment, marketing support, product quality and customer service, in addition to the sustainability attributes of a product. Stell pondered several questions during the long flight: Was third-party certification going to drive changes in the industry? Or, could FFD attract conscientious vendors and consumers? And, if so, could FFD's direct trade model ensure a sustainable supply of specialty coffee over the long term?

Company Profile

Portland Roasting Coffee Company was headquartered in the bustling central eastside industrial district of Portland, Oregon. The 20,000-square-foot facility contained roasting equipment, warehouse space, a coffee tasting facility and offices for 27 employees. PRC's core business was sourcing, roasting and distributing high-quality coffees to wholesale customers, including retail coffee shops, restaurants, businesses, food merchants and institutions. Consumers could purchase PRC coffees directly through the company's website. The company also sold coffee equipment and associated supplies, including a line of flavored syrups. Coffees were sourced from more than 20 different countries and FFD relationships existed with farmers and cooperatives in Guatemala, Costa Rica, El Salvador, Ethiopia, India, Papua New Guinea, Sumatra and Tanzania, as illustrated in Figure 6.5.

When Stell opened PRC in 1996, he chose to focus exclusively on the wholesale coffee business. Stell explained his original vision: "What we saw was a niche for small quality coffee roasters that had creative marketing, creative design and upscale packaging. We wanted to be synonymous with Portland and we wanted to buy sustainable products. Being as sustainable as possible has always been our motivation."

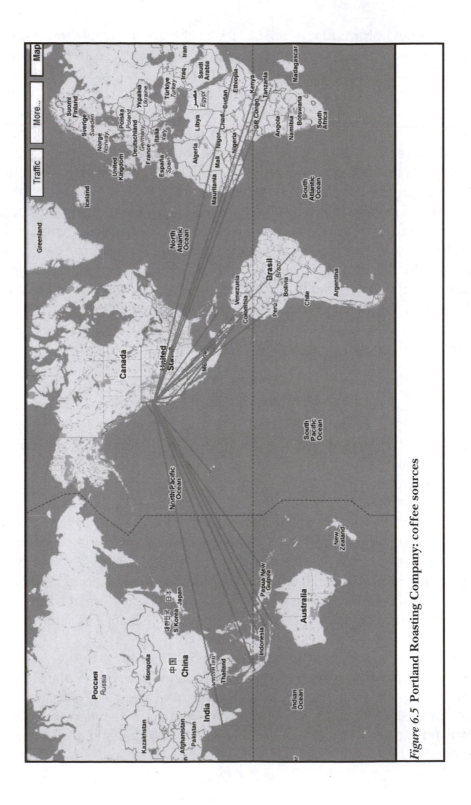

Figure 6.5 Portland Roasting Company: coffee sources

In its first year of operation PRC sold 40,000 pounds of coffee. Since then, PRC had experienced average annual growth of 20%. In 2007, the company sold 600,000 pounds of coffee, yielding approximately $5 million in revenues. After learning the pitfalls of having one customer represent 40% of total sales, PRC subsequently diversified across market segments and its largest customer now represented no more than 20% of total sales. In anticipation of continued growth—to hotel, mass grocer, university and other institutional accounts—PRC invested in new roasting and packaging equipment in 2008.

Coffee Production and Trade

Coffee is produced in more than 50 tropical countries, generally at or around 23.5 degrees north or south of the equator. Approximately 63% of coffee is produced in Latin America; 22% and 14% is produced in Southeast Asia and Africa, respectively. Similar to wine, coffee beans from different regions have distinct characteristics displayed in aroma, body, acidity and nuances of flavor. These variations are dependent not only on the appellation, or geographical location, but also the varietal grown and the manner in which the coffee is produced. The first flowers appear on coffee plants during the third year, but production is only profitable after the fifth year.

Coffee cherries typically ripen around 8 to 10 months after flowering and in most countries there is only one major harvest each year. Shade grown coffee often results in berries ripening more slowly, producing lower yields but with a higher quality and flavor. Ripened coffee cherries are typically harvested by hand, which is very labor intensive. Some coffee crops are picked all at once, but for better quality coffees only the ripe cherries are picked. For this reason, harvesting may be undertaken as many as five times during a season. The ripe berries have higher aromatic oils and lower organic acid content, lending to a more fragrant and smooth flavor. Because of this, the timing of coffee picking is one of the chief determinants of the quality of the end product.

After coffee is picked, it must be processed quickly to avoid spoilage. Each coffee cherry usually contains two coffee beans, covered by a silvery skin, a layer of parchment, a pectin layer, a pulp layer and finally the outer skin. These outer layers must be removed in one of two processing methods. The dry processing method is used in arid countries where water is scarce and humidity is low. Freshly picked cherries are simply spread out on large surfaces to dry in the sun. In order to prevent the cherries from spoiling, they are raked and turned throughout the day then covered at night. When the moisture content of the cherries drops to 11%, the dried cherries are moved to warehouses where they are stored. In wet processing, the freshly harvested cherries are passed through a pulping machine where the skin and pulp are separated from the bean. The beans are then transported to large, water-filled fermentation tanks for 12-48 hours, where naturally occurring enzymes dissolve the pectin layer. The beans are then removed from the tank and dried.

Most growers dry their coffee themselves and then sell their unprocessed coffee to intermediaries for milling. Intermediaries often make a large profit since small growers may not have direct access to buyers, and are thus forced to accept whatever price the intermediary offers. In order to compete against large coffee estates, many small growers—farming on just one to two hectares, as opposed to thousands of hectares—have formed cooperatives to help negotiate better prices from intermediaries, and to increase their market access. Milling involves a mechanical hulling process that removes the parchment layer from wet processed coffee or removes the entire dried husk from dry processed coffee cherries. The coffee beans are then graded and sorted by size and weight.

The intermediary sells its milled coffee beans to exporters or brokers who buy and sell coffee on commission, before passing it onto importers. Importers then sell the beans to roasters who roast, package and market the coffee to distributors and retailers. Roasting is generally performed in the importing country because coffee freshness diminishes rapidly after roasting. This way, the roasted beans reach the consumer as quickly as possible to ensure quality.

Large coffee importers and roasters purchase coffee futures and options traded on the Intercontinental Exchange (ICE). The ICE Futures US Coffee "C" contract is the benchmark for world coffee prices. The price of coffee has fluctuated dramatically, falling as low as $0.415 per pound in 2001 and reaching as high as $3.148 per pound in 1997. Price fluctuations are due to market influences such as natural disasters, supply surplus, transportation costs, political instability in producing countries and investor speculation.

For example, a frost in Brazil in 1975 and a drought in 1985 led to a sharp drop in coffee production and a significant increase in coffee prices. This price volatility is problematic for both farmers and commercial roasters, as it directly impacts profit margins and production costs. Just one year of low market prices can put a small farmer out of business. Coffee revenue is also a significant portion of the GDP for many equatorial countries. Burundi, Uganda and Ethiopia earn more than half of their export revenues from coffee alone. The economic disparity between producing and consuming countries, and the determination of a fair price, has long been a subject of debate within the coffee industry.

The Farmers' Perspective

Many countries with a climate appropriate for coffee production are in the developing world. This creates a unique set of challenges and opportunities for the coffee industry. Many of the tools, techniques, resources and technologies that farmers in the developed world use are either not affordable or not available to coffee farmers in developing countries. Unfortunately, there is also an inverse relationship between the quality of a coffee bean and the volume of beans that a coffee plant can produce. Finally, high quality coffee often requires more resources, time and attention in order to maximize the value of the bean. For instance, the beans mature at different times on the plant and must be hand-picked when they are ripe. Farmers must therefore choose to focus on either high quantity or high quality production strategies.

Unfortunately for many farmers, the harvest season is long, averaging two to four months. It then takes even more time to process the beans and get the finished product ready to ship. From the time a coffee cherry is picked to the time the bean arrives at its final destination, six months can pass. For most farmers, this is a long time to wait for payment, particularly when all of their costs of goods sold are incurred up front. This is a heavy financial burden for coffee farms of all sizes, but it particularly impacts small farms and the premium producers who have higher costs of production.

Historically, this is where the exporters have added value in the supply chain. Exporters will often finance the crop once it is ready to ship, or sometimes before the crop is harvested, depending on the needs of the farmer. Such arrangements allow farmers to pay for labor and processing before the crop has been harvested. These arrangements also enable roasters to purchase coffee beans as they need them as opposed to trying to buy all of their needs for the season. This, in turn, helps roasters maintain a more stable cash flow, and in some cases eliminates the need for expensive storage and warehousing.

Just one generation ago, many farmers had no knowledge of the value of coffee in foreign markets. Today, however, it is easy to look up prices on the Internet. Access to information is really benefiting the farmer since they know much more about markets, prices, promotions and perhaps most importantly, the value of consistent quality. Access to information has also led to a growing trend in direct trade between farmers and roasters. By reducing the number of middlemen, both the roaster and the grower can enjoy higher profits. Roasters like PRC can also add value to their product in the eyes of consumers by marketing the relationship and value they create for the farmer.

In addition to fluctuating coffee prices, farmers contend with many other challenges. The rising value of land for real estate development in many Central American countries, as well as competing crops, have pushed thousands of acres out of coffee production. In addition, the average age of coffee farmers is rising and the younger generation is not interested in following in the footsteps of their predecessors. Meanwhile, wage rates are also growing at an alarming rate, driving coffee production costs even higher. In Central America, the expansion of the Panama Canal is expected to drive up labor costs throughout the entire continent, as well.

The US Specialty Coffee Movement

Alfred Peet, an emigrant from The Netherlands, recognized the lack of quality coffee in the United States and opened his first coffee house in Berkeley in 1966. Peet's success inspired three college friends, Jerry Baldwin, Gordon Bowker and Zev Siegl, to open a coffee shop in Seattle's Pike Place Market in 1971, selling fresh brewed coffee as well as whole beans and supplies. They named the store Starbucks.

Other entrepreneurs began to recognize the market opportunity for roasting and selling wholesale specialty coffees to gourmet grocers and serving premium beans and fresh brewed coffee in retail coffeehouses. During the 1970s a small yet steadily increasing number of specialty coffee merchants opened businesses in cities along the East and West coasts and began making inroads into supermarket channels. The fledgling Specialty Coffee Association of America (SCAA) was formed in 1982 by 42 original charter members, at a time when specialty coffee amounted to less than 1% of total US coffee sales.

During a business trip to Milan, Starbucks' Director of Marketing, Howard Schulz, observed the popularity of espresso bars and visualized bringing the Italian café experience to America using premium coffee. In 1984 Schulz convinced Starbucks' owners to add an espresso bar inside an existing store. The concept was an instant hit.

Schulz left Starbucks the following year to open his own coffee shop, Il Giornale. With the backing of local investors, Il Giornale acquired Starbucks in 1987 and, as CEO, Schulz immediately embarked on an aggressive growth strategy driven by new store openings in major US cities. Starbucks went public in 1992 and the **initial public offering** provided the capital needed for rapid expansion domestically and internationally. Other large regional specialty coffee brands also experienced rapid growth during this time, including Gloria Jean's, Brothers Gourmet Coffee, The Coffee Connection, Seattle's Best, Caribou Coffee and Coffee People.

Following more than a decade of growth and consolidation among large retail coffee brands, the specialty coffee industry remained fragmented. The number of businesses providing products and services in the specialty coffee industry doubled to more than 26,000 between 2001 and 2009. By then, the SCAA boasted 1,918 member businesses consisting of retailers, roasters, producers, exporters and importers, as well as manufacturers of coffee processing equipment, in more than 40 countries. Among members, the SCAA identified at least 369 independent roasters in 2009. The percentage of adults drinking specialty coffee had grown from 3.3% to more than 17% in the past 10 years.

New Developments in the US Coffee Industry

By 2009, the US was the single largest consumer of coffee, buying close to 25% of total global output. US coffee sales had grown at an average rate of 23% every year since 2003 (adjusted for inflation) with retail coffee sales exceeding $6.5 billion in 2008. According to the National Coffee Association, 49% of Americans age 18 years or older drank some type of coffee beverage, and three-quarters of coffee consumed was made at home. Consumers were also buying less coffee by volume but paying more per pound, contributing to a growth in net sales.

Combined, Kraft Foods and Proctor & Gamble commanded more than 50% of the market for all roasted coffee sold in the United States and marketed numerous brands covering a wide spectrum of price points within various segments. However, these large companies were losing market share to smaller roasters. And, while Starbucks had grown into the largest specialty coffee company, followed by Peet's Coffee and Caribou Coffee, it was increasingly competing against national fast food retailers interested in gaining share; both McDonald's and Dunkin' Donuts had started selling their own brands of coffee and espresso drinks, for example.

In September 2007, the number of Starbucks customers fell in American stores for the first time in the history of the company, and in 2008 the company announced the closure of 600 stores. Meanwhile, foreign markets with consumers who had historically preferred to drink tea, such as in

England and much of Asia, had become large, growing market segments for many US coffee companies.

In conjunction with the industry trend toward higher quality, coffee roasters and retailers began promoting their coffees on the basis of sustainability. Wal-Mart launched six coffees under the Sam's Choice™ brand as part of its expansion of its eco-friendly and ethical product lines. Whole Foods launched its 365™ brand of coffee, noting fair trade practices and direct relationships with more than 40 growers. Kraft General Foods advertised that 30% of the beans that went into its Yuban coffee were officially certified by the Rainforest Alliance. Starbucks promoted its Shared Planet™ program, which had goals related to ethical sourcing, environmental stewardship and community involvement. Green Mountain Coffee Roasters, long recognized as an industry leader in environmentally friendly and socially responsible business practices, was ranked eleventh on the 2009 list of Forbes' 100 Fastest Growing Companies. In Stell's opinion, "Most of the growth in the SCAA is around sustainability, so whether it's Fairtrade, Organic, Utz Certified or Rainforest Alliance, sustainability is what's really moving our industry."

Certified Coffee

Within the coffee industry, the concept of sustainability was initially focused on concerns around the environmental and social impacts of large-scale coffee production. The International Coffee Agreement (ICA) of 1962 established a quota system that withheld coffee supplies in excess of market demand and also established quality standards in an effort to maintain stable prices and production. However, the initial ICA did nothing to address environmental or social concerns related to coffee production. There have been various renewals of the ICA, with the agreements of 2001 and 2007 focused on stabilizing the coffee economy through the promotion of coffee consumption, raising the standard of living for growers by providing economic counseling, expanding research and conducting studies on sustainability.

To address some of the shortcomings of the ICA, a number of worldwide coffee certification initiatives have been established to address what are commonly referred to as the three pillars of sustainability: economic, social and environmental development. In addition to promoting sustainability, certifications help with product differentiation. The leading certifications are summarized in Table 6.4. By 2006, certified coffees amounted to more

Table 6.4: Comparison of Coffee Certifications

Initiative	Fair Trade	Organic	Rainforest Alliance	Bird Friendly	4C	Utz Certification
Year Established	1970s	1973	1992	1997	2007	1997
Producer Focus	Small farmers	Mostly small farmers, some plantations	Mostly plantations, some small farmers	Mostly small farmers, some plantations		Mostly plantations, some small farmers
Fees to Producers	Cost of auditing and reinspection fee	Vary by certifier	Auditing costs plus annual fee based on size of farm	Cost of added days at inspection	Annual membership fee dependent on production levels	Auditing costs
Market Focus	All markets	All markets	All markets	All markets	Mainstream markets	All markets
Fees to Buyers	Licensed roasters pay US $0.05–$0.10/lb. Importers must provide pre-harvest financing when requested by coop	Vary by certifier from $700–$3,000/year	None	Importers pay US $100/year. Roasters pay US $0.25/lb	Annual membership fee dependent on import levels	US $0.01/lb
Standard Setting Body	Fairtrade Labeling Organizations International	International Federation of Organic Agricultural Movements	Sustainable Agricultural Network	Smithsonian Migratory Bird Center	Common Code for Coffee Community Association	Utz Certified
Monitoring Body	Autonomous non-profit certifier	Private certifiers regulated by state and accredited by NGO	Certification by member organizations	Private certifiers approved by initiative	Private certifiers approved by initiative	Private third-party certifiers approved by Utz Certified

Source: SCAA.

than 220,000 metric tons of coffee exports, or close to 4% of the world-wide green coffee market.

FAIRTRADE

As relayed in Chapter 6, Fairtrade's purpose is to enhance economic and environmental sustainability for farmers and their communities, guaranteeing a minimum purchase price to fully cover production costs and social premiums to enable investment in producer communities. The base price paid for Fairtrade coffee in 2009 was USD $1.26 per raw pound, with an additional $0.15 added for organic coffee. Importers purchase from Fairtrade producer groups as directly as possible, aiming to eliminate the middle man and help farmers compete in the global market.

For coffee, however, only cooperatives could participate in Fairtrade, excluding the large and small individual farmers who could not get certification on their own. Stell was concerned that a sufficient percentage of the price premiums were not making it past the producer cooperatives to the actual coffee farmers. Others in the sustainable coffee movement shared his concerns.

ORGANIC

The organic movement began in 1973 as a farming and certification system, focused solely on environmental issues. The USDA's National Organic Program sets guidelines for coffee roasters, who need be certified in order to market organic coffees in the United States. Organic certification regulates agricultural production practices, specifically aiming to eliminate the use of synthetic chemicals that are common in pesticides, herbicides and fungicides. In 2006, approximately 67,000 metric tons of organic coffee were sold throughout the world.

In order for coffee to be certified and labeled as organic in the United States it must be grown on land that has a buffer between the organic coffee plants and the closest traditional crop, and upon which no synthetic pesticides or other prohibited substances have been used for three years. The farmer must also have a sustainable crop rotation plan to prevent erosion and the depletion of soil nutrients. The initial amount of capital needed to grow an organic coffee crop is less than that for traditional coffee production since no synthetic fertilizers or pesticides are needed. However, organic methods typically yield smaller crops and thus organic farms tend to make less money relative to the size of their farm. While there is no set premium for organic coffees, the average price is roughly 20% higher than that for non-organic coffees. The premium is closely tied to the quality of the coffee.

Many small, family-owned coffee farms are organic by necessity since they cannot afford chemical pesticides and fertilizers. However, these small farms also cannot afford to pay for inspections to achieve certification, and therefore are unable to benefit by selling their beans for a higher price. Therefore, one common criticism of organic certification is that it focuses solely on environmental criteria while ignoring the social and economic aspects of running a business. Other certifications focus on sustainability by establishing social and economic criteria as well as environmental criteria.

RAINFOREST ALLIANCE

The Rainforest Alliance is a non-profit, tax-exempt organization whose mission is to conserve biodiversity through the promotion of sustainability in agriculture, forestry, tourism and other businesses. In order to be certified, coffee farms must maintain or restore enough natural forest cover to achieve 40% shade coverage, and there must be a minimum of 70 trees per hectare featuring 12 native tree species. The Rainforest Alliance social criteria focus on fair pay, health and safety benefits and schooling for local communities. If farms do not meet these standards, they can still be certified if they have a plan to meet these goals and are taking active steps to implement their plan.

The certification program is managed by the Sustainable Agriculture Network (SAN), a coalition of leading conservation groups in Belize, Brazil, Colombia, Costa Rica, Ecuador, El Salvador, Guatemala, Honduras, Mexico and the United States. The first coffee farms were certified through the Rainforest Alliance program in Guatemala in 1995. A common criticism of Rainforest Alliance certification is that a coffee with as little as 30% of its contents certified can be marketed with the Rainforest Alliance seal. In 2008, approximately 62,296 metric tons of Rainforest Alliance certified coffee were sold.

BIRD FRIENDLY®

Bird Friendly certification was started in 1996 by staff at the Smithsonian Migratory Bird Center (SMBC). The certification's criteria are based on ornithological research carried out by researchers in several Latin American countries and are focused on the biophysical aspects of shade on coffee plantations. SMBC requires that producers meet the requirements for organic certification first, and then meet additional criteria related to canopy height, foliage cover, diversity of woody species, total floristic diversity, structural diversity, leaf litter, herbs and forbs (flowering plant) ground cover, living fences, vegetative buffer zones around waterways and visual characteristics.

Bird Friendly certification does not address labor conditions. As Robert Rice with the SMBC stated in regards to the Bird Friendly certification, "It's a seal that just has a lot of scientific rigor behind it and people can rest assured that they're getting what they think they are paying for." The biggest challenge of Bird Friendly certification is related to the difficulty and cost of obtaining organic certification, which can require years of effort and expense. SMBC certifies farms for three years. In 2008, approximately 2,916 metric tons of Bird Friendly coffee were sold.

COMMON CODE FOR THE COFFEE COMMUNITY (4C)

The Common Code for the Coffee Community, also known as 4C, was established by the German Coffee Association (DKV) and the Deutsche Gesellschaft für Technische Zusammenarbeit (GTZ) with the goal of facilitating more sustainable coffee production. Building on best agricultural and management practices, the 4C code of conduct aims to eliminate the most unacceptable coffee growing practices while encouraging ongoing improvement.

4C distinguishes itself from USDA Organic, Fairtrade, Rainforest Alliance and Utz certifications by relying on an internal monitoring system incorporated into the initiative's business model, rather than third party compliance verification. 4C has no set price premiums, allowing free negotiation between 4C members with prices reflecting coffee quality and sustainable production practices. By December 2007, approximately 360,000 metric tons of coffee were 4C verified. However, only about 10% of the available verified 4C coffee was actually purchased by 4C members.

UTZ CERTIFIED

Utz Certified, originally known as Utz Kapeh, which means "good coffee" in the Mayan language, was founded in 1997 by Guatemalan coffee producers and the Dutch coffee roaster Ahold Coffee Company. Utz is one of the fastest-growing certification programs in the world, aiming to implement a global standard for socially and environmentally appropriate coffee growing practices, and efficient farm management. The program is focused on the mainstream market, and is open to all growers, traders, roasters and retailers across the entire supply chain.

Utz has a unique track-and-trace system, showing the buyers of a certified coffee exactly where their coffee originated. A roaster prints a code on a bag of coffee, which can then be used to trace a coffee all the way back to its originating farm online. Thus, the farm's story can be told and transparency ensured. The price for Utz coffee is determined via negotiation between the buyer and seller, a process with which the certification body does not interfere.

Utz has been criticized over weak environmental and social standards, a lack of pre-financing standards, and the lack of minimum guaranteed prices. Utz was primarily developed for European grocery chains for their own marketing purposes. Although Utz certification is not recognized worldwide it has slowly been gaining recognition in more countries, particularly in Japan where certification not only yields a premium, but is also necessary to meet the exacting standards of Japanese consumers. In 2008, 77,478 metric tons of Utz certified coffee were sold.

DIRECT TRADE AND FARM FRIENDLY DIRECT (FFD)

Direct trade is a general term for coffees that are imported directly from growers, rather than purchased through brokers at auction. Through a direct trade relationship, individual terms and prices can be negotiated. Growers typically receive a higher price using direct trade as no middlemen exist to take a share of the price. The FFD program, unique to Stell and PRC, pays above-market prices for premium coffees, and then pays an additional premium to finance projects that help improve the lives of farmers and their communities. A list of PRC's FFD projects between 2006 and 2009 is provided in Table 6.5. Other direct trade programs also pay premiums above Fairtrade prices to reward quality, but do not specify how these premiums are to be spent by growers.

PRC and Farm Friendly Direct

Stell and his team firmly believed in the FFD program they started in 2001 at the La Hilda Estate in Costa Rica. The program had evolved to include direct trade arrangements with farmers in Tanzania, El Salvador, Costa Rica, Sumatra (Indonesia), India, Papua New Guinea, Guatemala and Ethiopia. Stell strongly believed that because of FFD, consumers received higher quality coffee and farmers improved their communities and the natural environment. The program embodied his commitment to community and sustainability.

As the quality of coffee improved under direct trade, certain farmers were approached by other buyers, often offering higher prices. Stell and

PRC never tied growers into exclusive sourcing contracts, believing that a variety of buyers benefited the growers in the long term. Farmers had the choice of selling to the highest bidder, but tended to stay loyal to PRC, trusting that the company was making a long-term commitment and would pay stable prices over the long term.

Stell would typically sample different coffees from a broker until he found one that had the quality he desired. He would patiently work to find the original source of that coffee and then seek a direct trade relationship. Each FFD project was designed and implemented through a collaborative process between PRC employees, farmers and their communities, addressing some of the growers' most pressing needs. Projects were evaluated by how closely they aligned with the United Nations' Millennium Development Goals, the potential for improving farmers' lives, overall costs and visibility. Once a project was undertaken, PRC remained engaged to ensure that farmers and communities had access to the assistance and materials they needed to complete each project.

Table 6.5: **PRC's Farm Friendly Direct Projects**

Year	Country	Amount (USD)	Project
2009	World Water Day Tanzania	$28,000.00	Internship and pump donated
2009	Costa Rica	$4,200.00	Teacher's salary
2009	Papua New Guinea	$8,000.00	Women's literacy and book drive
2008	World Water Day	$16,000.00	Pump sponsor Ethiopia
2008	Costa Rica	$4,200.00	Teacher
2008	Carbon Neutral El Salvador	$2,000.00	Planted trees
2008	Guatemala	$3,000.00	Yield project with Andres
2008	Sumatra(Indonesia)	$500.00	School uniforms
2007	Guatemala	$3,000.00	Yield project with Andres
2007	Tanzania	$2,000.00	Agronomy Kit
2007	Costa Rica	$4,200.00	Teacher
2006	Costa Rica	$4,200.00	Teacher
2005	Costa Rica	$1,000.00	Internet setup and computer donated
2005	India	$500.00	School for the blind in Karnataka
2004	Papua New Guinea	$5,000.00	School built
2003	Guatemala	$12,000.00	Built water treatment for farm
	Total	$97,800.00	

Source: Portland Roasting Company.

Most FFD projects were short-term in nature and typically completed within one to two years. At that point, a new project was developed and implemented. FFD projects included building a school, paying teachers' wages, constructing a water treatment facility, installing water pumps, implementing a soil and leaf analysis program, supporting a local foundation to fund community needs and planting trees.

There were challenges to the FFD model. It took time to trace high-quality beans back to their farmers, and to build direct trade relationships. Farmers were often skeptical of foreign companies, and tended to be more comfortable transacting their business through local channels and cooperatives. Stell's teams were also able to travel to each farm at most once a year to meet with farmers and monitor projects. Also, certain projects required expertise outside of PRC's core business. In some cases, PRC chose to collaborate with NGOs to assist with project implementation, but this option was not always available or feasible.

Stakeholders began asking Stell for specifics on how much PRC invested in FFD projects. There were no internally mandated policies or formulas for determining how much money would be allocated to fund projects. Likewise, PRC had no formal guidelines for selecting or structuring projects, nor any metrics for measuring the success or effectiveness of a project. Kathleen Finn, a communications and marketing representative at PRC, believed that the FFD program should remain flexible and fluid, arguing that "the program supports sustainability and in order to best do so, the program itself needs to be organic. Sometimes a farmer growing coffee in a developing country like Guatemala or in another part of the world may be doing very well in relation to the rest of their community that supports them, so as a result sometimes the funds from proceeds going to the FFD program are best spent with the community versus the farmer. At other times the farmer needs support to meet quality standards or to help become more environmentally and/or socially sustainable. As a result, the program needs to be organic, flexible and transparent, and may need to change from crop to crop or farmer to farmer in order to meet local needs and be able to bring value to PRC and our clients."

The Farm Friendly Direct Supply Chain

With FFD, PRC worked to minimize the number of middlemen in the supply chain. The importer and broker still played a role by assisting with necessary functions like transporting, processing, storing, importing and financing.

However, PRC negotiated separate contracts with these intermediaries, assuring that the prices offered to growers were not impacted.

Containers carrying FFD Central American coffees were shipped into Oakland or Long Beach, California; FFD coffee from Papua New Guinea was shipped into the Port of Tacoma, Washington; and FFD Tanzanian coffees were shipped directly into the Port of Portland, Oregon. PRC coffee that was not part of the FFD program was typically purchased on the spot market through brokers who import coffee into various US ports and sell to roasters throughout the United States. Since coffee crops ripen at different times throughout the year, roasters must source coffee from different growing regions to ensure a sufficient quantity of beans to meet year-round demand.

After working with farmers to ensure best practices in growing coffee, PRC took on the responsibility of maintaining the beans on their long voyage to Portland for roasting. Storage and shipping conditions strongly impact the quality of a cup of coffee. For instance, if the beans absorb too much moisture, particularly over a long period of time, the coffee may take on a moldy overtone in the cup. Thus, shipping must occur right away. Temperature also impacts the quality of green coffee, as quick temperature changes cause condensation and fermentation of the beans. Good air circulation is therefore needed to keep humidity and temperature levels constant. Coffee transport time to Portland could be as little as three weeks or as long as four months.

ROASTING

Upon arrival at PRC, unroasted green coffee was stored in a climate-controlled warehouse environment. Samples were taken from each lot and inspected for defects. Defects could be attributed to the farm, the processing or the shipping, depending on the nature of the problem. Defects were quite common and only became a concern if their levels were abnormally high. Unusable beans were set aside to help PRC staff learn how to inspect coffee lots for quality. Although green coffee can last significantly longer than roasted coffee, it was important for green coffee to be roasted in a reasonable amount of time, again for quality reasons related to temperature and humidity. Coffee was stored in burlap bags. Bags of organic coffees were distinctly marked and kept separate from other coffees, conforming to certification standards.

The coffee roasting process heats green beans to a certain temperature for a specified length of time. Each coffee has a different roasting profile, designed to highlight different flavors in the coffee and ensure consistency in the final product. As subtle changes—such as fluctuations in ambient temperature or humidity—can affect the final product, every roast is slightly different. Therefore, while PRC's roasting equipment was electronically programmed, the process was also overseen by skilled roasters.

Most machines maintained a temperature of about 550 degrees Fahrenheit. The beans were kept moving throughout the entire process to keep them from burning as they roasted. When the beans reached an internal temperature of about 400 degrees, they turned brown, sugars started to caramelize and the oils locked inside the bean began to emerge. The hot roasted coffee beans were then quickly spilled out onto a tray where cooling fans returned the coffee to room temperature. After returning to a stable temperature, roasted coffee was ready for bagging and distribution.

At PRC, whole bean coffee for grocery distribution was packaged in bulk, as store customers filled their own bags at the point of purchase. Whole bean coffee bound for sale in small, prepackaged bags was simply packed and stored for distribution. Ground coffee was crushed to specified grind sizes, then bagged and stored. Bagged coffees were contained in sealed packages with valves to release the gasses produced as the coffee aged. The packaging also kept out air and slowed the coffee fermentation process. However, as gasses were let off, coffee also slowly lost its flavor.

Marketing and Product Differentiation

PRC used a number of different channels to market its coffee and services. It took leading roles in a wide variety of industry trade shows, conferences and sampling events. Through these channels PRC showcased its wide range of coffee blends and supporting products and services. PRC also worked with retailers on cooperative marketing efforts including customized labeling, storyboards, decorative packaging and colorful photography highlighting the FFD program. PRC also delivered its message to consumers through its website, relaying information on the company's history, products, the FFD program and other sustainable initiatives.

Because PRC was a small company relative to large scale roasters, it made every effort to provide superior customer service to clients. The company offered training programs for café staff, e.g., baristas, on preparing coffee beverages, along with technical support for clients using PRC espresso and drip coffee equipment. PRC also offered a range of online training videos available to anyone interested in the art of coffee making. In the PRC tasting room, PRC educated clients on the flavor spectrum of different coffee varietals and provided hands-on experience and training with its equipment available for purchase. In addition to ensuring quality for the end consumer, the training sessions provided PRC with a valuable opportunity to build personal relationships with café owners. Nick Doughty, general manager for Elephants Delicatessen in Portland, Oregon, emphasized that his business was about good coffee and good people. By doing business with PRC, he was able to bypass the hype of some of PRC's bigger-name competitors, getting high-quality coffee, training and equipment while working with people he liked.

One of the biggest differentiators for PRC was its focus on social and environmental responsibility. PRC was the first company to create a sustainability-based direct trade program. PRC's loyal clients indicated that the quality of the product and the company's sustainability innovations were the main reasons they chose to work with PRC. Telling the story of the FFD program, raising consumer awareness and being recognized for exceeding conventional certification standards were therefore integral to the success of PRC's marketing strategy.

Distribution

COFFEEHOUSES

PRC initially targeted small coffeehouses for distribution, in hopes they would serve PRC coffee to their increasingly sophisticated clients and help build the brand directly with consumers. However, coffeehouses were not an easy sell. Many of them purchased coffee in low volumes, yet had high expectations. Customer service was important to small coffeehouses, but the support required at times exceeded what even PRC could reasonably provide. Thus, the return on investment in the small coffeehouse distribution channel was low.

HOTELS

While most inexpensive hotel chains do not offer high-quality coffee to guests, many high-end hotels provide specialty coffee in rooms and restaurants as a way to enhance the guest experience. These hotels have a value proposition much different from low-priced chain hotels, offering personalized service with an emphasis on customer service, food and location. These hotels believed that the quality of coffee they offered their guests reflected their overall brand and quality proposition. PRC therefore targeted boutique hotels across the country.

INSTITUTIONS

From the beginning, Oregon institutions were strategically important for PRC's marketing effort. The company therefore cultivated key relationships with several of Oregon's largest universities, including Portland State University, Portland Community College and Oregon State University. These clients purchased large volumes of coffee from PRC and put its product in front of a high-priority market: young, conscientious consumers. PRC also sold its coffee and services to churches, large food distributors such as Food Services of America, casinos and medical centers like the Oregon Health and Sciences University. These clients were consistent, reliable purchasers that gave PRC good exposure. Thus, they had value beyond their purchasing of coffee and other products.

GROCERS

Finally, PRC sold a large amount of its coffee to supermarkets and grocery stores. Snell's team landed the Fred Meyer account, enabling it to create a pilot marketing and sales campaign in partnership with one of Oregon's largest supermarket chains. This gained PRC an unprecedented amount of floor space to create a unique shopping experience for the consumer and educate consumers about PRC's coffees and the FFD program. PRC also worked with small, gourmet food markets and grocers such as Zupan's Market and New Seasons Market, both of which had great potential for expansion.

Other Sustainability Initiatives

PRC's commitment to sustainability went beyond the FFD program. Beginning in 2006, an in-house environmental team was tasked with finding environmentally friendly alternatives for all of its operations. As a result, PRC encouraged composting, recycling, using post-consumer office paper and company-wide use of earth-friendly cleaning products. Employees were encouraged to ride bikes to work and PRC contracted with B-Line, a sustainable urban delivery service, to offer bicycle delivery of coffee beans and supplies to Portland clients. One of PRC's two delivery vans ran on biodiesel and the company declared that all new vehicle purchases would also be powered by biodiesel. The company began working with Trees for the Future with the aim of becoming a carbon neutral company through the purchase and planting of 16,900 trees.

Stell embraced these changes yet wanted to do even more. In 2007 PRC began distributing Ecotainer to-go cups. These cups had an interior bio-plastic lining made of corn and an outer layer of paper harvested from trees managed in accordance with Sustainable Forestry Initiative guidelines. The packaging for all bulk coffee sold to grocers and consumer bulk bags was 100% compostable. Under the proper conditions, these cups and bags could break down into water, carbon dioxide and organic matter. In 2009, PRC also sponsored a Walk for Water, which raised funds to benefit Water for All, a nonprofit organization dedicated to bringing clean water to families in sub-Saharan Africa. The inaugural event raised $28,000 and funded two wells in Yirgacheffe, Ethiopia, a coffee-growing region in Eastern Africa. PRC also signed the Global Compact in 2005 and since then has consistently promoted the Millennium Development Goals on cups, product packaging and the company's website.

Because of these efforts, the company received the 2005 SCAA Sustainability Award. It was also recognized by the City of Portland with a 2007–2009 RecycleWorks Award. More generally, PRC was a finalist for Roast Magazine's Roaster of The Year awards in 2006, 2007 and 2008.

The Future of Farm Friendly Direct

As the plane began its descent, Stell considered how the FFD program could improve the quality of life of Burundi's farmers and their surrounding community. However, he was unsure if the FFD program could give PRC the competitive edge needed to increase market share in the United States. Although Stell believed the FFD program was unique to the coffee industry and superior to mainstream certification programs in many ways, FFD was not verified by an independent third-party organization, and consumer awareness of FFD was relatively low compared with the Fairtrade, USDA Organic, Rainforest Alliance and Bird Friendly labels.

If PRC decided to implement independent verification of the FFD program, what criteria should be used to verify compliance and measure results? What other modifications could be made to FFD to ensure credibility, improve the program and distinguish it from the multitude of established coffee certifications? Should PRC also invest in certification of FFD coffees according to an established standard? If so, which certification should PRC select? And, from a marketing standpoint, in what other ways could the FFD program be leveraged to build the PRC brand and compel qualityconscious consumers to seek out and purchase FFD coffees? Would this be enough to give PRC an edge over its competition?

Discussion Questions

1. What should the government's role be in developing and/or regulating food labels, especially those dealing with credence attributes?
2. What is the funding mechanism for certification by most of the non-profit certification groups? What potential conflicts of interest can arise from these arrangements?
3. What are the apparent conflicts between organic certification and other, more comprehensive sustainability or carbon emissions certifications?

Additional Readings and Links

1. Eco-label verifier tool: http://www.greenerchoices.org/eco-labels/
2. Movies: *Food, Inc.* and *King Corn*
3. Michael Pollan. 2006. *The Omnivore's Dilemma.*

7

FOOD SERVICE

A recent job posting for a chef on a Disney cruise ship provides unique insight into the world of leisure industry food service. Cruise ships serve breakfast, lunch, dinner and snacks to travellers, so most chefs are expected to work a full eight to ten hours each day, or 70 hours per week during an eight-month contract. Prospective chefs must have a bachelor's degree in culinary arts and deep experience in various culinary specialties. Chefs are expected to do the following during a typical work day:

- Prep and peel vegetables, slice cheese and make salads for all meals and snacks to be consumed by the ship's 2,700 guests and 975 crew members;
- Work with a large and diverse crew—160 in the kitchen galley alone—representing over 50 nationalities; and
- Positively interact with guests on the ship and at port during food service times.

During the course of a typical cruise, a Disney cook will prepare over 10,000 meals and snacks each day. There are no days off during the contract, but the job is well-suited for those who love cooking, travel and life at sea.

Introduction

This chapter discusses the food service industry. We begin with an industry overview. We then assess commercial and noncommercial food service environments, exploring demand trends, common purchasing arrangements and supply chain operations. The distribution activities that support the food service industry are summarized. We conclude with an exploration of social and environmental issues in the food service industry today.

Industry Overview

More than 48% of food consumed in the United States is eaten away from home, at either a commercial food service establishment (e.g., at a restaurant) or in a noncommercial food service environment (e.g., at a school). Commercial food service is the primary entity in the food service sector, with approximately $580 billion in sales in 2009. Noncommercial food environments comprise about 10% of the US food service sector. For every dollar typically earned by a commercial food service vendor, 34 cents go to wages, 26 cents are spent on physical inputs (food products) and 26 cents are spent on transportation, trade or other activities. The restaurant industry alone employs 12.7 million people, or roughly 9% of the US workforce. Clearly, food service is a significant contributor to the domestic economy.

The breakdown of commercial and noncommercial establishments in the food service sector is illustrated in Figure 7.1. In the United States, restaurants are the most popular place to eat away from home, but the commercial industry also includes fast food, fast casual and other hospitality environments. Noncommercial vendors provide food service in institutional settings like schools, prisons, the military and hospitals. A robust network of distributors exists to move food between growers, processors and manufacturers to commercial and noncommercial vendors, as shown in Figure 7.2. All of these food service components are explored in detail herein.

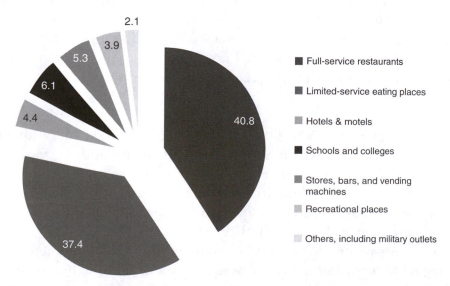

Figure 7.1 **Sales of food prepared away from home by outlet type, 2007** (Source: USDA ERS). *Note:* Data by percentage, 2007.

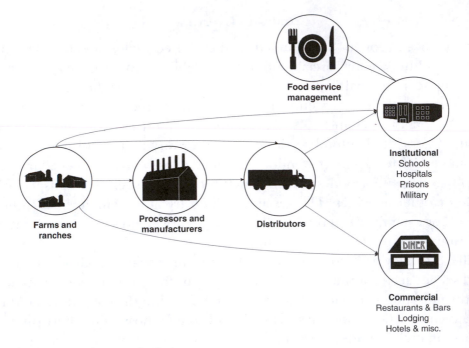

Figure 7.2 **Food service supply chain**

Commercial Food Environments

The commercial food service sector includes restaurants, fast food establishments and bars; travel and leisure vendors; vending machines; and take-out vendors, i.e., grocery stores or restaurants that sell ready-to-eat food. Sector earnings in 2010 are shown in Figure 7.3. The scale of these sites can range from small, family-owned restaurants that feed a few dozen people per hour to large hospitality venues such as stadiums, casinos, cruise ships, hotels and resorts, which cook meals for thousands of people per hour.

Restaurants

There are approximately 580,000 restaurants in the United States with a combined annual revenue of about $390 billion. Full-service and fast food restaurants make up about 77% of all away-from-home food sales. As defined by the industry, full-service establishments have wait staff and amenities such as ceramic dishware, non-disposable utensils and alcohol service. Fast food restaurants focus on convenience, and as such they have no wait staff, limited menus and sparse amenities relative to full-service restaurants. The fast food category has a sub-category termed "fast casual." These restaurants have higher quality food and amenities and, thus, their prices are slightly higher. Chipotle and Panera Bread are examples of a fast casual restaurant.

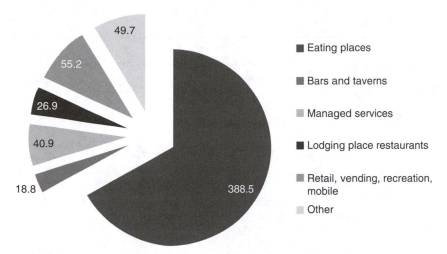

Legend:
- Eating places
- Bars and taverns
- Managed services
- Lodging place restaurants
- Retail, vending, recreation, mobile
- Other

Figure 7.3 **Sales in the commercial food service sector, 2010** (Source: USDA ERS). *Note:* In billions of dollars, 2010 estimate.

Most fast food restaurants have multiple units, or locations. McDonald's, for instance, has about 14,000 locations in the United States and approximately 32,000 locations in other countries. Subway currently has about 34,000 locations in over 90 countries. As a result, the supply chain that supports these multi-unit enterprises relies on bulk ingredients, such as flour, beef, potatoes and tomatoes, which are processed by a company's central supply facility or a sub-contracting facility into basic products like buns, fries, burger patties and chicken nuggets. Many food items are prepared with ingredients that preserve a food's freshness and visual appeal. Flavorings and additives are also used to improve the food's consistency, texture and taste.

After initial processing, meal and drink components are shipped to individual restaurants for final preparation. Therefore, individual locations typically have standardized equipment and cooking procedures. A restaurant's staple products are typically made in anticipation of an order; e.g., burgers or brewed coffee. Other products, particularly customizable or perishable products, are typically made on demand. Examples of on-demand food include pizzas that are assembled and baked, Starbucks Frappuccinos®, and deep-fried foods like chicken nuggets and french fries. To ensure a consistent level of product quality, prepared products are almost always thrown out after a certain holding time expires.

The demand for fast food has grown by roughly 6% since the mid-1980s while full-service restaurant demand has stayed flat, as shown in Figure 7.4.

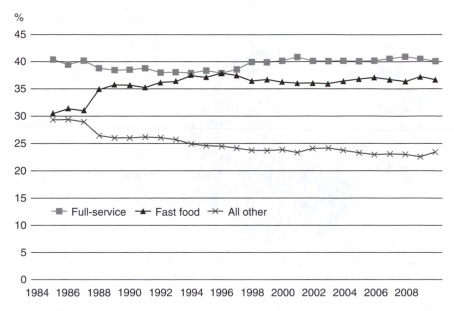

Figure 7.4 **Demand in the commercial food industry, 1984–2008** (Source: USDA ERS).

The growth of the fast food industry is often attributed to its convenience-oriented approach. Tactics like building close to consumers' homes and work places, adding drive-thru windows and expanding into non-traditional locations like retail stores and campuses are proving the convenience strategy to be a success. Additionally, the price point for fast food makes it affordable for most people. For instance, while the recent economic downturn caused most restaurants to lose sales, fast food establishments lost less revenue than full service restaurants. Average yearly sales declined 2.7% for fast food, versus 7.1% for full service restaurants.

Today, the fast food industry is being criticized for the poor nutritional quality of its food, which is typically high in sodium, fat, sugar and additives. Popular books and movies, such as *Fast Food Nation* and *Super Size Me*, have brought to light the connection between fast food and obesity, as well as other illnesses. Not surprisingly, many consumers are wanting to eat healthier restaurant food. A 2010 survey conducted by the National Restaurant Association indicated that 56% of adults said they are more likely to visit a restaurant that offers food grown or raised in an organic or environmentally friendly way. Additionally, 70% claim they are more likely to visit a restaurant that offers locally produced food.

Other Hospitality Venues

Demand trends in the non-restaurant commercial food service sector have varied. In the last 20 years, hotels have seen their market share drop 1.5% and stores, bars and vending machines have seen a drop of 2.1%. Casinos, which once used inexpensive buffets or complimentary food and drink as strategies to draw in gaming traffic, have seen their food and beverage profits increase sixfold since 1995. Today, many casinos function like full-scale entertainment centers, with multiple restaurants and other amenities keeping guests "in house."

In the events industry, many sports stadiums and convention centers have shifted away from the time-honored tradition of hot dogs, peanuts, draft beer and soda. Instead, these facilities are anchoring their concessions with branded fast food and fast casual chains. High-concept foods like gourmet hot dogs and burgers, sushi, house cut fries and local microbrews are also making inroads. As fans still want to limit their time away from the game, however, these restaurants must still move people through lines as quickly as possible. Thus, just-in-time food production strategies are being employed. The efforts to transition the recreational food service market are paying off; stadiums and parks have increased their market share by 1.5% in the last two decades.

Noncommercial Food Environments

Noncommercial environments are primarily large-scale or institutional settings, such as public and private schools, prisons, the US military and hospitals. Because most of these environments use a standard set of purchasing and contracting methods, they are relevant to the food industry and are therefore discussed here. Private institutions have considerably more leeway than do public institutions with regard to their purchasing and contracting strategies. Often, they also have more funding. However, many private institutions tend to follow the government purchasing model due to their scale and thus benefit from the potential savings and convenience of purchasing from one contractor.

Government Institutions

Each year, the US government buys a substantial amount of food from a variety of channels. Government purchasing supports commodity prices in domestic markets, feeds US military personnel, enables hungry children to obtain a nutritious meal and bolsters supplies of domestic and global food aid, among other outcomes. Government purchasing channels vary by food type. Bulk commodities, such as unprocessed grain, are typically procured directly from producers or processors through competitive bidding and commodity support programs. Food such as ground beef, fruit and infant formula may be purchased directly from manufacturers or through contracts with vendors.

To obtain a government contract, applicants must go through a competitive bidding process. The General Services Administration (GSA) acts as the central procurement agency for the federal government, but purchasing is also driven by individual agencies, some of which have their own centralized procurement department (e.g., the Defense Logistics Agency within the Department of Defense). Thus, the government has different contractor databases and frequently has different contracts up for bid. Many agencies prefer long-term contracts known as Indefinite Delivery/Indefinite Quantity contracts (IDIQ) and Blanket Purchase Agreements (BPA). IDIQ and BPA contracts give agencies consistency and predictability; they give a chosen supplier a competitive advantage but also a very aggressively priced contract to fulfill. Prime Vendor contracts (long-term contracts with supply chain contractors who take over procurement activities) are also used most by large government agencies.

Government contract provisions often push forward certain policy goals and thus influence agencies' purchasing decisions. Examples include "buy American" and small, minority- or women-owned and disadvantaged businesses provisions. The competitive Request for Proposals and Request for Quotations processes drive price points. Policy goals and price points are balanced in the decision-making process, so having the cheapest offer on the table may not ensure a contract win. Note that contract provisions can also exist at the state level, often aiming to support local industries or locally owned businesses. For example, public entities in Oregon that purchase food through the State can buy up to $5,000 of locally grown products per transaction as long as those products are within 10% of the cost of an out-of-state product.

PUBLIC SCHOOLS

During the Great Depression, the federal government began distributing surplus farm commodities to schools with a high percentage of undernourished children. By the 1940s, food donations were augmented with cash for kitchen equipment and staff. In 1946 Congress passed the National School Lunch Act, which established the National School Lunch Program (NSLP) "as a measure of national security . . . to safeguard the health and well-being of the Nation's children and to encourage the domestic consumption of nutritious agricultural commodities and other food." A related program, the National School Breakfast Program (NSBP), was established in 1975.

NSLP and NSBP meals are available for purchase by all schoolchildren, but the program is targeted at kids from households that are near, at or below the poverty level. If children are from such a household, they can receive a free or reduced-price lunch. They are also eligible for a free or reduced-price breakfast and afterschool snack, and milk. Today, more than 30 million children in the United States eat school lunch five days a week, 180 days a year. When it began, NSLP cost taxpayers $70 million. Today, the program costs taxpayers close to $10 billion.

The program is administered by the United States Department of Agriculture (USDA), which also administers other domestic hunger relief programs, like food stamps. The USDA allocates commodities to schools depending on their availability. These commodities range from protein items like ground beef, chicken and cheese to grain products like flour and cornmeal. Schools are allocated a certain amount of food each year; schools can order additional amounts of certain grains and dairy products if they wish. The average school lunch costs about $1.92 to prepare and serve, including the value of the donated commodities in the meal. Commodity products generally amount to about 10% of the meal cost and one-third of the caloric value per meal.

Because the USDA's reimbursement rate for meals is very low, and because the USDA must provide schools with shelf-stable products, most public schools have a limited ability to source nutrient-dense foods like fresh produce. Therefore, many schools were and are having trouble meeting children's nutritional requirements. Congress passed the "School Meals Initiative for Healthy Children" in 1995. This policy required school food to provide one-third of a child's recommended daily allowance of calories, protein, calcium, iron and vitamins A and C, while keeping fat below 30%. In addition, schools had to limit foods of "minimal nutritional value," such as candy and soda. Two-thirds of cafeteria planners reported that the guidelines influenced their school menus.

Serving healthy meals is still difficult for schools, however. Diminishing budgets, soaring food costs, heavy processing of commodity staples and the lure of off-campus fast food are, today, barriers to healthy meals for children. This has become a hot button issue for parents and policymakers as obesity rates among children have doubled in the last ten years, and tripled for adolescents. Recent studies show that 27% of US children are overweight and that one in three children born in the year 2000 will develop diabetes. These rates are even higher if the child is Hispanic or African American.

Increasingly, state and local governments are taking matters into their own hands. In 2004, Chicago Public Schools banned vending machines in elementary and middle schools, and required that snacks in high school vending machines meet nutritional standards. Oakland, California banned junk food in vending machines in January 2002. Taking aim at school vending services is no small matter; vending contracts often contribute substantially to a school's bottom line. For instance, Oakland's ban cost them an estimated $650,000 in annual revenue. A 2003 survey by the Texas Department of Agriculture estimated the total annual revenue received from vending contracts by schools in the state at more than $54 million, including cash receipts and the value of non-cash benefits (scholarships, sponsorships, merchandise, etc.).

Recent changes to procurement rules are allowing and encouraging local governments to explore the Farm to School concept. This initiative connects K-12 schools with local and regional farms, helping the schools source fresh produce for meals. In addition to increasing fresh fruit and vegetable consumption, Farm to School aims to improve nutritional education. It also supports local businesses through more direct purchasing. In 2010 there were an estimated 2,224 Farm to School programs in the United States impacting nearly 9,000 schools. This trend is expected to continue, with 34% of schools across the country serving locally sourced foods either occasionally or every day, and an additional 22% planning similar programs.

PRISONS

Correctional facilities in the United States house close to two million prisoners, the highest prison population worldwide. While most of the facilities are managed by federal or state entities, private prisons are a growing trend. Today, ten private prisons exist in the United States, housing 62,000 people. It's estimated that approximately 360,000 people will be incarcerated in private prisons within the next ten years. Prison food budgets are as tight as those for schools, if not tighter. For example, New York estimates that it costs $2.65 per day to feed an adult prisoner; one day of full meal reimbursement (free breakfast, lunch and snack) for a child in the public schools costs taxpayers $5.30.

Prison food service is most commonly outsourced to private providers, who are typically members of the Association of Correctional Food Service Affiliates. The largest companies in the industry are Good Source Corrections, which serves approximately 1,600 facilities at the federal, state and county level and feeds over 80% of the nation's inmate population; Aramark's correctional services division, which feeds over 300,000 inmates in over 600 correctional facilities; and Sodexo, which manages 450 prison kitchens. Aramark and Sodexo are also major food service providers at US colleges and universities.

As with other institutions, the drive to outsource food service to private corporations at correctional facilities is motivated by cost. For instance, Kentucky estimates that it saves over $4 million per year outsourcing food production at its correctional facilities to Aramark. However, the prison food service sector has few regulations and quality requirements, so the cost savings that are being passed on to government are being obtained by reducing portion sizes and lowering ingredient quality. Many prisoners suffer adverse health problems due to the lack of fresh and healthy food. Additionally, substandard portions and poor food quality can lead to prisoner violence.

Kentucky has had two food-related prison riots in the past three years. In the most recent riot, prisoners at the Northpoint Training Center set fire to the prison canteen and kitchen. Other states are cutting costs by eliminating meals, such as in Georgia, where state prisons no longer serve lunch on weekends. In these cases, prisoners with friends and families supplement their diets through care packages or by purchasing food from the canteen or vending machines. In New York and Florida, 12% to 15% of inmates eat outside the cafeteria each day. This benefits food service contractors as they are paid based on prison head count rather than meals served, so the vendor's profits actually increase if prisoners eat elsewhere.

On a positive note, more prisons are starting gardening programs. These programs have been shown to reduce violence and improve prisoner mental health, improve the nutritional quality of prison food and give prisoners a skill set that is valuable in the outside world. Today, organic gardens exist in prisons like San Quentin (California), Rikers Island (New York) and McNeil Island (Washington). Wisconsin has a substantial prison gardening program, with gardens at 28 correctional facilities each producing as much as 75,000 pounds of produce per year. More states are supporting "buy local" initiatives for prison food service as well, which directly impacts the quantity of fresh produce purchased in many states.

MILITARY

Although the US military represents less than 2% of overall US food sales, it is a significant purchaser, supplying food products to both domestic and foreign bases and ration kits for men and women on active duty. Prior to 1940, each branch of the military was responsible for its own food procurement and distribution activities. In 1941, perishable food procurement and distribution activities were shifted to one organization, the Market Center System (MCS) of the Army Quartermaster Corps. MCS hires private industry experts as food buyers and supply chain managers, supplementing the work of Army personnel.

Each branch of the service decides whether to manage its own domestic food service activities or to contract out these services. Currently, the Air Force operates its own 270 dining facilities and flight kitchens, serving more than 90 million meals each year. Additionally, the Air Force manages more than 300 non-government funded food and beverage operations, such as golf course and bowling center snack bars and clubs, which generate more than $193 million in sales. The Navy and Marine Corps, however, contract with Sodexo for food service at dining facilities on the east and west coasts. Sodexo is currently the only large food service operator used at domestic bases.

Internationally, the military receives food through a long and complex supply chain. Most packaged, non-perishable food is purchased from US manufacturers and distributed through the Defense Supply Center Philadelphia

(DSCP) Prime Vendor program. Most food is purchased from American growers and producers, as required by the Buy American Act and the Berry
Amendment. Food procurement for places such as Iraq and Afghanistan has
been excluded from the Berry Amendment due to operational considerations,
but most non-perishable food is still acquired from US manufacturers.

Suppliers ship their product to their closest US Prime Vendor distribution
center, which packages food for shipment. Shipping containers are moved by
truck to port, then loaded onto a US-flagged ocean vessel. Transit to the destination port typically takes 40 to 50 days. At the destination point, containers
are loaded onto trucks and transported to the foreign-based Prime Vendor distribution facility, where they are unpacked. The food is stored at the Prime
Vendor facility until it is ready for delivery to base or to a military installation.
When an installation places an order, the food is packed onto pallets and
shipped via truck to the installation, where it is again unloaded and stored
according to the installation's dining facility protocol. Typically, perishable
food items like fresh produce, dairy products and baked goods are not shipped
from US manufacturers. Rather, they are procured directly or from the Prime
Vendor in each country.

The dining facility operation at foreign bases has largely been contracted
to civilian companies, and these companies' personnel are often drawn from
the local population or from other foreign countries. Consequently, the Defense
Logistics Agency has contracted out delivery of more than $10 billion worth of
food to US troops and other government personnel serving in Iraq, Afghanistan,
Kuwait and Jordan since the start of the second Gulf War. The contracting job
is complex. The Prime Vendor must be capable of supplying "all chilled products, semi-perishable foodstuffs, frozen fish, meat and poultry, other frozen
foods (fruits, vegetables, prepared foods, etc.), dairy and ice cream products,
fresh and frozen bakery products, beverage base and juices (for dispensers),
beverages and juices (non-dispenser), fresh fruits and vegetables and non-food
items." In addition, the vendor must deliver government-furnished food kits,
rations and related operational items. Some fresh food can be obtained locally,
but much of it must come from the United States, according to typical Prime
Vendor contract provisions.

"Meals Ready to Eat" (MRE) are the individual rations bought by the US
military for service members to use in the field, when conditions for full food
service are not possible. MREs are produced exclusively in America from
US-grown ingredients. MREs have changed significantly since they debuted
decades ago. A very limited selection of canned or tinned goods used to be the
norm. Today, servicemen and servicewomen have a range of entrées from which
to choose and receive larger servings; 24 complete MREs and 150 additional
menu items are available. Food may also be supplied in or with biodegradable

materials (e.g., forks, napkins, etc.). The internal cost of a case of 12 MREs is $86.98, or approximately $7.25 a meal.

Hospitals

After schools, hospitals are the largest institutional food purchaser in the United States, spending $12 billion a year on food. Privately owned hospitals comprise the majority of all facilities (70%) with the remainder owned by city, county, state or federal governments. Most hospital meals are served in cafeterias frequented by employees and visitors. Food is also served in patients' rooms.

Public hospitals have limited budgets and thus often struggle to provide meals that meet nutritional requirements. Private hospitals with more funding are moving toward the "room service" model for patient food, where patients can order high quality items off a menu. Like most institutions, hospitals often hire food service management firms, like Aramark, and tend to buy from brokers and distributors who source food from across the country and throughout the world. Given concerns about hospital food quality, a number of hospitals throughout the country are now debuting Farm to Hospital programs that are bringing fresher, healthier food to medical facilities and giving local farmers new market options.

Food Service Management

As noted, many public and private institutions today outsource their final food production and service activities to food service management companies. This trend is especially true for complex institutions with multiple departments and locations, e.g., the military; universities; large, campus-based corporations, etc. Services offered by food service management companies typically include centralized food production, multi-site catering and food-related environmental management. Today, management companies are also taking on nontraditional activities like housekeeping, laundry, uniform management, facilities management and employee, patient and student transportation.

In 2009, the three largest food service management companies were the Compass Group, Aramark and Sodexo, with annual sales of $9.1 billion, $8.4 billion and $7.7 billion respectively. Their overall and sales by segment data are shown in Table 7.1. Together, these companies held over 18,000 food service contracts in 2009. These companies have grown by targeting a range of institutional clients, as shown in Table 7.2, and by taking on activities beyond basic food service.

The Compass Group focuses predominantly on food service in businesses and schools. While Aramark and Sodexo also focus on these clients, Aramark services more sport and leisure clients than its competitors and Sodexo has a

Table 7.1 **Largest Food Service Management Companies, 2009**

		Compass Group	Aramark	Sodexo
2009 North American Sales ($B)		9.1 B	8.4 B	7.7 B
2008 North American Sales ($B)		8.9 B	8.9 B	7.6 B
2009 Sales by Segment Category (%)	Business/Industry	37	25	30
	Healthcare	26	19	27
	Education	22	28	25
	Sports/Entertainment	12	19	–
	Corrections	–	5	–
	Vending/ OCS	–	5	–
	Other	3	–	18

Source: Forbes.com.

bigger presence in health care. Recently, Sodexo divested its 17% stake in the publicly traded Corrections Corporation of America after university students opposed to large-scale incarceration—particularly the privatization of prisons— boycotted the Sodexo-operated facilities at a dozen US and Canadian campuses. The food service management industry is extremely concentrated; the fourth-largest company in the market made 75% less than Sodexo in 2009.

As funding for public institutions dwindles, arguments are increasingly being made to outsource public food service activities to private companies to save on costs. However, many have voiced concerns about this practice, particularly parents of schoolchildren and advocates for prisoners and labor unions. For-profit food service companies largely achieve reduced costs for government

Table 7.2 **Segments Served by Food Service Management Companies**

	Colleges/ Universities	Airports	Business Services	Health-Care	Military Bases	Travel Plazas	Convention Centers	Stadiums/ Cultural Facilities
Compass	X		X	X				X
Aramark	X		X	X			X	X
Sodexo	X		X	X	X			
HMS Host		X				X		
SSP America		X						X
DNC		X						
Area USA		X						
AAFES						X		
Self-Operated	X				X			
Independent Contractors	X				X			

by minimizing the nutritional and quality aspects of food, and by paying minimum wages or offering minimal to no benefits to workers relative to what they once received. Clearly, the issue of privatizing formerly government-managed activities is highly political, with public health, social justice, economic policy and business concerns at stake.

As an alternative example of food service management, Bon Appétit Management Company, a division of the Compass Group, has made a concerted effort to source sustainable, local foods for the 400 cafes it manages across the United States. Bon Appétit introduced environmental sourcing early on and is one of the few major companies to have invested the time, energy and money necessary to develop effective, category-specific procurement policies. For instance, specific programs exist for meat, egg and dairy procurement, addressing animal welfare and antibiotics issues; the company has a separate set of non-negotiable standards for seafood purchasing. The company has been sourcing locally grown produce for over a decade. It also takes an active role in supporting farm workers' rights. Bon Appétit's clients include eBay, Nike and the Getty Center, as well as many colleges and universities. The company has received numerous awards for its work from organizations such as the Natural Resources Defense Council, the Seafood Choices Alliance, the Humane Society of the United States and Food Alliance.

Distribution

Wholesale distributors supply food service companies with items for use in the kitchen and items for use by end consumers. There are tens of thousands of distributors comprising this industry in the United States, generating combined annual sales of approximately $670 billion. Firms in this industry are classified as either broadline or specialty distributors.

A broadline distributor sells many types of food-related products from a global selection of producers, some stocking as many as 180,000 different items, or stock keeping units (SKUs). Their profitability depends on bulk purchasing and economies of scale in distribution. Broadliners purchase products in bulk from manufacturers, food brokers and consolidators. As they receive orders from food service companies, they break up these bulk shipments. Individual orders are built and then delivered to the appropriate food service company. This cycle is shown in Figure 7.5. Larger broadliners tend to have multiple distribution centers each stocking 5,000 to 10,000 SKUs. Larger distributors also offer supplementary services such as inventory financing, food industry trend analysis, menu analysis and design, and food show and product showcasing.

Only 120 distributors in the United States can be classified as broadliners, and at this scale, the industry is concentrated. The top 50 distributors in 2009

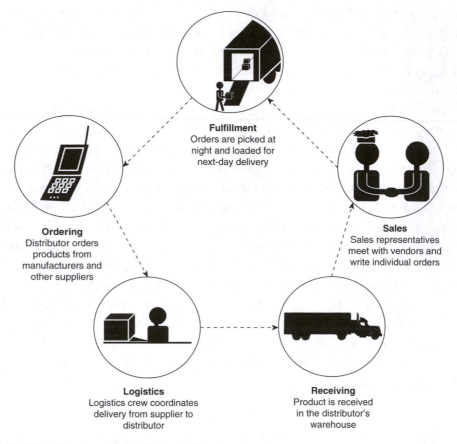

Fulfillment
Orders are picked at
night and loaded for
next-day delivery

Sales
Sales representatives
meet with vendors and
write individual orders

Ordering
Distributor orders
products from
manufacturers and
other suppliers

Logistics
Logistics crew coordinates
delivery from supplier to
distributor

Receiving
Product is received
in the distributor's
warehouse

Figure 7.5 **Distribution supply chain and business cycle**

earned $96 billion in revenue, or about 14% of overall sales in the sector. Revenues for the top five broadliners are shown in Table 7.3. Clearly, Sysco and US Foods dominate the market, earning a combined $55 billion, or more than half of the total sales of the top 50 distributors.

The remaining companies in the market are specialty distributors. Specialty distributors sell category-specific items, like beverages, or specialize in highly regulated categories, like alcohol. They may focus on a particular niche, designing their sourcing and distribution processes to maximize the quality of their products in that niche, e.g., locally grown produce, specialty meats, live seafood, ethnic foods, etc. Specialty distributors can also sell non-food items such as paper products, restaurant glassware, service materials, equipment and furnishings. Smaller companies succeed by focusing on the particular needs of a specific geographical area.

Table 7.3 **Largest Food Service Distributors, 2009**

Company	Ownership	Number of Distribution Centers	Revenue ($B)
Sysco	Publicly traded	125	36.85 B
US Food Service	Privately held	100	18.96 B
Performance Food Group	Privately held	25	10.10 B
Gordon Food Service	Privately held	12	7.14 B
Food Services of America	Privately held	11	2.65 B

Source: Forbes.com.

SALES AND PRICING

Salespeople in the distribution industry are commonly referred to as distributor sales representatives (DSRs) or marketing associates (MAs). They are typically paid on commission by the distributor. The sales team is a vital information link between food manufacturers and restaurant or food service vendors. Manufacturers develop new food products and thus have a strong knowledge of cost trends, supply issues and innovations in their specific category or area of expertise; the DSR passes on this information to food service purchasers. Likewise, food service vendors directly observe trends in consumer preferences and feed that information back to the sales force, who then funnel it back to the manufacturers.

Distributors frequently have different prices for different food establishments. Generally, a food service vendor is charged a product's base cost (the invoice cost), plus a markup. The markup is set by the DSR and varies based on vendor size, number of delivery windows available, delivery site requirements, order size, order entry mechanism (electronic, phone or fax), rebate considerations and account type. A typical "street" account is a basic relationship between a restaurant and a DSR that has no purchasing constraints. A "program" or primary vendor account is a committed or contracted relationship where the vendor must purchase a minimum number of products (often 70% to 80% of all of its purchases) from a single distributor. A street account typically pays the invoice cost plus a 35% markup, while a program account pays cost plus 8% to 14%. Sysco's purchasing relationship with Wendy's is an example of a low percentage program account. Wendy's is Sysco's largest account, making up 5% of its total sales. Thus, Sysco offers Wendy's a highly favorable pricing structure relative to a single unit restaurant. Wendy's is the only fast food chain using an outside distributor.

Food sale income is not the only revenue source for distributors. Distributors also make off-invoice income from manufacturers, as shown in Table 7.4.

Table 7.4 **Types of Off-Invoice Income for Distributors**

Type	Description
Growth Programs	Manufacturer drops the per case cost of a particular product as a distributor reaches a certain dollar-volume sales target.
Bonus-on-Bonus	Manufacturer gives a distributor a supplementary bonus for achieving a specified dollar-volume growth target.
Rebate	Manufacturer gives a distributor a percentage of the total volume of their purchases as a year-end sales allowance.
Pickup Allowance	Manufacturer gives a distributor an allowance (often added to the end-of-year rebate) for picking up a less-than-truckload amount.
Prompt Payment Discount	Manufacturers offer distributors discounts for prompt payment.
Income From Shows	Manufacturers pay distributors to promote their products at food shows.
Advertising	Manufacturers pay distributors to advertise their products in promotional materials.

Source: EPA.

These revenue sources include special pricing, rebates and incentives that are not passed along to the client.

SUPPLY CHAIN CHALLENGES

The food service industry has 740,000 different types of enterprises, from small one-unit restaurants to national chains with thousands of locations. Distributors fill more than 200 million food orders per year; in turn, they place approximately 26 million orders each year with manufacturers. While some companies have sophisticated ordering and supply chain management technologies, many vendors still rely on manual inventory and ordering systems. Thus, the supply chain in this sector has a number of costly inefficiencies.

In the 1990s, an industry-wide food service consortium published a report specifying supply chain improvements that could save the industry roughly $14.3 billion annually. Five strategies were articulated: equitable alliances, category management, electronic commerce, demand forecasting and logistics optimization. The program, named Efficient Foodservice Response (EFS), is based on the same principles used for the grocery industry's Efficient Consumer Response initiative; that is, reducing inventory and costs in the supply chain and improving customer service.

The goal of equitable alliance is to forge better relationships between operators and distributors; this could reduce existing or perceived practices—particularly arbitrary pricing and margin squeeze—that adversely affect both food service companies and distributors. Category management offers distributors and customers a way to balance variety and cost by matching consumer demand to food service menus and ingredient assortments. E-commerce, demand forecasting and logistics optimization could automate time-consuming manual processes and minimize inventory in the supply chain, thereby lowering consumer prices or enabling more profits in the industry.

A lack of trust between supply chain members and slow technology adoption in the industry have limited implementation of the concepts, the latter three in particular. For instance, in the 1990s, 20% of US food service orders were processed electronically. By 2002, only slightly more than half of the industry used e-commerce technology, lagging far behind other industries. Today, most broadline distributors can accept electronic orders and many offer monetary incentives to get more users to buy electronically.

Social and Environmental Issues

Because almost half of the meals consumed in the United States today are prepared away from home, the social and environmental impacts of the industry are worth assessing. Concerns about nutrition, food waste and food sourcing are most significant in this regard. These issues are explored below.

Nutrition

As consumers eat more of their meals away from home, they lose the ability to control the nutritional and caloric content of their meals. Not only are restaurant portions significantly larger than home portions, but away-from-home food tends to be more caloric and less nutritious than similar meals prepared at home. In particular, eating food away from home leads to a reduced consumption of fruit, vegetables and whole grains and an increased consumption of calories from saturated fat. For each meal eaten away from home, the typical adult consumes an extra 134 calories, contributing to an average weight gain of 2 pounds per year. People who eat fast food more than twice a week increase their risk of obesity by close to 50%.

To counter this problem, many restaurants are offering healthier menu options. Even fast food chains have added vegetable salads and fruit-based items to their menus. For instance, Starbucks began offering healthier meals— including hot oatmeal, a protein plate with a cage-free hardboiled egg, a whole-wheat bagel and a whole grain muffin—to its menu in response to consumer demand. These meals provide more protein and fiber and less fat and sugar than the average bakery fare. Starbucks also set 2% milk as its default milk option and reduced the size of some of its pastries.

Required nutritional labeling is also affecting restaurants. Most consumers underestimate the caloric content of restaurant meals by 30% to 50%. In an effort to encourage healthier eating, several state and municipal governments have either passed or introduced legislation requiring chain restaurants to provide caloric content and other nutritional information at the point of sale. In most cases, the legislation applies to multi-unit restaurants with 10 to 20 locations, requiring disclosure of calorie, fat, carbohydrate and sodium content per serving for standard menu items. The information must also be posted on menus or menu boards.

In an effort to combat obesity, the federal government recently moved to establish a uniform, national standard for calorie information disclosure. Chains with 20 or more restaurants will likely soon be required to disclose, in a clear and conspicuous manner, the number of calories in standard menu items, possibly adjacent to the item's listing on the menu. While not required yet by law, the Food and Drug Administration is in the process of formulating these regulations. Some fast food chains have decided to tackle the issue proactively. Subway, for example, lists calorie data for many of its sandwiches on its drink containers, while Burger King and McDonald's provide similar information on the back of their placemats, on in-store posters, in pamphlets and online.

Food Waste

Commercial and institutional food waste has a significant environmental impact, and yet has received less attention in the popular press than other food service issues. Recently, researchers assessed carbon emissions data for whole chickens, canned tomato and fresh potato products bought through institutional food channels. They compared their environmental impact using various types of environmentally friendly packaging; their impact if purchased locally versus using broadliners' standard supply lines; and by assessing their food waste before and after preparation. For all the products, reducing food waste most significantly reduced emissions, compared to other sustainable purchasing methods.

Most food waste is not recycled, as shown in Table 7.5. In fact, less food waste is recycled today (2.5%) than in 1995 (3.4%). Of the 32 million tons of food waste generated each year in the United States, therefore, almost all of it goes to the landfill. Restaurants, grocery stores, institutional food service establishments and residences generate the most food waste, respectively. The food service industry estimates that 4% to 10% of food products become waste before reaching the consumer, through spoilage, value-added processing activities, and so forth. Food service does donate some edible food to the needy; composting is also an increasingly popular option. Composting companies work with high-volume commercial and institutional food producers to recover their food byproducts.

According to the Environmental Protection Agency (EPA), which has developed a food recovery hierarchy model, food waste reduction efforts should most focus on reducing source waste in the food supply chain. This model is shown in Figure 7.6. To counter the huge food service waste problem, analytical

Table 7.5 **Food Waste, 1995 and 2008**

	1995	2008
Food Waste		
Generated	14.1 M tons	31.8 M tons
Recycled	3.4%	2.5%
Yard Waste		
Generated	30.6 M tons	32.9 M tons
Recycled	22.9%	64.7 %

Source: EPA.

tools have been developed to measure and monitor food waste in food service settings. Several commercial programs exist. The EPA also has free waste auditing tools and a Food Waste Management Cost Calculator on its website.

Sourcing

Food service operators are increasingly looking for local and regional producers to supply goods for their operation, particularly Farm to School, Farm to Hospital and Farm to Prison programs. It can be very time consuming for a food service buyer to track down the appropriate local foods needed for a specific venue. In response to this market need, support services are springing up to help purchasers in their efforts.

FoodHub is an Internet service that essentially works like a supplier and buyer dating website. Farmers will put up a profile of their operation and list

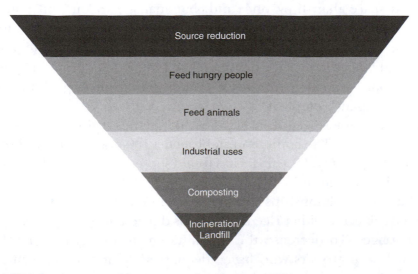

Figure 7.6 **EPA food recovery hierarchy model** (Source: EPA).

the items they have for sale, while the food service operator posts their profile and lists their food needs. The service has a search function and can automatically generate suggested matches based on a buyer or seller's criteria. FoodHub's geographical scope, today, covers food buyers and sellers in Oregon, Washington, Alaska, Montana, Idaho and California. The developers of FoodHub believe their system will one day open doors for many new vendors, enhancing their distribution opportunities.

Company Profile: HOTLIPS Pizza

HOTLIPS Pizza is a family-owned pizza chain in Portland, Oregon that began making pizzas in 1984. Ten years ago, the current owners bought out other family members to transform the business into an environmentally friendly, gourmet pizza restaurant. Today, HOTLIPS has five pizzerias in the Portland metropolitan area. In 2005, the company started a soda brewing operation to produce fresh and seasonal fruit sodas (pear, apple, raspberry, strawberry, blueberry and other flavors). Recently, the company added a mobile oven that travels to farmers' markets and regional festivals to sell its products.

HOTLIPS' mission is "to preserve culture and celebrate humanity through our rich culinary traditions and by joining with others in finding new, sustainable ways of doing business." The company's operations reflect this mission: HOTLIPS is particularly committed to addressing pollution and energy consumption issues. For instance, its kitchens today occupy 20% less space than they once did, but manage to put out almost as much pizza. Its ovens also capture residual heat that is then used to boil water for dishwashing. All restaurants compost their food waste and use bicycles and electric cars for delivery. The owners take pride in "pushing the envelope," soliciting new ideas and engaging in insightful dialogue with the company's employees.

One important aspect of HOTLIPS' operation is its food miles strategy for food sourcing. The company established a 100-mile radius for produce and meat purchasing. HOTLIPS has found success with its food-mile policy is due to its realistic and fair purchasing strategies. For instance, the company has close relationships with its 30 to 40 ranchers and farmers, who are often subject to wide price fluctuations due to natural supply surpluses and shortages. To decrease the risk inherent in this system, HOTLIPS identified local growers who have adequate scale and a complementary variety of products and offered them fixed prices and renewable annual contracts. The contracts factor in the cost of living to guarantee the growers a profit. Thus, when one grower has a shortage, the other growers' products will meet HOTLIPS' demand. Close communication also helps the network manage surpluses. Local sourcing and strong grower relationships give HOTLIPS more than just supply predictability; they also allow them to better plan their menu and tell the story of their food. Connecting customers to the land is an integral part of the company's brand and marketing strategy.

Despite its clear position on sustainability issues, the company has at times struggled to align its environmental commitments with customer expectations. Simply put, customers expect certain ingredients on their pizza, some of which can only be procured from a distance or frozen to ensure a year-round supply. Examples include pineapples, which are sourced from Hawaii and are one of the biggest contributors to HOTLIPS' food miles, and tomatoes, which are not a local field crop in winter. The company experimented with ingredient alternatives, but consumers did not respond well to the substitutions. Alternatives have also been explored for salad packaging, but the company found that customers prefer clear plastic containers. When customer choice dictates an environmentally unfriendly outcome, efforts are made to educate consumers about the implications of their choices.

HOTLIPS' values have led to considerable innovation in the food service supply chain. While its procurement method is not the cheapest available, it ensures high quality ingredients, benefits local farmers and gives the restaurant a predictable supply of ingredients. The company is profitable, is growing and has a much smaller environmental footprint than its competition. It is also playing an important role in educating consumers about the impact of their food choices.

Discussion Questions

1. Other chapters have discussed the increasing popularity of organic and local foods. What challenges do commercial food service providers face in incorporating these foods into their menus?
2. What are some of the barriers to improving the quality of foods served in public schools and prisons? What are the benefits and drawbacks of privatizing food service in the public sector?

3. Describe where the food service supply chain is concentrated and where it is not. What are the benefits of concentration for supply chain partners and consumers? What are the drawbacks?

4. Research how food waste is handled in your community, either online or by calling local companies or waste agencies. Does a system exist in your community to divert food waste from landfills? If so, describe the system and explain its outcomes (i.e., amount and percent of food waste diverted). If not, explain the barriers to implementing such a system.

Additional Readings and Links

- The USDA's Food and Nutrition Service agency coordinates distribution of US-grown commodities to government programs nationwide. The Food Distribution Program website explains this process in detail: http://www.fns.usda.gov/fdd/

- Let's Move is the USDA's initiative to combat childhood obesity in schools: http://www.letsmove.gov/chefs-step-1.php. Farm to School, a nongovernmental movement, has a different but related agenda: http://www.farmto-school.org/

- Bon Appétit Management Company is a unique, sustainable food service vendor. Their website details their purchasing policies: http://www.bamco.com/

8

FOOD MANUFACTURING AND LOGISTICS

Frito-Lay, a well-known manufacturer of snack products, is committed to improving the sustainability of its product line through energy and water conservation, and through waste and emissions reductions. In service of this goal, its plants employ numerous production methods that are unique and innovative in the industry, including solar concentration to heat cooking oil, solar electricity, water reclamation and recycling, biomass boilers, stack heat recovery and food scrap recycling. The company has set a goal of having all of its plants be "zero landfill" by 2011. In May 2010, the Frito-Lay facility in Casa Grande, Arizona won the Manufacturing Plant of the Year award from the Arizona Manufacturers' Council and the Arizona Chamber of Commerce, in recognition of its sustainability and community programs.

As a division of PepsiCo, a publicly traded company, Frito-Lay is ultimately responsible to its shareholders, and not the general public. It must therefore support share price and profits, making its efforts to become sustainable particularly noteworthy. However, not all of its efforts have been met with high praise. In April 2009, the company adopted a 100% compostable bag for its SunChips brand snacks. In spite of their environmental appeal, the bags had a drawback: they were noisy. So noisy, in fact, that detractors started a Facebook page deriding them. Sales of SunChips dropped a reported 11% in 52 weeks, and in less than 18 months the bags were pulled off the shelves. Not to be deterred, Frito-Lay acknowledged the issue and has indicated that the search is on for a new bag material, one that is both environmentally and consumer friendly.

Introduction

This chapter details two primary topics in food supply chain management: food manufacturing and logistics management. Food manufacturing actually entails two concepts: processing, which is the modification of food to prepare it for consumption, and manufacturing, which is the creation of entirely new products from raw or already-processed ingredients. Logistics encompasses everything from the transportation of raw, processed and finished goods to inventory management in the factory or warehouse. Seamless integration of manufacturing and logistics is important in the food industry, as it lessens inventory in the supply chain and enables faster product delivery.

This chapter assesses trends in food processing, manufacturing and logistics. We then explore common processing and manufacturing techniques, discuss traceability and examine sustainability issues related to processing and manufacturing activities. We explore common transportation and inventory management methods in logistics. We conclude with a study of industry-specific initiatives designed to increase efficiency and sustainability in logistics.

Industry Trends

Food processing and manufacturing are critical activities in the food supply chain, as most foods need some form of processing to be eaten. Food processing is defined as the manipulation of raw agricultural goods into food products that retain many of the original product's characteristics. Vegetable freezing and canning, cattle slaughter and packaging and milk pasteurization and bottling are all examples of food processing. Food manufacturing is the creation of entirely new products out of a given set of ingredients. Bread, cheese and ice cream are examples of manufactured food products. Although the industry recognizes the formal distinction between processing and manufacturing, the terms are often used interchangeably.

Profit margins are generally low in the food industry, and the same is true in the processing and manufacturing sector. Thus, the sector is susceptible to the same challenges faced by other producers in the food supply chain. Slow growth in developed countries, increasing input prices, the need to enhance technology and pressures to automate are key challenges impacting processors and manufacturers. Consequently, consolidation is a decades-long sector trend, as illustrated in Table 8.1. Consolidation facilitates efficiency in processing and manufacturing activities, helping the sector manage its challenges better, but it also has the effect of eliminating small- and mid-sized producers.

The United States is the largest consumer and producer of processed food in the world. The top 100 food manufacturers make approximately 75% of

Table 8.1 **Number of Food Processing Plants, Companies and Sales Concentration**

Census Year	Plants	Companies	Top 50 Share of Shipment Value (%)
1963	37,521	32,617	32
1967	32,517	26,549	35
1972	28,193	22,172	38
1977	26,656	20,616	40
1982	22,130	16,813	43
1987	20,624	15,692	47
1992	20,798	16,075	50
1997	21,805	17,221	51
2002	23,338	18,696	53

Source: S.W. Martinez.

the processed food sold in the United States, and the top 20 manufacturers make about half the processed food consumed in America. Globally, the four largest food manufacturers are Nestlé, Tyson Foods, Kraft Foods and PepsiCo, with respective sales of $28 billion, $26 billion, $24 billion and $22 billion in 2009. However, most of these sales are in America. Thus, no one food manufacturer dominates global processed food sales. For instance, Nestlé sells only 3% of the world's packaged food, and the top 25 companies worldwide account for less than 25% of global packaged food sales.

The market for processed food in the United States is growing steadily but slowly, with the largest growth occurring in fruits, vegetables and snack foods. US industry has invested heavily in technology and automation, aiming to increase output and lower costs. As noted, consolidation has also facilitated this goal. In the United States, consolidation tends to create production clusters in certain geographical areas. For instance, the US poultry industry is concentrated in northwest Arkansas, northern Alabama and northern Georgia, where several major processors are located.

International expansion is becoming an important growth strategy for food processors, particularly in crowded markets. International expansion improves and stabilizes overall sales by mitigating economic fluctuations in regional markets. As North America, Japan and Western Europe approach market saturation and population stagnation, companies from these regions are seeking new markets in Latin America and Asia. US Companies are leading this race.

Challenges to going global exist. Although almost all food consumed in the world undergoes some amount of light processing before consumption, the developing world does not seem to share the industrialized world's taste for highly processed and manufactured goods. Additionally, food companies abroad tend to focus their offerings and specialize in a few select products, which is different from the US way of doing business. As an entry strategy into new markets, global leaders are tending to focus their attention on specific, highly concentrated markets in certain countries and regions.

Processing and Manufacturing

Processing and manufacturing entail a range of activities, often performed in rapid sequence or even simultaneously. Pathogen destruction, physical modification of a food product and packaging are key components of processing and manufacturing. As noted elsewhere in this textbook, eradicating and keeping pathogens at bay is critical to safe food production, as is the need to prevent spoilage. Thus, certain pathogen management and food preservation techniques—namely heating and cooling—are often deployed repeatedly or sustained throughout the food production process. These and other processing and manufacturing activities are explained below.

Pathogen Destruction and Food Preservation

Most food processing entails some sort of pathogen destruction and preservation activity, which alters the chemical makeup of food or its environment. Application of pathogen-destroying and preservation techniques often begins in the field, milk house or slaughterhouse. As noted, these activities are often sustained or reapplied during processing to keep food safe and fresh. Different techniques may be employed as food moves through the production process and thus its safety or preservation requirements change. Common techniques include thermal processing (heating, cooling or both), irradiation, pressurization, pickling and curing.

THERMAL PROCESSING

Thermal processing is one of the most common and important food processing techniques. Heating increases the temperature of food, and is typically achieved through boiling or baking. Heating is extremely important from a food safety perspective, as high temperatures kill most pathogens. Heating is also often used to develop a food's taste, flavor and texture. Cooling entails chilling or freezing food, and is key to keeping pathogens at bay once they have been eradicated, and to preventing spoilage. Cooling can also be used to develop a particular attribute in a food product. Of all preservation methods, freezing may be the best way to preserve nutrients. Freezing techniques include immersion in cold liquids, high-pressure shift freezing and freeze-drying, in which foods are simultaneously subjected to extremely low pressure and temperatures. Many products undergo both heating and cooling during food processing. An example of this is pasteurized milk.

IRRADIATION

Another common preservation technique is ionizing radiation, or irradiation, which uses high-energy electrons, gamma radiation or x-ray to eliminate contaminants. Irradiation is common in the meat, grain and produce industries, as it can kill bacteria, fungi and insects. It is also efficient. For instance, gamma radiation from cobalt-60 can sterilize an entire pallet of food at one time. Ultraviolet radiation utilizes light just beyond the visible region of the electromagnetic spectrum to address food pathogens. UV radiation also is employed to disinfect food processing environments.

OTHER TECHNIQUES

High pressure food processing exposes food to extremely elevated pressures to kill microbes. High pressure processing may or may not use heat to assist in this process. Pulsed electric field processing (PEF) is an emerging technology that uses short electrical bursts to deactivate microbes. PEF has little to no detrimental effect on food quality, and can be used for processing liquid and semi-liquid food products.

Physical Modification

Processing and manufacturing almost always involve some degree of physical modification to a raw food product to prepare it for consumption. Common physical modifications in food processing include polishing, trimming, cutting, grinding and milling, among many others. If done, these activities happen before foods are packaged. As noted, food processing activities tend to be somewhat basic in nature, retaining the characteristics of the raw base product, e.g., milk is bottled, grains are milled, apples are polished. Therefore, many food processing activities have already been described in the food-specific chapters presented earlier in this book.

Food manufacturing is more involved than food processing, as the resulting foods are distinct from their raw ingredients. Thus, blending, mixing and baking are common activities in a food manufacturing environment. Food manufacturers use recipes to guide the cooking process; many recipes have numerous inputs. Due to uncertainty in pricing, quality and material supply, a manufactured food product may have several recipes associated with it, each requiring a slightly or altogether different process. This heightens the need for logistical expertise, such as inventory management. Note that processed foods often go on to a food manufacturer for incorporation into multi-ingredient products.

In the last few decades, food manufacturing processes have become similar to generalized manufacturing processes. Food products are "designed" to achieve a very specific marketing and branding objective. Agricultural products are conceptualized and referred to as industrial inputs: proteins, carbohydrates, fats, flavors, colors and so on. The use of already-processed ingredients in food manufacturing simplifies production control and gives companies flexibility in where they locate their manufacturing facility. It is no longer a requirement that plants and factories be located in agriculture-producing regions, although doing so can be a strategic advantage in some sectors.

Manufacturing companies carefully design their product line to work in harmony with their production environment, and vice versa. Some food products, such as bread, necessitate expensive, heavy equipment and have relatively inflexible, flow-oriented processes. Their long, sequence-dependent manufacturing processes prod companies to develop product lines with minimal variation, e.g., wheat bread, white bread and buns. An example of a large bread bakery is shown in Figure 8.1.

Other plants are extremely modular in nature, designed for quick transition between products—e.g., potato salad one day, artichoke spread the next. However, even small-scale, batch production processes are designed with efficiency in mind, as minimizing the extent of transition between products helps maximize efficiency and thus profits. Standardized equipment and processes, as well as automation, allow for high-volume implementation of single-purpose activities. This volume is strategically necessary, enabling a business to take advantage of economies of scale and increase capacity utilization even when the overall product line has substantial variation.

Figure 8.1 **Manufacturing process at a large bakery** (Source: iStock).

While the food industry is becoming more akin to other manufacturing environments, input characteristics do separate the food industry from other industrial operations. The nature and source of raw materials in the food industry frequently cause variation in supply, quality and price due to unstable yields, as does crop seasonality. Food processors tend to be more susceptible to these market fluctuations than food manufacturers, as their suppliers tend to be primary producers, like farmers or ranchers. The sensitivity of food products to their processing environment can also create yield and processing time variation. For example, yeast-based breads can be highly impacted by ambient temperatures and humidity, thus creating variation in output yield and timing.

Packaging

Processed and manufactured foods are packaged using a variety of materials. Common packaging materials include glass bottles and jars; plastic bottles, jugs and tubs; paper cartons and boxes; aluminum cans; plastic and mesh bags; and hybrid packaging, such as foil and paper cartons. Packaging materials for processed foods need to withstand a fairly rigorous packing, distribution and handling process. Sometimes, products are double-packaged to reduce damage during production and shipping, e.g., cereals may be bagged and then boxed. This type of packaging can also maintain food safety and improve marketability. Many packaging methods have been discussed extensively in earlier, food-specific chapters. Common packaging methods that have not already been discussed are described below.

CANNING AND JARRING

Canning and jarring combine food preservation and packaging activities into one. Food is cleaned and undergoes minor physical processing (e.g., trimming or chopping) and is then sealed in an airtight container and heated to destroy pathogens. Canned foods with high acidity (pH below 4.7) or high water activity (the relative availability of water in a substance), such as fruits, tomatoes and pickled products, typically last 18 to 24 months on the shelf. Low-acid and low water activity foods can last two to five years on the shelf. Canning and jarring are commonly used to preserve and market seasonal fruits and vegetables, fish and meat products, noodles and heat-and-eat meals, like soup.

ASEPTIC PROCESSING AND PACKAGING

Aseptic processing is a comparatively new processing and packaging technique. Aseptic processing pumps flash-sterilized food into pre-sterilized containers—often cartons or tubs—and then vacuum seals the container. This process obviates the need for post-packing heating, as the entire product is already sterile.

Aseptic processing is appropriate for liquid and semi-liquid foods like juice, pudding, yogurt, liquid eggs, sauces, broths and soups. Aseptically packaged foods can be very efficient to ship and store, thus they are becoming increasingly popular in the food service industry. The technique is also often used for natural and organic products, like soymilk, because it requires few additives and preservatives and because the sterilization process is quick, enabling less destruction of product nutrients.

FROZEN FOOD PACKAGING

The packaging used for frozen foods is paramount to their sale and safety. Frozen food packaging must be moisture- and vapor-proof to prevent evaporation and freezer burn, and able to withstand the packing, freezing, storage, transportation and post-sale thawing processes. Frozen food packaging may also need to withstand the cooking process. Indeed, recent packaging innovations are enabling new product designs, like ovenable packaging, in which a product is packed and frozen, then bought and cooked in the same package. Frozen food packaging materials can include plastic, aluminum and paper.

Traceability

Modern food processing and manufacturing practices have increased the length and complexity of the food supply chain and the number of handlers involved in the chain. Enhanced traceability efforts are responding to these risks, aiming to provide clear, valid information about the origin and handling history of a particular ingredient or product. Many variables affect the availability and reliability of data, however, as products move through the manufacturing process.

Food manufacturing companies use both manual and automated processes to track ingredients and record food handling activities. The best production control systems employ unique codes to identify specific ingredients that are used in a given process. The ingredients are then tracked as they move through a processing operation. For such a system to work, however, information about the product must move with the product through the control system. Technology is greatly enhancing this effort, and vastly expanding traceability in the food supply chain. However, robust tracking technology is expensive, therefore many manufacturers still manually organize their information.

Recent legislation may push manufacturers to improve their traceability efforts. The new Food Allergen Labeling and Consumer Protection Act (FALCPA) requires food products to have "plain English" label descriptions of any ingredients that contain derivatives or components of the eight major food allergens: milk, eggs, fish, crustacean shellfish, tree nuts, wheat, peanuts and soybeans. Such information can only be provided by maintaining good information about a product's path through its supply chain, which in turn is bound to necessitate a traceability process and technology upgrades.

Sustainability

Current food processing and manufacturing methods are environmentally problematic. Food waste, packaging waste, energy waste and water use and contamination are the sector's most pressing environmental concerns. Some federal laws and regulations have changed the way food processors do business. Nonetheless, more must be done to reduce the impact of the food manufacturing industry on the environment. Recent relevant federal statutes are summarized in Table 8.2.

FOOD WASTE

Food waste is an enormous issue in processing and manufacturing. According to the United Nations Environment Programme (UNEP), more than half of the food produced worldwide is lost, wasted or discarded due to inefficiency and mishandling in the food supply chain. According to the UNEP, 14% of waste occurs during processing. Up to 25% of all fresh produce in the United States is thought to be lost between the field and the table. Globally, about 33 million tons of fish are estimated to be lost, discarded or spoiled every year. Food waste can include skin, bones, rinds, seeds and other unusable parts of an animal or raw plant. Typically, these are all discarded after processing is complete. New initiatives in food waste composting are helping to alleviate this issue in some areas of the United States, but the number of large-scale, commercial composting facilities—which have special infrastructure and processes designed to handle hard-to-compost items, like bone—are limited.

PACKAGING WASTE

Packaging materials also generate waste. Although many packaging materials are recyclable—e.g., plastics, glass, steel, tin and aluminum—many non-recyclable packing materials are still used in food production. Packaging materials can also be difficult to recycle if contaminated with food, or if the local infrastructure doesn't exist to recycle a specific material type. In recent years, environmental groups, city councils and consumers have advocated for the reduction of non-recyclable food packaging, in an effort to reduce at least some packaging waste.

ENERGY WASTE

The food production process, inclusive of farming, processing and transportation, accounts for about 8% of total US energy consumption—the rough equivalent of about 68 billion gallons of gas per year. Roughly 27% of that

Table 8.2 **Federal Environmental Regulations**

		Regulations
Resource Conservation and Recovery Act (RCRA)	Non-hazardous solid waste	Prohibits open dumping of solid, nonhazardous wastes
	Hazardous waste	Producers of hazardous waste must keep records, obtain FDA permit to treat, store, or dispose of hazardous waste
	Universal wastes	Provides for widely generated hazardous wastes: dead batteries, pesticides, mercury lights, switches and thermostats
	Underground storage tanks	Initial design, construction, operation and notification requirements; release detection and reporting; system closure requirements
	Used oil	Varies by state
Clean Water Act (CWA)	Industrial facilities	A "point-source" of pollution; discharge into waterways and wetlands is regulated
	Agricultural facilities (some)	Irrigation return flow is exempted; may be a significant source of pollution
Clean Air Act (CAA)	Title I: Air Pollution Prevention and Control	Carbon monoxide, lead, nitrogen oxides, particulate matter (PM), ozone, sulfur dioxide. Fossil fuel emissions (industrial ovens, boilers, etc.); PM from solid size reduction, cleaning, roasting, cooking; VOCs from fryers, ethanol use, lubricating oils
	Title III: Air Toxics	Organic and inorganic hazardous air pollutants (HAPs), defined in Title III
	Title IV: Acid Deposition Control	Sulfur dioxide and nitrogen oxide, acid rain
	Title V: Permits	Combined emissions from boilers, receiving areas, cooking, grinders, waste treatment, fryers, fermentation, dryers, etc., may require permits
Pollution Prevention Act (PPA)	Pollution sources (opposed to waste reduction or clean-up)	Process control. Reduction of resource use and waste

Source: Food Processing Environmental Assistance Center, EPA.

energy is estimated to be wasted through inefficiency, such as truck idling at warehouses and docks. Gaseous emissions are also produced during the food manufacturing process, including the creation of odorous volatile organic compounds (VOCs).

Energy-intensive manufacturing comprises about 40% of the value of processed food. The main contributors to this problem are heating and cooling systems, such as ovens, steam systems, refrigeration systems and freezers, which consume 75% of the energy used in food manufacturing. Motorized mixers, grinders, pumps and other equipment account for another 12% of energy used. Heat, ventilation, lighting and other physical support systems use about 8% of energy in the production process. Clearly, while these activities are not overtly wasteful, energy efficiencies could contribute profoundly to natural resource conservation and save producers billions.

WATER USE AND CONTAMINATION

Food processing accounts for 75% of water used in industrial countries and 25% of water used worldwide. Water can be an ingredient, a cleaner, a mode of transport for raw ingredients or an agent in the sanitation process. The food industry negatively impacts water quality in several ways.

Organic pollutants deplete oxygen, as measured by biochemical oxygen demand, which is a measure of oxygen required by microbes to break down organic content. They also increase suspended solids, i.e., organic and inorganic particles, and increase nutrient loading, or the nitrogen and phosphorus compounds that promote excessive algae growth in water. Pathogenic organisms from animal processing can be released into water during processing operations. Ironically, chemicals used to promote food safety, such as chlorine and pesticides, can also leave residuals in water.

Any of these pollutants—or adulterants—can enter the water supply through direct agricultural runoff or through the sewer systems at processing and manufacturing facilities. In addition, the practice of spraying liquefied manure onto fields in amounts that exceed fertilizer requirements can contaminate water supplies. Manure can run off during spring thaws and rainstorms, or percolate into groundwater supplies, contaminating wells and springs.

Logistics Management

Logistics encompasses numerous activities that occur throughout the food supply chain. Generally, logistics is divided into control, execution and value-added activities. Control activities include transportation oversight, inventory management, production management and physical network administration. Execution consists of warehousing and the actual transport of goods. Value-added activities include certain manufacturing operations, such as packaging and labeling. The specific activities performed in each of these categories are detailed in Table 8.3, and key topics in the industry—transportation, inventory management, warehousing and packaging—are discussed below.

Transportation

Approximately 200 billion metric tons of food are shipped internationally each year. Of this, 60% goes by sea, 35% by land and 5% by air. Food in the

Table 8.3 **Common Logistics Activities**

	Logistical Activities	
Control	Transportation Oversight	Routing and scheduling, mode and carrier selection, price negotiation, tracking
	Inventory Management	Business forecasting, stock management, tracking
	Production Management	Planning and material processing
	Physical Network Administration	Site analysis and selection
Execution	Warehousing	Receiving, storage, pick and pack operations
	Transportation	Shipping and delivery
Value-Added Activities	Selected manufacturing operations: e.g., packaging, labeling	

Source: Author.

United States often travels 1,500 miles or more from farm to factory to table. Domestically, most food is moved by land, i.e., by truck or rail. An estimated 4% of every dollar spent on food in the United States goes to cover transportation costs. For reasons that should be clear, increasing transportation efficiency is an industry priority.

Water transport is the most common method used to transport food. An advantage of ship transport is that it is inexpensive. A disadvantage is that it is slow. Ships also require waterways and ports, and specialized equipment for loading and unloading. Local and regional food transport can rely exclusively on land-based modes of transit. Transporting food by land can be cost effective. However, drawbacks to rail and truck travel include higher loss and damage rates, and a high environmental impact, particularly for trucks. Commodities, fruits and vegetables typically travel by these methods.

Air transport is generally used for high-value or extremely perishable products, like lobsters or rare wild mushrooms. Air transport's primary advantage is speed, but cost is a major disadvantage. Intermodal shipment, i.e., shipment methods that combine two primary modes of travel, like train-ship, air-truck, train-truck, etc., is most common in international transportation. Intermodal methods can be effective in linking areas of agricultural production, which may have limited transportation access, to transportation networks. It is worth noting that fuel for international air and water transport is not taxed, effectively providing incentives for these methods.

While cost is a critical factor in the decision to use a particular shipping method in the food industry, time-based competition and just-in-time inventory management practices have made speed and reliability key considerations as well. Producers must also consider the type and quantity of food being shipped, labor costs and capital investment required to purchase loading or shipping equipment before selecting a method.

Fluctuations in demand, capacity shortages and driver issues are challenges the food transportation industry faces daily. Additional concerns include maintaining the cold chain or appropriate temperatures, sanitation, proper loading and handling and avoiding cross-contamination, or the transfer of contaminants from one food product to another. Highly sensitive products require consistent communication during transportation, and manufacturers and shippers must document food safety control procedures. Food also needs to be secured during shipment to prevent intentional tampering.

Inventory Management

Inventory management is uniquely difficult for food processors and manufacturers. As in other industries, material shortages can stop production. However, excess inventory can lead to storage, perishability and cold chain maintenance problems. The use of preprocessed and shelf-stable ingredients can help minimize these issues.

Processors typically have large product lines for which inventories must be maintained. Although manufacturers have much smaller product lines, they tend to have long ingredient lists, for which inventories must also be maintained. For example, Kettle Chips, a potato chip manufacturer, uses hundreds of flavorings and a variety of packaging materials to produce a relatively simple line of potato chips.

Inventory has four primary purposes: localization, decoupling, supply and demand balance and buffering. Localization situates processing and manufacturing close to raw materials. For example, frozen orange juice is processed in Florida and California where the majority of oranges are grown. Most of the processing occurs at the peak of the orange season and the frozen juice is stored in that location until needed. Fresh oranges and juice must be sent out to distributors during the orange season.

Decoupling improves process control. Large food manufacturers employ continuous-flow production methods that require time-consuming changeovers between operations, so producing and stockpiling products in large quantities ensures availability. Warehousing finished products provides flexibility in fulfilling orders. However, adoption of just-in-time production has reduced overall inventory for production throughout the food supply chain over the past two decades.

Balancing supply and demand addresses the discrepancy between seasonal material supply and year-round consumption. The freezing or canning of vegetables exemplifies this idea, as does concentrated juice. Maintaining an inventory of these products is cheaper than importing them for just-in-time production.

Buffering refers to safety stock, or inventory that fills the gaps during unanticipated spikes in demand or delays in production. The amount of safety stock held by a manufacturer or distributor is based on the degree of risk a producer is willing to take on with regard to inventory shortfall.

Information technology and management systems have significantly changed the practice of inventory management with regard to distribution channel efficiency, cost-effectiveness and responsiveness. Electronic data interchange (EDI) and efficient consumer response (ECR) today link supply chain partners to enable efficient inventory flow-through across a supply network. Radio frequency identification (RFID) allows identification and tracking of merchandise while materials are being handled and in transit. RFID is a hands-free identification and tracking technology that uses a radio transmitter and a reader to tag items and track information. RFID can efficiently manage both quantity and quality information about food products, but today it is primarily used at the pallet and case level due to cost and practical considerations for its use at the grower and retailer level. Inventory replenishment is now often triggered by point-of-sale information.

Warehousing

Warehouses systematically store and track inventory on a large scale. "Inventory" can be the supplies needed for a processing or manufacturing process (e.g., food ingredients or spare machine parts). "Inventory" can also refer to final products that are waiting to be shipped to customers. In the manufacturing industry, warehousers break down inventories from suppliers and then distribute a select set of goods to manufacturers, helping them meet their production requirements. They also provide value-added services like cross-docking (the practice of receiving goods and immediately re-combining and re-shipping them, without intermediate storage), produce ripening, lot control and distribution. Warehouses also enable companies to accommodate seasonal production and demand and stockpile supplies for large-scale or continuous production.

Strategically located warehouses help stabilize prices by buffering fluctuations in material and product availability and improving transportation efficiency. These activities can reduce the overall carbon footprint of the supply chain. Warehouses are often located at transit junctions, such as ports, airports and rail terminals, and along major highways. Warehouses can be specialized or compartmentalized to accommodate issues such as safety or perishability.

Packaging

Packaging can be considered an activity of manufacturing or of marketing and advertising. Food packages serve several functions: containment, protection and preservation, distribution, communication (identification and advertising) and convenience. Packaging is one of the most labor-intensive steps of food manufacturing, yet it is necessary—particularly for consumer goods. New concepts include "smart packaging" such as food quality labels that indicate time and temperature, and use-by date indicators. There are now smartphone applications that allow consumers to read bar codes on packaging and trace produce that comes from participating farms.

Legally, food packages must indicate the name of the product, weight or volume of product within, ingredients and nutritional information. Consumer packages frequently incorporate logos, pictures, recipes and serving suggestions. As elaborate as they may be, the packages the consumer sees on the shelf are only one aspect of food packaging. Primary packaging, such as a plastic bag insert, holds the food, while secondary packaging, usually cardboard boxes, hold the primary packages and display product information. Certain foods like potato chips have no secondary packaging; the consumer sees and buys the primary package (the bag). Tertiary packaging generally consists of corrugated shipping boxes, and quaternary packaging references palletized loads or containers. These terms are sometimes simplified as industrial (tertiary and quaternary) and consumer packaging (primary and secondary).

Reducing Carbon Emissions in Transportation

As consumers become more aware of the sources of their food, one immediate concern they raise is the "food miles." This in turn forces food companies and logistics providers to find ways to reduce the carbon footprint of transportation. Logistics has become a competitive weapon for supply chains to bring product to market in the right quantity, at the right place and time.

Transportation accounts for as much as 14% of energy use within the food industry. Therefore, corporations and governments are taking initiatives to reduce the carbon emissions and pollution associated with commercial transportation. SmartWay[SM] is a branding collaboration between the Environmental Protection Agency (EPA) and the freight sector designed to reduce carbon dioxide and other emissions, and improve energy efficiency. The SmartWay[SM] brand identifies energy-efficient products and services. Recently, the EPA awarded $3.4 million to help small trucking companies reduce fuel costs and emissions and $20 million to develop financing programs for cleaner trucks, school buses and non-road vehicles and equipment.

The Clean Cargo Working Group is an international collaboration between manufacturers, freight carriers and forwarders. It includes more than 25 leading multinational manufacturers, retailers and freight carriers, which collectively move nearly 60% of global container cargo. Member companies include Coca-Cola, Wal-Mart, Chiquita, Nike and Starbucks, among others. The group's goal is to integrate environmentally and socially responsible business principles into transportation management.

Wal-Mart has recently launched its "Sustainability 360" initiative to implement drastic changes to address environmental issues in business practices, particularly the reduction of material use and waste in the supply chain. It set goals to reduce its logistics function's carbon emissions by 25% in 2012 and improve fleet efficiency by 25% by 2015, which if achieved, will result in $310 million in savings. Not to be outdone, Tesco (UK) has stated that it will reduce its distribution network's emissions by 50% by 2012. Its supply chain includes 29 warehouses and over 2,000 vehicles. The company has adopted carbon footprint labeling for many of its products and has additionally committed to reduce packaging by 25% in the coming years.

Transportation-Related Food Safety

Food transportation involves several industry-specific safety concerns, specifically the prevention of spoilage, microbial contamination and tampering. Hazard Analysis and Critical Control Point (HACCP) plans, detailed in Chapter 2, therefore also cover manufacturing and distribution.

With regard to spoilage, food products must be properly packaged and handled during transportation. Transfer points are the most vulnerable parts of the distribution chain, and particular care must be taken when food is palletized, loaded and off-loaded, or switched between transportation modes.

In April 2010 the Food and Drug Administration (FDA) announced plans for implementing the Sanitary Food Transportation Act of 2005. The act gives the FDA broad authority to regulate food transportation, and federal regulations will govern sanitary practices by shippers, receivers, motor and rail carriers and others involved in transporting food. The FDA identified 15 areas of concern and specifically advised food shippers to focus on temperature control, sanitation, packaging, training and communication among partners in the distribution process.

Logistics Outsourcing

Many food companies are outsourcing some or all of their logistics activities, from transportation and warehousing to inventory control. The decision of whether and how many functions to outsource is influenced by product characteristics

Table 8.4 **Reasons for Logistics Outsourcing**

Service Improvement	Cost Reduction and Risk Management	Focus on Corporate Core Competencies	Operational Flexibility
• Better handling logistics complexity • Unique service available from 3PL providers	• Avoidance of capital investments • Hedging against uncertainties associated with logistics-related IT technology • Cost reduction and risk management	• Delegation of non-critical activities • Leverage unique skills and expertise in transportation and storage (e.g. Hazardous material handling) • Reducing internal operations complexity	• Access to various technology upgrades and competition from 3PL providers • Hedging technological uncertainties • Handling growth and expansion to new markets

Source: Author.

(size, weight and volume), network characteristics (national vs. international), processing characteristics (production cycle time), market characteristics and firms' core competencies. Table 8.4 summarizes the key influences affecting the decision to outsource logistics services.

THIRD-PARTY LOGISTICS (3PL)

Third-party logistics services can include any or all warehousing and transportation activities: freight consolidation and distribution, cross-docking and in- and out-bound shipment management, as well as the associated tracking, documentation and follow-up, freight bill payment and auditing and product packaging. 3PL companies generally own and operate shipping fleets or warehouses, or contract for these services on behalf of their clients. They may or may not offer additional value-added services.

3PL companies maximize asset utilization in a number of ways. Client firms avoid capital investment by sidestepping the risks of owning transportation equipment and warehouses, allowing manufacturers to concentrate on core competencies and potentially reducing or eliminating in-house logistics departments. 3PLs serving the food industry are, of necessity, sensitive to the perishability and fragility of the goods they handle, their clients' and customers' need for timely deliveries, and the variable volume imposed by seasonality and marketing activities such as promotions.

FOURTH-PARTY LOGISTICS (4PL)

Fourth-party logistics providers are non-asset based supply chain managers. They are independent and do not own shipping resources, e.g., trucks, warehouses, etc. They are essentially IT consultants who oversee all of their clients' logistics activities on both the supply and demand sides of the business, while outsourcing the physical operations. 4PLs are less common in the food industry than elsewhere.

Logistics and Distribution for Niche Markets

Logistics and distribution for niche markets are challenging due to higher costs and the lack of logistics infrastructure. Niche markets include certified organic food products (frozen foods, processed poultry, meat and dairy), kosher foods (meeting religious specifications and made under rabbinical supervision), and products for special dietary needs (e.g., gluten- or other allergen-free, low- or no-sugar, low-sodium, etc.).

Producing and moving niche food products is more complex and expensive than moving conventional products. Niche farmers, processors and manufacturers deal in smaller volumes, and must keep niche products separate from bulk commodities to maintain their unique characteristics. For example, producers of niche grains (and the products made from them) must have these grains blended, sorted and cleaned separately from the undifferentiated versions. This special handling is more expensive because it is done in smaller batches and may require additional equipment preparation.

Traceability is particularly important in logistics management of niche products. Consider, for example, organic potatoes. Given the need to preserve product integrity through each link of the supply chain, the handling, distribution and marketing are distinct from those used with conventional potatoes. One organic potato packing plant in Minnesota processes potatoes for several growers. The warehouse stores, washes, packs and ships certified products. To ensure traceability, individual lots are separated by coding indicating the variety and the grower. Imprinted bag fasteners include lot numbers for traceback purposes.

Niche markets are often supplied by small family farmers and small growers. These businesses do not always have cheap and timely access to the facilities necessary to process their products. Several states, including Vermont, Washington and Kentucky, have set up mobile units to help small growers process their products on-site. In Vermont, flash-freeze units are set up to allow growers to quickly freeze fruits and vegetables for later resale. The units extend a grower's season and make those products more available year-round to specialty food producers looking for additional sources of local ingredients. These units allow farmers to plan higher production levels in anticipation of expanding markets.

Modeled after fruit and vegetable mobile units, United States Department of Agriculture (USDA)-inspected mobile field slaughter units have been implemented to allow farmers and ranchers to process and inspect meat right on the farm, rather than going through the time and expense of moving their animals to USDA slaughterhouses. The mobile slaughter unit bridges the gap until these small producers become large enough to afford to support a local USDA processing facility. This has the added benefit of reducing the transportation of livestock, which in turn reduces animal stress. Lastly, reducing transportation also reduces fuel consumption, air pollution and emissions.

Case Study: Trailblazer Foods

When Rob Miller pulled up to the strawberry farm and looked over the fields, he saw Bill Wheeler, director of Purchasing, Planning and Logistics for Trailblazer Foods, walking towards him with a worried look on his face. "Will they be able to pick and pack the berries today?" asked Rob. Bill nodded, "Yes, I think the rain will hold off until tomorrow, but I'm getting increasingly worried about how we're going to double the volume of strawberries for next year." Rob responded, "Well, we didn't know how we were going to meet the first year's commitment, but in 8 months you created a working supply chain for our new organic strawberry spread that met our customers' tough quality and volume expectations. I have complete faith that you can double that volume this year." Bill smiled, "Yes, we did pull that one out of our hat, so let's hope that we can repeat that trick again."

The two men walked over to the processing shed and discussed various scenarios. They agreed that they had built positive relationships with growers, processors and transportation providers over the past year. Hopefully, their planning and these valuable relationships would help them meet the challenge of sourcing almost 5 million pounds of fruit, moving it from California to Oregon quickly and processing that product within the six-month strawberry growing season.

Company Background

Trailblazer Foods is one of the largest manufacturers of jams, jellies, preserves, and syrup in the western United States. It was founded by Gary Walls, who grew up picking berries as a child, managed local berry fields as a young adult, and later started his own blueberry farm. Eventually, Walls went on to develop the first fruit-based syrups for Elmer's Restaurants, an all-day breakfast restaurant chain. He incorporated his business as Trailblazer Foods in 1984, with the intention of producing a wide range of fruit-based products.

Miller Family Holdings acquired the majority and then remaining interest in the company in 2000 and 2002, respectively. As the president of the company, Rob Miller continued to expand the company's product lines and capabilities, adding capital equipment and facility upgrades to enable more production of co-packed and private label foods. Trailblazer also obtained organic processing certification from Oregon Tilth and the USDA in 2005, and Kosher processing certification from KOF-K International in 2008.

Today, Trailblazer produces branded, private-label and co-packed products including fruit jellies and preserves; punch and drink concentrates; Italian syrups; savory sauces, BBQ glazes and marinades; pancake and waffle syrups; pasta sauces and fruit fillings and toppings.

Manufacturing Capabilities and Products

Trailblazer's manufacturing capabilities are currently oriented toward high-volume production of sugar- and corn-sweetener-based recipes and other non-oil based wet products. The company has three branded product lines: Nalley Lumberjack Table Syrups, typically used for pancakes and waffles; Walls Berry Farm preserves, including a wide range of berry and other preserves available in traditional and organic varieties; and a punch concentrate called Portland Punch, which is made from loganberries and raspberries.

While Trailblazer's own brands are sold to major retail customers such as Safeway, Wal-Mart and Costco, the company sells its fruit toppings, syrups and preserves to all major US food service distributors, including Sysco, US Foodservice and Food Services of America. Additionally, Trailblazer produces private label and co-packed products for many companies, and produces specialty items such as Trader Vic's drink mixes and Boyd Coffee's Italian syrups. Each day, the company produces over 40 tons of jam, jelly, and preserves; 40 tons of syrup; 8 tons of pie filling; and 25 tons of sauces and marinades.

Operations

The company has a food manufacturing facility located outside of Portland, Oregon with a daily capacity of 100 tons. Main equipment includes vacuum pans, premix kettles and standardization kettles for cooking, filling and capping stations with the ability to fill various types of packaging and container sizes (2 to 128 ounces), pasteurization and cooling systems, packaging stations for labeling individual and case containers, and fully automated palletizing stations. Because the equipment is designed to handle a consistent product at high volumes, they are able to produce at relatively low costs for the industry. But, because of this high volume production design, clients looking for co-pack production must commit to 10,000 pound minimums.

The Strawberry Spread Challenge

In 2008, a customer approached Trailblazer to see if they could produce a co-private label "super-premium" organic strawberry spread. To achieve the desired quality, appearance, and taste, the customer required 100% fresh organic strawberries, almost 50% more fruit than traditional preserves, and 100% organic sugar as a sweetener. In order to achieve the appropriate jam quality, the berries had to be picked and packed in jars within 72 hours. This product involved a radically different approach to fruit sourcing, logistics and trucking than previously used by the company.

FRUIT SOURCING

Many Trailblazer fruit products were based on fruits grown in the Willamette Valley and neighboring areas. As the largest producer of raspberries and other berry varietals in the United States, Oregon is a prime location for many of Trailblazer's main product categories. Historically, Trailblazer had been able to leverage the location for much of their fruit. But the new strawberry spread would require almost 3 million pounds of fruit. Oregon not only has an extremely limited season for strawberries, but due to the small number of growers, low volumes, and highly fragile fruit, organic strawberry producers can only supply the local fresh consumer market.

As a result, Bill Wheeler was forced to look out of state to get the needed strawberry quantities and still meet the 72 hour door-to-door requirement. This task required identifying organic strawberry growers in California with a high quality and volume product and covering a large enough geographic spread to source strawberries over the six-month growing season. Additionally, there was the question of whether the overall supply of available strawberries was big enough to support their needs without driving up the price of organic strawberries with increased demand. At the time, 33 million pounds of organic strawberries were potentially available in California, with Trailblazer needing 10% of that capacity. Bill spent several months talking to growers and touring their fields, reviewing growing practices, identifying and testing strawberries to see which varieties produced the appropriate flavor and color profile. Eventually he found almost 30 California growers to support the project.

FRUIT LOGISTICS

With 72 hours to move the fruit from the fields in California to the processing facility in Oregon, logistics would play a significant role in the success of the project. Growers and packers need to be in constant communication with their respective trucking companies to make sure the fruit was transported from the fields to the packer and the packer to Oregon in a timely manner. The logistics also required communication with the multiple growers, the trucking company and the production people, and the equipment and technology to handle strawberry volumes that ranged from 20,000 to 480,000 pounds of raw fruit per week, depending on the season. Finally, contingency plans had to be in place for rain-destroyed product, truck breakdowns and other transportation delays, and factory scheduling overrides.

PEOPLE

One of the biggest challenges, often overlooked by those undertaking the development of a new supply chain, is the difference between people and industry cultures. This challenge was quickly apparent to Bill and Rob as they developed the fresh organic strawberry supply chain. On the one hand, the strawberry growers and grower co-ops are traditionally independent and used to selling to a commodity market that sets their price. Therefore, building trust was difficult. In this case, Trailblazer often offered more money and a commitment to buy product at the end of the season, as they were an unknown entity in the California arena. Trailblazer was also unaccustomed to processing fresh fruit to their client's exacting standards. The design of the new supply chain required them to be much more flexible with their scheduling than with previous products, due to perishability and quality concerns.

Conclusion

After their first year running the operation, Bill and Rob realized that they could be successful, with all involved parties making a decent profit. But, as they discussed on their walk, would they be able to handle the increased volume? How would this potentially affect the price of strawberries, relationships with growers and their ability to handle the increased volume in their supply chain? Could the factory be flexible enough to handle twice the volume? What new potential challenges lay around the corner?

Discussion Questions

1. How are food manufacturing processes becoming similar to other manufacturing processes? How does food manufacturing remain distinct?
2. Why might traceability be difficult to maintain during the manufacturing process? How can traceability efforts be enhanced during manufacturing?
3. What is the purpose of inventory in food supply chain management?
4. Research the supply chain and the production practices used to create one of your favorite manufactured food products. What are its ingredients? Do you know from where these ingredients came? What were the likely pathogen reduction, processing and preservation techniques used to create the product? How is it packaged, and why do you think that method of packaging was selected by the manufacturer?

Additional Readings and Links

- Cohen, Fiona. March 2009, 2009. "Big Changes to Seattle's Recycling Program." A summary of Seattle's food waste composting program: http://www.seattlepi.com/local/404368_recycle30.html.
- McTigue Pierce, Lisa. January 1, 2009. "Packaging Trends 2009 Roundtable: No Trade-Offs." This article provides an in-depth, practical assessment of sustainable packaging trends in large food manufacturing environments: http://www.foodandbeveragepackaging.com/Articles/Cover_Story/BNP_GUID_9-5-2006_A_10000000000000506505
- Gabert, Krystal. "Sustainable Snacking." A write-up of Kettle Foods' sustainably designed facility and operations: http://www.foodmanufacturing.com/scripts/Products-Sustainable-Snacking.asp

9

FOOD RETAILING

Webvan launched in 1999 as an online grocery store, promising delivery within a 30-minute window and prices competitive with supermarkets. The brainchild of Louis Borders, founder of Borders Books, Webvan was once valued at $8.4 billion and hailed as an innovator in the grocery world, and a rising hero in the new Internet environment.

But in 2001, shortly after its launch, the company filed for bankruptcy. It wasn't just the dot-com bubble that killed Webvan. Internet shopping was in its infancy and the infrastructure required to support operations was not matched by sales: Webvan's business model in effect called for three infrastructures to be built from scratch—an electronic shopping system, a dedicated grocery distribution network and a home-delivery network. Webvan was also overly ambitious. Its plans included a $1 billion warehouse contract with Bechtel, a $1.2 billion acquisition of rival HomeGrocer.com and a proposed expansion to 26 markets over a two-year time span. Webvan's investments were all made long before the market for online grocery shopping showed any promise of sufficient demand. Ultimately, Webvan overreached, and could not compete with traditional grocers.

In contrast, grocery giant Tesco took an incremental approach to launching its online grocery service. In business since 1919, Tesco is one of the world's largest grocers. Its online sales capacity has been building slowly over the last two decades, leveraging the company's existing infrastructure—distribution centers, employees and equipment—to balance sales with necessary investments. Tesco's branding of its online grocery experience also differed from Webvan's. Tesco positioned its online grocery service as a convenience, versus a stand-alone shopping method, enabling it to charge for delivery. By utilizing its existing infrastructure and supply chain to satisfy growth, and by pricing its services to reflect actual costs, Tesco successfully created and is expanding its online presence.

Introduction

In this chapter, we provide an overview of the retail grocery industry in the United States. We review industry trends and discuss the important issues of inventory and information management. We also assess significant retail strategies, including those related to perishable goods, product differentiation and organics, among others. We conclude with a discussion of international food retailing.

Industry Overview

Consumers in the United States support a $400 billion retail grocery business. Nearly 40,000 companies operate approximately 70,000 grocery stores, not including convenience stores. Retailers earn very thin margins, so efficiency and product sell-through are critical to their success. Supermarkets introduced their low-markup, high-volume retail model in the 1930s; eighty years later, that same approach still dominates the industry. Industry growth depends on supply chain efficiency, competitive pricing, innovation and overseas expansion.

Consumers today get their food from both traditional and nontraditional sources. Traditional sources include supermarkets and small grocers, which may buy their supplies from wholesalers like SuperValu or retail cooperatives like Associated Wholesale Grocers. Integrated wholesale-retail operations are another traditional retail channel. Kroger is an example of an integrated wholesale-retail operation; it owns several grocery chains across the United States and operates food manufacturing and distribution centers nationwide.

Nontraditional retail outlets include drug stores and convenience stores. Farmers' markets and specialty food stores, which sell highly differentiated products such as wines, cheeses and local produce, are also considered nontraditional. At the other end of the nontraditional spectrum are wholesale clubs and supercenters, like Costco, Sam's Club and some Wal-Mart and Target stores. These operations typically combine wholesale purchasing and retail sales, similar to large grocery chains, but they sell a large volume of nongrocery items in addition to food.

Mass Merchandisers

Table 9.1 lists the sales share of food-at-home expenditures from both traditional and nontraditional outlets between 1994 and 2005. The entry and growth of mass merchandisers in the food industry is notable. Their competitive force is exemplified by Wal-Mart, which has risen from the nation's tenth largest food retailer in 1996 to number one today. Wal-Mart accomplished this by opening hundreds of supercenters that combine large food and drug stores with other merchandise in one location. Attracting customers with low food prices, Wal-Mart and Costco now attribute about 30% of their sales to groceries.

Table 9.1 **Share of Food-at-Home Expenditures by Outlet Type, by %**

	1994	2001	2005
Traditional Grocery Retailers			
Supermarkets	59.2	62.7	58.2
Convenience	3.1	2.9	2.9
Other grocery	16.6	3.5	3.6
Specialty food stores	2.8	2.3	2.7
Total Traditional	81.7	71.4	67.4
Nontraditional Grocery Retailers			
Supercenters and warehouse clubs (e.g., Costco)	3.9	11.7	17.1
Mass merchandisers(e.g., traditional Wal-Mart)	1.8	2.2	1.8
Other stores (e.g., Walgreens)	9.0	9.6	8.7
Home-delivered and mail order	2.4	4.1	4.0
Total Nontraditional	17.1	27.6	31.6

Source: S.W. Martinez.

Table 9.2 lists the major grocery retailers in the United States in 2008. Mass merchandisers occupy two of the top three sales positions. Their popularity is putting incredible pressure on traditional retailers. It is also profoundly influencing the dynamic of and operations in the entire food supply chain. Mass merchandisers are dominating food marketing and supply chain management at the expense of the traditional wholesaler, and at the expense of others in the supply chain.

Table 9.2 **Top US Grocery Retailers*, 2008**

Company Stores	Estimated Sales in Billion $	Number of Stores
Wal-Mart	167.2	4184
Kroger	66.3	3269
Costco	39.8	394
Supervalu	37.4	2514
Safeway	36.0	1518
Publix	22.8	1044
Ahold	21.8	735
Target	21.4	1682
Delhaize Group	15.8	1594
HE Butt	12.7	289
Aldi	10.9	1304
Meijer	10.8	190
Whole Foods Market	7.7	264
Winn-Dixie Stores	7.1	521
Tengelmann (A&P)	6.6	434

*Note that estimated sales are the Estimated Grocery Equivalent Sales in the US market.
 Source: R.A. Cook.

Mass merchandisers focus on everyday low pricing (EDLP), and their volume buying puts distributors and producers at a distinct disadvantage. Mass merchandisers can impose standards to which suppliers must conform. Their knowledge of a supplier's business also allows the merchandiser to determine the price they will pay, as opposed to the supplier. Large retailers today are thus wielding power over prices paid to suppliers and shippers, as well as prices paid by the consumer—a win-win for the retailer.

To stabilize prices and supplies, large retailers are also increasingly relying on contract buying. Contracts encourage suppliers and shippers to grow and consolidate, in order to meet demand, but also make them dependent on high volumes to sustain their businesses. As retailers are exerting greater buying power, they are also pushing suppliers to pay for aspects of business for which retailers once paid. These include marketing, inventory services, third-party safety certifications and reusable shipping containers.

Other Industry Influences

Other nontraditional grocers are also changing the dynamic of sales in the industry. About 90% of all groceries were sold through traditional grocery stores in 1988; that number fell to 55% in 2005 and to below 50% by 2008. This is occurring because drugstores such as Walgreens and CVS offer convenience by providing essentials such as milk and snacks to busy consumers. Indeed, these companies have recently opened new stores and expanded their grocery selections. Drugstores now account for almost 5% of food sales in the United States.

Internet grocery sales have also grown slowly but steadily over the past decade. With 2008 sales of roughly $3.75 billion, the online segment is small but expanding. Market share forecasts project that online food retailing will soon comprise an estimated 2% of total food sales. However, sales are not expected to reach above 5%. Top online grocers in the United States include Peapod, Safeway, Fresh Direct, ShopFoodEx and Amazon. In the UK, Tesco first offered online groceries in 1994. Today the company accepts Internet orders and provides local delivery through one-third of its 690 stores. This effectively puts 91% of the British population within a half hour of a Tesco. The company dominates the online market in the UK with a 41.5% share.

Lastly, changing lifestyles are influencing the food retail industry in the United States. Americans are significantly increasing their consumption of restaurant and takeout food. Although retailers are changing the way they do business in an attempt to recapture share—vastly expanding their selection of ready-to-eat meals—they are still losing sales to the food service industry. Food store sales have now been in decline for decades; less than 40% of total food sales in the United States today are attributable to food stores, down from 45% only a decade ago.

Consolidation

Because of the low profit margins on most groceries, companies must move large quantities of product to generate profits. When combined with the general decline in food store sales, the purchasing and distribution efficiencies of large food retailers makes price competition difficult for smaller companies. Thus, consolidation has transformed the retail food industry in the past two decades, as it has nearly every other aspect of the food supply chain.

Big companies have become even larger in recent years, mainly by acquiring local and regional chains and expanding into new territories. The 50 largest grocery chains today capture more than 60% of the market. Recent major supermarket mergers and acquisitions include Kroger's $12.75 billion acquisition of Fred Meyer, which had itself previously acquired Smith's Food & Drug Centers and Quality Food Centers; Albertsons $12 billion acquisition of American Stores Company; and Ahold's acquisition of Giant Food Stores.

Inventory and Information Management

The retail supply chain fundamentally consists of inventory selection, wholesale buying, logistics (shipping, handling and stocking), marketing and retail pricing. Inventory management influences all of these supply chain elements, and is thus of primary importance in the retail industry. There are three general components of inventory management: assortment, allocation and replenishment. These concepts are described below. Information management's role in inventory management is also summarized.

Assortment

Assortment is the decision as to which brands and products should be stocked by a retailer. Assortment is influenced by a number of factors, including consumer preference, available shelf space, product availability, product competitiveness, supplier recommendations and the potential for revenue beyond product sales—e.g., slotting fees. Assortment is also strongly influenced by retail strategy. For example, some stores rely on private labels as a cornerstone of their assortment and revenue strategy, while others avoid private labels, as they are only able or prefer to stock name brands.

Another example is the decision about how many products to stock. The average retailer carries an average of 40,000 stock keeping units (SKUs). When a large retailer's assortment of goods is much smaller than this, the retailer is anticipating that average daily demand per item will be relatively large. The smaller variety enables high volume purchasing from suppliers, which in turn reduces prices, stabilizes product demand and results in less waste in a product category. An example of this is Costco, which stocks 4,000 different items. Compare this to Wal-Mart, which stocks more than 100,000 items, clearly employing a different assortment strategy.

Allocation

Allocation refers to the amount of shelf space that each product gets. The allocation of space to products in a retail environment is incredibly important for both retailers and suppliers. Retailers devote prime store and shelf space to highly appealing products that drive traffic and build retail brands. Produce, for example, is a key store differentiator in a competitive market, thus it is often given prime "real estate" in the store environment—right next to the front door. For suppliers, good product visibility on the shelves is critical for driving sales and building market share. No supplier wants their product languishing on the top or bottom shelf of a retailer's store; in addition to low revenues for the supplier, a languishing product will not be carried by a retailer for long.

Shelf space is so important that many retailers charge suppliers slotting fees—additional charges to display products on their shelves. Food retailers claim that these fees guide them in shelf space allocation and help balance the risk of product failure, while food processors and manufacturers counter that the fees are merely a way of increasing retail profits at their expense. In some cases, slotting fees account for more retailer profit than actual product sales. The fees can be a barrier for small producers that cannot afford the "pay to play" arrangement, particularly because slotting fees tend to be higher the more "choice" a particular store or shelf space is.

Allocation for perishable products is particularly tricky. Because customers almost always choose the freshest products on the shelf, managing their inventory is more complicated than managing inventory for nonperishable products. Perishables with too much shelf space often end up with multiple batches, i.e., multiple date codes, on the shelf. This over-allocation leads to last-in-first-out (LIFO) selection. Of course, from a supply chain point of view, first-in-first-out (FIFO) sales are optimal. In limited display space environments, grocers often split inventories between the shelf and back room storage. A retailer can then control the inventory on the shelf by managing shelf space allocation and replenishment from the back room.

Replenishment

Replenishment is the decision of when and how much to reorder, thus it goes hand-in-hand with forecasting. Retailers want to have as accurate a forecast as possible, as an accurate forecast minimizes inventory in the pipeline. This, in turn, reduces cold chain management and storage costs, as well as spoilage and loss costs. At the same time, retailers do not want to underestimate demand, i.e., have a forecast that underserves actual replenishment needs. Underestimating demand results in a stockout, which reduces retailer revenue and gives the customer a lack of supply predictability.

Accurately predicting demand can be very difficult in the food industry. Long-term demand varies widely between products, and is heavily influenced by factors like perishability, seasonality and promotions. Holidays in particular spike demand for particular products, e.g., hot dogs, hamburgers, buns and baked beans at 4th of July. All retailers engage in some form of forecasting. Retailers may do the work themselves, or they may use the services of a category manager. A category manager typically works for a supplier and projects demand for all of the items in a given food or product group.

To manage inventory effectively, retailers and suppliers employ various inventory management and replenishment strategies. Demand substitution and risk pooling are two internal strategies that can be employed to influence consumer demand. Cross-docking and direct delivery are external supply chain strategies that can optimize the replenishment process.

DEMAND SUBSTITUTION

Demand substitution involves adjusting prices to temporarily change consumers' demand patterns. For example, retailers often offer discounts on fresh meat products before they reach their expiration date, which increases demand and clears the shelves before spoilage occurs. Yield management is a version of demand substitution and works well for retailers with multiple outlets. Real time demand is forecasted for particular products across stores, and prices are adjusted as needed to match supply with demand.

RISK POOLING

Risk pooling is a concept that helps companies with multiple retail locations set inventory at an appropriate level. It seeks to reduce demand variability by aggregating demand across locations, based on the assumption that high demand from one customer will offset low demand from another. The reduction in variability makes it possible to reduce safety stock and overall inventory. Risk pooling allows companies to use central warehouses with lower inventories to replenish multiple locations. This strategy is most effective when the demand across various retailer locations is highly correlated.

CROSS-DOCKING AND DIRECT DELIVERY

Cross-docking and direct delivery can reduce delivery lead times, minimizing inventory in the pipeline and improving product freshness. Cross-docking is a value-added process that often occurs in distribution centers, and is a logistical alternative to warehousing. Incoming goods from trailers or rail cars are transferred onto outbound trucks as quickly as possible, usually during the course of one employee's work shift. Materials are separated into smaller packages, recombined, sorted and then shipped to different retail destinations with minimal stay at the distribution center. Buying products locally, and direct delivery, can also reduce lead times. For instance, local bakeries can bake and deliver bread daily.

Information Management

Today, retailers monitor inventory and manage replenishment activities both manually and through automated store ordering systems. When employed, automated systems can greatly improve and streamline the inventory management process, as they allow retailers to collect and share data with different tiers of the supply chain in real time. Radio frequency identification (RFID) is a key technology advancement in the industry, and is influencing the entire food supply chain. However, due to its expense and some practical limitations, RFID today is primarily used by the food industry at the pallet and case level. This application of RFID technology is explained in Chapter 8.

Retail Strategy

Because retail margins are so thin, and because competition in the industry is fierce, retailers are constantly refining their business model to increase—or maintain—their share in the market. This section discusses several topics that are essential to retail strategy today, including perishable goods; natural, organic and local products; ready-to-eat and import products; store format and layout; and generalized revenue enhancement strategies, such as private label and loyalty cards. Strategies in online retailing are also described.

Perishable Goods

Grocery stores, including warehouse stores, superstores, neighborhood stores and convenience stores, sell products that can be classified under one of three general categories: perishables, nonperishables and other items. Perishable goods, mainly fresh produce and meats, drive retail profits and are growing in terms of sales, SKUs and consumer draw. Perishables represent one of the last competitive advantages traditional grocers have over low cost supercenters, such as Wal-Mart. Because perishables are time-sensitive, their inventory management is particularly critical. Figure 9.1 illustrates the per capita consumption of common perishable food products in the last eight years in the United States.

PRODUCE

Produce is a particularly important facet of the corporate image, and thus a particularly important perishable good. In addition to drawing customers,

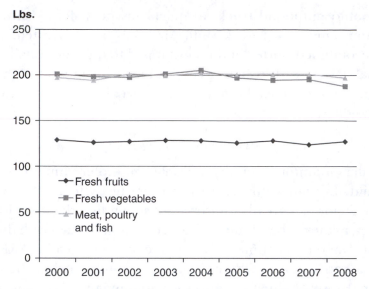

Figure 9.1 **Per capita consumption of key perishable goods, 2000–2008**(Source: USDA ERS).

fresh produce helps drive profits, accounting for 12% of sales and 17% of retailer profit, on average. Produce sales also encourage incremental sales in other departments, acting as ingredients and complements to other products. Retailers therefore invest additional effort to showcase fruits and vegetables and to offer a good selection and prices.

In recent years, small and large retailers have devoted more overall floor space and SKUs to produce. Sales and profits have grown accordingly, as illustrated in Tables 9.3 and 9.4. In response to consumer demand for convenience, retailers are also growing their selection of value-added fruit and vegetable products; e.g., fresh-cut produce. To differentiate themselves from competitors, retailers are also pushing suppliers to provide new and exotic varieties of produce, and improve traceability and environmental accountability in the supply chain. The challenge for suppliers is to meet all these criteria reliably on an ongoing basis.

MEAT

Development of new meat products has increased consumer demand in all three segments of the meat industry: pork, beef and chicken. As with produce, meat's perishability necessitates accurate inventory management. Increasing consumer concern about meats' origins and handling practices has also increased consumer interest in traceability in the sector. Although the adoption of automated inventory management technologies, such as RFID, might therefore benefit retailers, the meat industry is embracing such technologies

Table 9.3 **Produce Department Share of Total Profits by Firm Size, by %**

	Up to $1.5 B	>$1.5 B	All Retailers
1996	15.9	14	14.6
2001	18.4	14.9	15.9
2006	21.1	17.7	18.7

Source: D.J. Perosio, E.W. McLaughlin, S. Cuellar and K. Park.

Table 9.4 **Number of Retail Store Produce SKUs by Firm Size**

	Up to $1.5 B	>$1.5 B	All Retailers
1996	436	426	430
2001	592	562	574
2006	706	636	664

Source: D.J. Perosio, E.W. McLaughlin, S. Cuellar and K. Park.

slowly, a demonstration of the fact that collaboration between partners in the food supply chain is still often limited.

The meat industry is highly concentrated in the United States. Packers therefore strongly influence retailers' meat prices, although they can also give retailers promotional opportunities that would not otherwise be possible given meat price fluctuations. To generate revenue on meats, retailers stimulate sales through in-store promotions, coupons and frequent buyer discount cards. In particular, feature pricing is a markdown from a product's shelf price at the checkout. Such price control and sales promotions put small and independent meat producers at a disadvantage; these and other processing issues mean that small-scale and independent meat producers often avoid selling their products through standard retail environments.

Natural, Organic and Local Foods

Growing demand for natural, organic and local food has changed the retail landscape. Growing demand has stimulated the fast growth of fresh format stores that target niche market segments. For example, Whole Foods specializes in natural and organic products, and grew by 159% between 1999 and 2004 and 70% between 2005 and 2009, in part through acquisitions of other natural food chains, like Wild Oats. However, while natural food stores have entered the retail sector as a major force, conventional supermarkets now represent the largest outlet for organic food sales.

Growth in natural, organic and local food sales has been so robust that the sector has attracted supercenter players. For instance, Wal-Mart has begun to offer locally grown and organic products and recently launched its "Heritage Agriculture" program, which encourages farmers within a one-day drive of any of its warehouses to grow crops to sell in their stores. The grocery industry is well aware of the "Wal-Mart effect" that drives low costs and expands markets, so this shift may be a bellwether for retailers.

Concerns about the "corporatization" of the local and organic food movement have begun to surface among producers, and were exemplified in a protest against the "farmers' markets" held in Albertsons stores during the 2010 Labor Day weekend. About 200 Albertsons stores in Idaho, Washington and Oregon displayed "Farmers' Market" signs in their produce sections. The Farmers Market Coalition, a national trade group, protested and formally adopted the longstanding, commonly recognized definition of a farmers' market: an event that consists primarily of farmers selling their products direct to consumers. Clearly, there will be much debate about the role of natural, organic and local products in the retail industry as the definition of sustainable agriculture evolves.

Other Forms of Product Differentiation

With consumers seeking convenience, food retailers are increasingly competing against restaurants and food service establishments. Consequently, they are selling more prepared and ready-to-eat foods in the retail environment. Among the fastest growing products are prepackaged produce and salad products and prepared meats and poultry. Many supermarkets offer hot and cold takeout meals, which have high profit margins.

Retailers are also targeting growth with specialty and imported foods. As American customers seek out new food experiences, specialty and imported foods are becoming important competitive tools. The imported food and beverage market continues to expand, rising from $46.5 billion in 2002 to $76.8 billion in 2009. Sourcing these products can pose a challenge; retailers must often establish relationships with several distributors of imported and specialty foods to tap this market.

Store Design

Conventional supermarkets are changing their layouts to lure customers to high margin sections: bakery margins average 40%; deli, 38%; and produce, 30%. Thus, these sections are accounting for an increasing percentage of store floor space. Bakeries are today often the largest store section, averaging 2,100 square feet. Retailers are also often creating deli areas that have dining space, and expanding natural foods sections. Many retailers also have large health and beauty products sections, and 68% of new stores have pharmacies.

Nonfood services, like party planning, flowers and DVD rentals, are also being accommodated in grocery stores.

Some chains are also fundamentally evolving the traditional retail store format, e.g., combination food and drug stores and warehouse stores. Stores are also decreasing in size. The typical new grocery store today is less than 49,000 square feet; this is a decline from the average new store construction size in recent years, given the supercenter trend. Overall, supermarkets today average 45,000 square feet in size. This is because many older stores are still in use.

FLOOR LAYOUT

A store's layout is extremely important because it influences in-store traffic, consumer behavior, efficiency and the overall mood of the store. Studies have shown that layout affects consumers' perceptions of price appropriateness, and their purchasing decisions. Figures 9.2 through 9.4 depict three major types of store layout. In practice, retailers often customize and adopt a mix of these three designs.

The grid layout is a rectangular arrangement of displays and long aisles running parallel to one another. The grid facilitates routine and planned shopping behavior, providing flexibility and speed in identifying and locating products. It is widely favored by the grocery sector because most grocery customers have planned their purchases.

The freeform layout is an asymmetric arrangement of displays and aisles, with a variety of different display sizes, shapes and styles. In this pattern, customers can move in any direction within the store. It is more frequently used by large department stores. The freeform layout increases the amount of time that consumers spend in the store and makes it easier for them to browse.

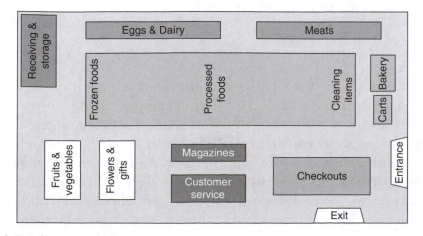

Figure 9.2 **Retail store: grid layout**

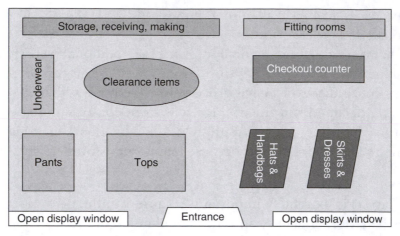

Figure 9.3 **Retail store: freeform layout**

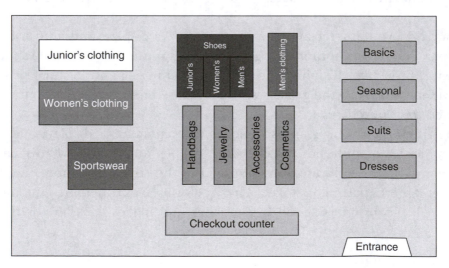

Figure 9.4 **Retail store: racetrack/boutique layout**

In the racetrack, or boutique layout, the floor is organized into separate areas, organized around themes. It leads the customer along a predetermined path to visit as many sections or departments as possible and the main aisle facilitates customer movement through the store.

In an online shopping environment, studies found that customers prefer a hierarchical, tree-like structure in virtual stores. This reflects the grid layout in concept, which was perceived as the easiest to use. The logic behind the other two layouts does not offer the ideal customer shopping experience in virtual stores.

Other Revenue Strategies

PRIVATE LABEL

Since 2003, the United States private label market has expanded by almost 60%, compared to 23% for the overall US retail food market. Even small chains carry private label goods that offer retailers lower prices but higher margins than national brands. Private label now accounts for 24% of the market by volume and 19% of market value. Larger supermarket chains have been steadily upgrading the quantity and quality of their private label offerings. For example, Kroger carries about 7,500 store brand items. Other examples of private labels include H.E. Butt's Central Market Organic, Albertsons Essensia premium line and Publix line of branded Hispanic products.

In addition to improving margins, private labels strengthen the relationship between customer and retailers. As retailers improve the quality of private label products and offer competitive pricing and marketing, these products will pose a greater threat to national brands. In response to the proliferation of store brands, national brand manufacturers have adjusted product quality and wholesale price. If retailers cannot easily match the quality of a national brand, the large brand manufacturers maintain quality and discount their wholesale price to ensure distribution.

LOYALTY CARDS

Loyalty discount cards have been implemented by almost every major grocery chain in the United States. By tracking purchasing habits and histories, stores can group customers by how much and how often they purchase. This information helps target the most desirable customers and cater to their needs and allows customers the opportunity to take advantage of attractive price reductions. But the cards are under attack from consumer advocates who claim that the personal data and shopping information collected violates privacy rights. Stores disclose their use of data in legal sections of signup forms for loyalty cards, but consumers are often unaware, provoking ongoing debate between stores and advocacy groups.

DISTRIBUTION

Depending on their scale, food retailers may or may not own their own distribution center. If they do, these centers receive and redistribute merchandise, usually to stores within 250 miles of their hubs. For example, Kroger is one of the largest US food retailers, but it is also one of the largest food distributors. It runs its own bakeries and dairies and leverages its distribution hubs to supply all of the grocery stores it owns and operates—a number of chains with different names across the country. The largest chains leverage their distribution systems to increase revenue by providing replenishment services for other grocers.

Online Strategy

On average, shoppers tend to spend twice as much online as offline when making food and beverage purchases. Thus, when this market can be served effectively, revenues can be high. Five types of shoppers favor online groceries: very busy or very wealthy consumers or those with young children who need convenient, one-stop shopping, with a wide range of products at low prices; the carless population, which prefers alternative transportation or is carless by necessity; the less-abled and elderly for whom driving and shopping are difficult chores; technology fans who prefer computer shopping to the in-store buying; and "lifestylers," for whom online ordering can provide hard-to-obtain items, like specialty and imported foods or organic produce.

There are two models for online retailers: bricks and clicks and pure play. Brick and click stores, like Tesco, rely on existing infrastructure to offer online grocery services; i.e., their physical stores handle the logistics of their online sales. Orders are picked and packed at stores near customers and delivery vans take groceries to consumers. The bricks and clicks model is an extension of an existing business, requiring comparatively minimal capital investment. It adds convenience to its service offerings by leveraging existing supply chain infrastructure.

Webvan represented the pure play model. Like Amazon, which now owns the Webvan name, a pure play entity is created as a virtual store, supported by physical warehouses but no retail locations. Amazon, which offers a large line of food products through its grocery department, has recently begun to offer grocery delivery services similar to those of Safeway and the former Webvan, under the name Amazon Fresh. Using its existing warehouse infrastructure and technology, it offers local fresh food delivery in the Seattle metro area.

International Retailing

While the population of industrialized nations has stabilized, populations in lower income countries are expected to grow over the next 25 years, particularly in urban centers. Global retailers are positioning themselves to follow this relocation of demand. The number of supermarkets has been growing in developing countries throughout Africa, Asia and Latin America in the past two decades. Table 9.5 lists the largest grocery retailers in the world as of 2005. Table 9.6 summarizes the factors for the rapid growth of supermarkets in the developing countries.

With the rise of the middle class in developing countries, markets are shifting from fragmented, local outlets—such as village markets acting as wholesalers and retailers—to larger, centralized wholesale markets supplying retail operations. The changes started in dry goods such as grains and legumes, and have

Table 9.5 **Largest Grocery-Based Retailers in the World, 2005**

Group	Country of Origin	US Banner Sales	Net Sales	% Grocery Sales	% Foreign Sales
Wal-Mart	USA	338,774	312,427	44.9	22.4
Carrefour	France	117,175	92,597	74.1	52.4
Metro Group	Germany	83,237	69,260	47.4	51.7
Tesco	UK	77,171	69,631	73.4	23.1
Ahold	Netherlands	76,774	55,307	84.0	82.0
Seven & I	Japan	69,237	35,324	72.0	34.0
Kroger	USA	63,702	60,553	70.5	0.0
Rewe	Germany	56,527	51,832	76.4	30.5
Costco	USA	56,456	52,935	60.2	20.5
Casino	France	53,842	28,347	74.7	41.8
Aeon	Japan	51,478	40,230	59.4	8.2
Auchan	France	51,273	38,216	62.0	47.0
Edeka	Germany	50,131	41,266	85.4	6.7
Schwarz Group	Germany	49,726	45,802	82.5	43.3
Aldi	Germany	48,773	45,008	83.3	44.7
Albertsons	USA	42,457	40,358	68.3	0.0
Safeway	USA	42,078	38,416	75.5	16.1
Leclerc	France	39,539	35,424	63.0	5.6
ITM	France	36,556	37,724	66.0	10.0
Tengelmann	Germany	33,024	29,986	65.7	50.8
Woolworth	Australia	31,086	27,090	70.5	8.7
Sainsbury	UK	30,606	30,178	76.1	0.0
Coles Myer	Australia	30,150	27,853	52.0	0.6
Loblaw	Canada	24,994	22,943	77.4	0.0
Delhaize	Belgium	24,836	18,600	76.9	77.1

*Retailers with 40%+ of sales in grocery, ranked by sales in US$ million, 2005. Source: S. Burt, K. Davies, J. Dawson and L. Sparks.

Table 9.6 **Factors for Supermarket Diffusion in Developing Countries**

Demand	Supply
Real mean per capita income growth during the 1990s, along with the rapid rise of the middle class; entry of women into the workforce increases demand for processed foods to save on cooking time.	Saturation and intense competition in home markets and much higher margins to be made by investing in developing markets motivate western retailers to make foreign direct investment in developing markets.
Supermarkets, often in combination with large-scale food manufacturers, reduce the prices of processed products.	A full or partial liberalization of retail sector and foreign direct investment undertaken in many developing countries in the 1990s and after.
Rapid growth in ownership of refrigerators shifted shopping from daily shopping in traditional retail shops to weekly or monthly shopping. Growing access to cars and public transport reinforced this trend.	IT technology advancement in retail procurement logistics technology and inventory management (e.g. efficient consumer response, enterprise resource planning tools) drive costs out of the system.

Source: T. Reardon, C.P. Timmer, C.B. Barrett and J. Berdegue.

continued with perishables—fruits and vegetables, meat, fish, eggs and dairy. One factor driving change is economies of scale in production. Of the fresh food categories, supermarkets first gain a majority share in commodities such as potatoes, then in sectors experiencing consolidation in processing and production, often led by meat and poultry. Supermarkets' fresh food market share is roughly one-half of their shares in packaged foods. Overall, this market consolidation reflects the changes that have transformed American markets in recent decades.

Many of those changes will present great challenges—even to the point of market exclusion—for some small farms, processors and distribution firms, but may offer great opportunities as well. As income grows in these economies, market integration proceeds through long-distance trade and specialized production. Improvements in roads and urbanization accelerate integration and consolidation. As a result, supermarkets expand beyond the middle class in capital cities and penetrate deeply into rural food markets. Supermarkets, for instance, have now spread well beyond the largest coastal cities in China and to smaller towns and the more remote interior.

As supermarkets grow, their global food system relies increasingly on industrialized production and centralized distribution networks run by relatively few companies. In international expansion, grocers must consider both the geographical and cultural distance between their home market and the country it intends to enter. Grocery retailers are well advised to lean toward markets that offer a close cultural fit and numerous operational advantages. Where there is a large cultural distance, populations are most sensitive to food item differences, particularly meat and cereal products. These types of cultural factors affect retailers' decisions regarding how to adapt to local needs, the degree of standardization versus local market adaptation and operational autonomy. In recent years, companies have aimed for integration and coordination of operations at the regional level to attain economies of scale.

For instance, Carrefour takes a decentralized management approach as a critical internationalization strategy as it expands in China. The company grants the local management team significant autonomy. According to their Annual Report, "Carrefour not only exports its unique retailing expertise to the countries in which it operates, it also strives to adapt to their specific environment at every level." The company relies on a decentralized organization comprising over 50 international operating units. Each develops its own format and product lines for their country of operation. This operating method relies on local initiative, providing a good match between merchandise, store layout and customer expectations.

Conclusion

The retail food business today faces unprecedented challenges: stagnating populations are limiting growth, new formats are increasing competition and consolidation among retailers and their suppliers has made the marketplace more homogeneous. The largest retailers are exerting increasing control over their supply chains to drive prices down. Meanwhile, smaller chains and traditional food stores are responding by increasing their specialization. While new technologies, such as RFID systems, could increase efficiency, smaller stores and chains often cannot afford their initial costs. Whatever their strategy, all retailers are under pressure to sell more for less.

Producer Profile: Fred Meyer and Richey's Market

Fruit and vegetable retailers face purchasing challenges every day. The products they sell are perishable, mandating rapid inventory turns. Many items require special handling, storage and frequent inspections to assess quality and safety, and customers are demanding more choices, such as natural and organic fruit and vegetable products. The growing demand for social and environmental sustainability creates both opportunities and challenges for retailers. This trend in turn mandates changes to how retailers manage logistics and inventory, supply chain relationships, product branding, store management and pricing. In this case, we assess the fruit and vegetable management decisions made by two Pacific Northwest retailers: Fred Meyer and Richey's Market.

Fred Meyer and Richey's both have outlets in Corvallis, Oregon—a college town with a population of 54,880 and a student population totaling 20,320. Given its location, Corvallis has a high proportion of college-educated residents. Fred Meyer is located in close proximity to the university and a significant portion of the school's student housing. The store tends to attract student shoppers in addition to local residents. Richey's is located 1.7 miles from the university. Although it is in a student residential area, the store focuses on serving local residents, thus its customers are primarily middle aged and elderly locals who have been loyal shoppers for years.

Fred Meyer is a regional company that is a Kroger subsidiary. Kroger is one of the largest retail food companies in the United States. Fred Meyer became a part of Kroger in 1998. Its modern, full service grocery store also sells electronics, clothing, toys and miscellaneous durable goods. The Corvallis store spent $3.8 million on a renovation in 2005. Its furnishings are modern, and its lighting is designed to highlight certain high-value products. The store's aisle width is average for a modern grocery store, allowing two carts to easily pass one another. The store's look is modern, clean and upbeat.

By comparison, Richey's is a small, family-owned grocery and deli. Jack Richey and his brother Herman came to Oregon from Oklahoma in the late 1940s, followed by their two brothers. They opened the first Richey's store in 1962 in downtown Corvallis, and opened a second store in Albany, Oregon soon after. Over the next 10 years they opened an additional store in Corvallis and two more in Albany. The family-owned business became a corporation in 1970. Since then, the three stores in Albany were sold, and two of the stores in Corvallis were either sold or closed.

The remaining Richey's store carries a high percentage of generically branded merchandise on the shelves, along with a few name brand items. The store was built in 1963, and is located in a single story, older, leased building with multiple long aisles and a tile floor. The store has the look of a traditional grocery of the 1980s. The produce department has several dedicated areas. One section consists of a refrigerated, multitier rack used for juice and bagged salads and dressings. Another area is a long multitier rack for conventional produce. In the center of the department are three dry racks for conventional produce and fruit. The south wall consists of a special section used only for organic fruits and vegetables.

Product Sourcing and Store Management

FRED MEYER

The buyers and the Vice President of Produce at the distribution center in Clackamas, a suburb of Portland, determine the selection of produce available. However, the corporate buyers for Fred Meyer, located in Cincinnati, set the price for produce, and all large produce contracts are executed at this corporate level. Regional Fred Meyer offices have the freedom to make decisions regarding ads and promotions independently. Coordination between each individual Fred Meyer store regarding purchasing is almost nonexistent. Corporate buyers give guidelines on product placement within the produce department, but local stores can vary the location depending on local needs. Local managers are allowed to place order quantities at the store level.

The Portland Fred Meyer distribution center sources its local produce and vegetables from many companies, including Organically Grown Company (OGC). OGC is the largest wholesaler of organic produce in the

Pacific Northwest with offices in Eugene and Portland, Oregon and Kent, Washington. The Fred Meyer in Corvallis sells the highest volume of organic produce and vegetables of all Fred Meyer locations in Oregon. There are about 100 organic items available from the Clackamas distribution center. Store buyers are also able to order approximately 58 different items from OGC in Eugene if those items are not available from the distribution center.

RICHEY'S

Richey's does well selling conventional produce, but carries very little organic produce. Its main customers are composed of local residents and are loyal shoppers. They tend to be middle aged or older and do not have a high demand for organic products. Tony Richey, son of founder Jack Richey, is the current produce manager. Tony places orders with United Salad and Unified Grocers, two of the region's primary distributors of conventional and organic produce. These distributors make deliveries five days a week, so Tony orders small amounts frequently and the store has a rapid turnover of products.

Richey's is known for its high quality produce and vegetable products. This is one reason why the store has a loyal customer base. Besides purchasing from United Salad and Unified Grocers, Richey's uses half a dozen local produce growers including limited production from one of their own farms, which grows rhubarb and squash, during its harvest season. One major local supplier is Dennison Farms, a 20-acre farm located just north of Corvallis that is the largest organic grower in the area. Another supplier is Green Gables, outside of Philomath, Oregon, which provides strawberries when they are in season. Because Tony orders these products from local suppliers, particularly hot or wet weather can cause supply problems. Tony keeps an eye on the weather and talks to local growers to manage inventory. He relies on his experience and past knowledge to estimate which fruits and vegetables are coming into season.

For both Richey's and Fred Meyer, the end of the growing season for local, domestic and international produce is a constant source of problems. Produce shipped toward the end of the season or after weather damage may be subpar. Inspections occur at both the distribution center and at the store level. A USDA representative must certify the produce when disputes between the distribution center and the grower/supplier occur. This can be expensive so questionable produce is often sold to a third party that sorts and resells the produce in good condition.

End of an Era?

In recent years, several factors have forced the Richey's owner to decide to close the last store in Corvallis. No one in the fourth generation plans to take over the family business. As family members such as Tony near retirement age, it is difficult to manage the store's day-in and day-out workload. In the meantime, Richey's is facing fierce competition from Fred Meyer, national grocers such as Safeway and Albertsons, farmers' markets and CSAs that also supply high quality produce and vegetables. These stores all compete for higher income customers and young customers attracted to product quality but also wanting one-stop shopping and broad product choices. In 2009 and 2010, Trader Joe's and Market of Choice entered the Corvallis market, further diluting the customer base and creating more competition. While the city encouraged Richey's to build a new store in the south side of the city—an underserved area without a grocery store—the family turned down the proposal because the capital investment was too high.

Fred Meyer also feels the competition heating up. While the store was renovated several years ago and is competing with the national chains in town, the entry of Market of Choice imposes a direct threat to its relatively upscale produce and vegetable positioning. At the same time, Fred Meyer corporate is streamlining produce and vegetable merchandising operations and decision processes, reducing the decision-making autonomy of store managers. With the loss of autonomy for everyday decisions, its ability to compete with smaller, niche stores offering quality products and a more personal shopping experience is in question.

Discussion Questions

1. What does the retail grocery industry look like today? Who are the key operators in the industry and what forces are influencing the industry's present and future?
2. How does consolidation at the retailer level impact consolidation in other realms of the food supply chain?
3. What are the key components of inventory management? How do they work?
4. Consider the strategy at work in your local grocery store. What might be the store's assortment, allotment and replenishment strategies? What is the logic behind the store's layout? What other strategies might your local grocer be employing to maximize revenue?

Additional Readings and Links

- The Progressive Grocer's website provides useful industry information, primarily articles and resources, to readers: www.progressivegrocer.com
- The Packer is a useful web resource for those interested in produce, providing readers with industry data and information on commodities: www.thepacker.com

10

FOOD AID AND HUNGER RELIEF

On January 12, 2010 a magnitude 7.0 earthquake devastated Haiti's capital city, Port-au-Prince. The quake destroyed the country's already-meager infrastructure, knocking out communications, crumbling the airport control tower, ruining the port and blocking roads with rubble. At least 200,000 people died and survivors faced starvation, dehydration, disease and untreated injuries. In many places reserves of food, water, hygienic supplies and medicine were ruined, so the demand for new goods was immediate.

First responder support came from Haiti's neighbor, the Dominican Republic, which opened its airport to relief flights, accepted Haitian patients into its hospitals and sent in heavy equipment to move rubble and clear roads. In addition, the Dominican Republic dispatched ten mobile kitchens, 110 cooks and sufficient provisions to prepare 100,000 meals a day. However, additional support was needed.

Many relief agencies already in Haiti, such as the American Red Cross and key United Nations agencies, were crippled because of ruined supplies and staff deaths. Emergency coordinators tried to fly new supplies and relief personnel into Haiti's airport, but the airport was ill-equipped to handle the volume. Lacking communication, most planes were unable to land and the few that could crowded the tarmac, waiting to be offloaded. There were few forklifts, no one to run those that were available, and no place to receive and organize the stalled cargo. As a result, supplies and support personnel were extremely delayed in getting to the desperate Haitians.

Introduction

This chapter examines international food aid and hunger relief activities. We begin with an overview of food development programs, which address the long-term needs of a region or population. We then discuss the disaster relief supply chain, which pertains to the short-term, emergency needs of a region or population. We conclude by comparing food aid supply chains to commercial food supply chains, and discussing the importance of collaboration and cooperation in the hunger relief field.

Food Development Programs

Even without an identifiable trigger event, such as Haiti's natural disaster, there are millions of people around the world suffering from chronic hunger and malnutrition every day. More than 20 million children suffer from severe or acute malnutrition in the developing world, and an estimated 5.6 million children under the age of five die from malnutrition each year. Poverty, disease, political conflict, war and corruption are key factors in the global hunger and malnutrition problem, as is a lack of infrastructure in some countries to sustain farming and food distribution activities.

Development agencies work to alleviate these problems, providing food aid as well as education, economic assistance and medical care to people in need around the world. Two issues are most salient with regard to food development programs: the need to supply actual food to hungry people, and the challenge of developing long-term food security through self-sufficiency. Complications associated with food development programs include ensuring that hungry people receive nutrient-dense foods when they receive direct aid, versus nutrient-poor foods; and preventing long-term market disruptions in recipient countries, i.e., avoiding the creation of artificial market forces that drive down prices on locally grown foods.

Food Aid

In 1961, the United Nations General Assembly and the Food and Agriculture Organization (FAO) of the United Nations co-sponsored one of the first food development agencies, the World Food Programme (WFP). Initially an experimental program, its founding premise was to support self-sufficiency through education and capacity-building in developing countries, and to divert agricultural surpluses from the developed world to countries in need during times of crisis. Today, the WFP uses commodities, cash and services contributed by UN member states to support social and economic development programs and to provide emergency relief services. Other well-known government agencies, such as the United States Agency for International Development (USAID), the European Commission on Humanitarian Aid and Civil Protection (ECHO) and the United Kingdom's Department for International Development (DFID) partner with the WFP to help it achieve its objectives. Nongovernmental aid organizations also provide relief services. Major nongovernmental organizations are listed in Table 10.1.

In 2009, WFP delivered just over 10 billion pounds of food to the hungry, feeding more than 100 million people in 75 countries. The food supplied came primarily from the developed world. Just under half was donated, and the remaining food aid was purchased with cash. Over 84 million recipients of WFP's aid were women and children. Internally displaced persons, refugees and people affected by HIV and AIDS were also key recipients. While 2009 saw the WFP serving more individuals than is normal, the program on average still feeds more than 90 million people each year.

Because food aid supply lines are long, the food provided to recipients needs to be shelf-stable. As an example, the WFP food ration typically consists of some combination of cereal, pulses (beans and peas), vegetable oil, salt, sugar, high energy biscuits and bread, often sourced from commodity surplus programs in the developed world. While these products alleviate hunger, they have also been critiqued for their lack of nutrients. Figure 10.1 illustrates the food donations received by the WFP, which are high in low-nutrient grain and cereal products. Recently, humanitarian relief groups such as Médecins Sans Frontières (MSF) have urged policymakers to improve the nutritional quality of the food delivered to aid recipients. Specifically, MSF has suggested that agencies like WFP invest in newly developed, ready-to-use therapeutic foods that can help malnourished individuals recover quickly.

An example of one of these products is Plumpy'nut, a peanut paste that is packed with vitamins and calories. The product is specially formulated to re-nourish starving children and help them gain weight rapidly. The product's manufacturer is Nutriset, a private French company, which sells 90% of its supply to the United Nations Children's Fund (UNICEF). In 2009, Nutriset

Table 10.1 **Major Humanitarian and Relief Organizations**

Name of Organization	Total Program Expenses 2008	Countries of Operation
American Red Cross (including international programs)	$3,322,460,000	186
Feed the Children	$1,055,503,509	119
UNICEF	$391,948,122*	190
World Vision	$838,733,000	100
CARE USA	$608,629,000	66
Catholic Relief Services	$596,540,000	100+
Save the Children Federation	$424,146,000	50+
International Rescue Committee	$243,647,000	40+
Oxfam America	$51,470,000	120
International Children's Fund	$31,586,168	31

*2010. Source: Better Business Bureau.

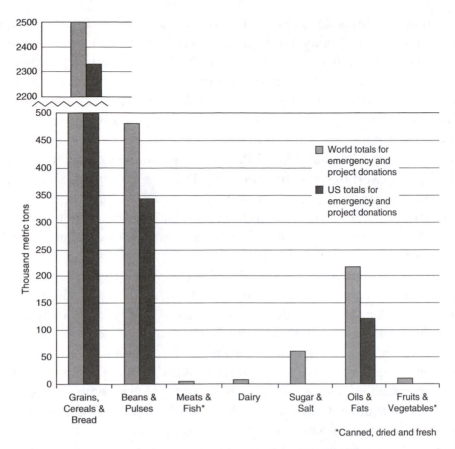

Figure 10.1 **World food donations** (Source: World Food Programme).

produced about 3 million pounds of Plumpy'nut and related products, generating $66 million in sales and high profits. Nutriset has licensed producers in 11 African countries to make its product, and has plans to open more production franchises in developing countries. Through local production, Nutriset hopes to reduce shipping costs and thus prices, while assisting developing countries. However, many food aid organizations have urged the company to go further, allowing anyone to make the product without having to pay a licensing fee. Such a fee can be cost-prohibitive for small producers, impacting supply and thus, access.

Self-Sufficiency

Despite the clear benefits of direct relief, many acknowledge that food aid organizations can negatively impact regional development over the long term. Constant assistance can destroy a delicate local economy by undercutting small businesses, thereby obviating the need for production and trade in supported industries and thus, opportunities for wages and economic growth.

An example of this is, again, Haiti. In 2010, former US president Bill Clinton apologized before the Senate Foreign Relations Committee for his administration's role in exporting cheap US rice to Haiti, undercutting local growers. Haitian farmers supplied 47% of the country's rice in 1988, but by 2008, that figure had dropped to 15%. The lack of a viable food production base in Haiti, resulting in the decline of agricultural jobs, negatively affected its economic health, even before the country had a natural disaster. After the 2010 earthquake, Haitian President René Préval, an agronomist, called for an end to free food in an effort to staunch its decline. This was an immensely unpopular decision in the impoverished country. Instead, WFP, in tandem with Préval's government, began offering food and cash to Haitians who were employed on community improvement projects, such as clearing rubble and installing drainage systems.

Preventing aid dependency is a goal of all development agencies. Therefore, programs exist that aim to increase the self-sufficiency of impoverished nations, villages and people. The list of development needs is often long. In addition to basic farming and agricultural capacity, many countries need a viable supply chain to deliver their agricultural products. Both tangible goods, such as production equipment and supplies, and soft skills, such as farming knowledge, logistical capabilities, technical know-how and political skills, are essential. Social innovation and entrepreneurial skills can also help leverage a basic supply chain into a robust, economically significant local asset.

One successful capacity-building example is Working Villages International, which is using sustainable agriculture practices to enhance lives and facilitate village autonomy in sub-Saharan Africa. The program provides hands-on training in organic and environmentally appropriate growing practices. It works with villagers, many of whom are refugees displaced by years of civil war, to clear land, dig irrigation canals, plant seeds, train people in animal traction and build drying pads and barns for crops. The program also trains participants to manufacture building products, and teaches them construction techniques to help build new villages. Finally, the nonprofit agency works with villagers to build up their non-agricultural commodity infrastructure (e.g., looms, kilns, bakeries, etc.) and associated skills, which assists with the functioning of daily life. After it has finished working with a community, the group stays on in an advisory role, offering support as needed to the fully-functioning and independent village.

A unique for-profit example of capacity building is the e-Choupal initiative, created by ITC Limited, a large Indian company specializing in the international trade of agricultural products. The e-Choupal program has changed the role of middlemen in the traditional Indian agricultural supply chain—some of whom once took advantage of asymmetric information, distorting prices at the expense of farmers—by building an electronic, web-based infrastructure across India that can be easily accessed by farmers. The access gives farmers information on everything from growing practices to market prices, and enables e-commerce. The information transparency, improved access to supplies and knowledge, and more direct access to the world market have enabled many Indian farmers, even those in remote villages, to have more control over their operations and, in turn, enhance profits.

Disaster Relief

Direct food aid comes in two types: development aid, which is long term and generalized in nature, as discussed, and disaster relief, which is event driven and temporary. The goal of disaster relief is to protect and assist a civilian population in the event of a natural or manmade disaster; because people require immediate support, being able to quickly assemble or reconstruct food and other supply chains is essential. Natural disasters include storms, floods, droughts and other environmental events. Manmade disasters include wars, political conflicts and other civil actions that disrupt access to basic needs, such as food and shelter. Human activity can also exacerbate natural events, e.g., excessive development in flood-prone areas, or post-natural disaster riots.

In recent years, an increasing percentage of food aid has been used for disaster relief, as compared to development aid, because more catastrophes are occurring. Additionally, just-in-time practices in the food industry are making people more vulnerable to disaster; inventory in the pipeline is now more limited, reducing potential reserves in the face of immediate demand. The globalization of the food supply chain has also introduced vulnerability. If one link in a particular chain fails, an entire network could lose access to one or many necessary goods.

The average number of events requiring disaster relief between 2000 and 2004 was 55% higher than during the previous four-year period. This reflects a decades-long trend that has influenced how large agencies use their resources. For example, in 1993 the WFP used approximately 60% of its resources on emergency events. Today, the WFP spends 87% of its resources on disaster relief, leaving only 13% for development aid. Disaster relief is also impacting business. Many companies are assessing their supply chains to determine the risks of and remedies to disruption.

The Disaster Relief Process

The emergency response process has three basic phases: ramp-up, sustainment and ramp-down, as shown in Figure 10.2. During ramp-up, emergency needs are assessed and assets and staff are deployed. Sustainment occurs when a disaster response is in full swing and has reached its maximum scale: aid is

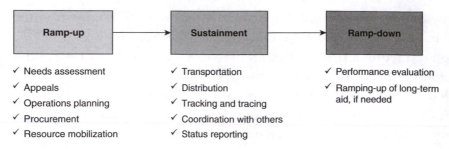

Figure 10.2 **Emergency response process**

being distributed, personnel are on-site and the relief chain is operating at capacity and with maximum efficiency. Ramp-down involves the reduction of emergency assistance and the withdrawal of relief personnel from a disaster zone. Ramp-down frequently occurs in conjunction with the ramp up of long-term development aid and assistance, which helps restore critical, permanent infrastructure to a given population in a stricken area.

The emergency response process has little variation, the exception being variation in the ramp-up phase of disaster relief. Disasters can be divided into two categories: slow-onset or rapid-onset. Slow-onset disasters, such as droughts and famines, give emergency workers a bit of lead time to plan, thus the needs assessment process can occur in a calm and orderly fashion. Rapid-onset disasters, such as the earthquake in Haiti, give relief workers little to no time to anticipate and assess needs. Thus, ramp-up for a rapid-onset disaster must occur very quickly.

Because many disasters are rapid-onset, management agencies may develop plans or relief concepts for certain locations before disasters occur, particularly areas that are disaster-prone or areas that may be difficult to serve due to fundamental instability (social unrest, poor infrastructure, etc.). Several global distribution networks, stocked with reserves of food and other supplies, also exist to facilitate ramp-up wherever it needs to occur.

The Relief Supply Chain

Figure 10.3 depicts a general model of a centralized relief supply chain. Supplies are proactively sourced and stored in strategically placed warehouses located around the world. When an emergency strikes, both stored and freshly sourced supplies are sent to the location in need. After arriving at port, they are sorted and stored at a central warehouse, which then sends supplies as needed to local distribution centers. Relief workers in the field get their supplies from the distribution centers. The response cycle that accompanies this supply chain can be divided into five phases, described below: assessment, appeals, operations, coordination with other relief organizations and reporting.

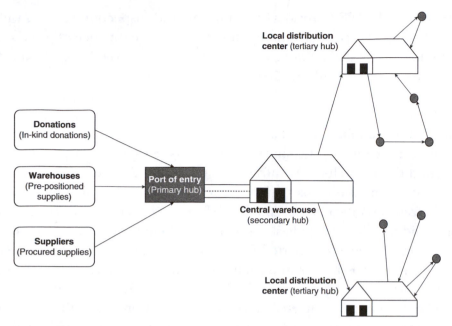

Figure 10.3 **Typical disaster relief supply chain** (Source: Beamon and Balcik 2008).

ASSESSMENT

Assessment occurs within the first 24 hours of a crisis. Humanitarian organizations gather facts about the population in need and the distribution landscape, and estimate supply requirements. Estimates cover nutrition, water, sanitation and health care needs. When calculating needs, organizations factor in early reports on casualties and damages, although they know that the numbers can change rapidly.

APPEALS

Appeals for support occur simultaneously with assessment—usually within 36 hours of a disaster striking. Appeals management focuses on donor solicitation and the collection of cash and supplies. In-kind donations (goods and services) are checked to see if they are appropriate and needed, and if so, they are moved into the relief supply chain. In-kind donations that are not relevant for a particular emergency are stored in central warehouses for later sorting and use. Cash donations are managed through a separate, non-supply chain process.

Donations that are received through the appeals process augment supplies that are already in the relief supply chain. The UN Humanitarian Response Depot (UNHRD), managed by the WFP, supports several relief organizations by pre-positioning supplies in disaster-prone regions around the world. There are five UNHRDs, located in Italy, Ghana, the United Arab Emirates, Malaysia and Panama. Participating organizations pre-position relief supplies at the

UNHRDs and the WFP provides warehousing and inspection services without charge. Though it represents an ongoing expense, the practice of pre-positioning supplies offers the advantage of reducing transportation costs and time when supplies are critically needed.

OPERATIONS

Supply chain planning, mobilization and actual delivery in the country or geographical area in need comprise operations. Supply chain planners assess field conditions, including infrastructure, weather, cultural constraints, political situations and worker safety concerns. As soon as is feasible, resources are mobilized and international and local shipping capacity is mustered to move supplies and people. As supplies arrive in the afflicted country, they go through customs and are then transported to warehouses near the disaster site. At this stage, information is just as important as supplies: accurate inventories help predict replenishment needs and facilitate performance evaluations when a disaster response is complete. In-country operations typically enlist local personnel to distribute resources. Inventories are again verified before distribution and receipts are generated as goods are used or handed out.

COORDINATION

Coordinated effort between relief organizations is critical, particularly for a major relief effort in which hundreds of organizations are often at work. All organizations require facilities, communication equipment and the ability to move people and supplies, yet competition for local goods and services can inflate prices compared to normal conditions. Pooling resources when possible minimizes duplicated effort. It can also prevent the misallocation of human resources, placing skilled workers where they are most needed. Because of its importance, coordination and collaboration are discussed in more detail later in this chapter.

REPORTING

Reporting is ongoing during a disaster. The flow of accurate information and data between partners, and up and down the relief chain, enables a coordinated response. External reporting—sharing data with the public—can also increase donor contributions by illustrating the effectiveness of relief efforts in progress and explaining the depth of need remaining. Finally, data management enables performance assessment after an emergency is over, which can facilitate efficiency improvements in the future. Unfortunately, the lack of communication and data infrastructure makes data collection in some disaster areas particularly difficult. Reporting can also be hampered by a lack of training for field employees.

The Decentralized Relief Chain

Although the basic, centralized relief chain has been in place for decades, relief experts are constantly innovating, trying to improve upon the efficiency and effectiveness of the traditional chain. One recent innovation is the decentralized relief supply chain. An example of a decentralized relief supply chain is shown in Figure 10.4, in comparison to a centralized supply chain, and described below.

The International Federation of the Red Cross (IFRC) decentralized its supply chain in 2005. This new chain was put to use during the Yogyakarta earthquake in Indonesia in 2006, with outstanding results. The IFRC had pre-positioned inventory at three Regional Logistics Units (RLUs) in strategic locations: Dubai (serving Europe, the Middle East and Africa), Kuala Lumpur (serving Asia and Australia) and Panama (serving North and South America). The three RLUs served as intermediaries, linking the IFRC's Geneva headquarters, national Red Cross societies, suppliers and field workers. In terms of inventory management, the IRFC in essence created a push system, which was then followed by a pull system. The decentralized supply chain reduced air transportation time during the emergency phase (the first few weeks). After the emergency phase, the IFRC was able to replenish materials more economically by using previously existing transportation methods as needed—by ship, for example.

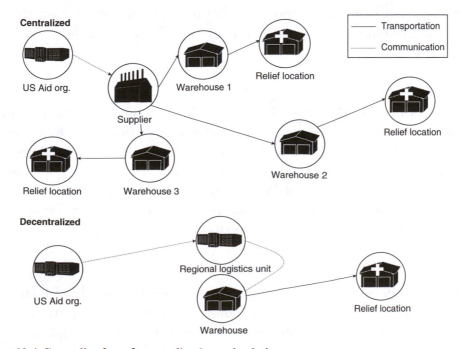

Figure 10.4 **Centralized vs. decentralized supply chain**

Lessons in Disaster Relief

Every disaster is unique, which makes systematizing and optimizing the response process very difficult. Different types of calamities create different types of relief challenges. Culture, languages and politics also add variation to the disaster response effort. Only recently has supply chain management been recognized as a core function of humanitarian relief. Relief agencies, universities and private institutions, such as the Fritz Institute, are now studying and evaluating the unique challenges of disaster relief management, aiming to improve logistical and technological expertise in the field. Often, mistakes in one disaster response can offer lessons for the next. Table 10.2 highlights lessons learned in recent disaster relief efforts.

Aid Supply Chains vs. Commercial Supply Chains

As should be evident, food aid supply chains are very different from commercial food supply chains. The differences are most significant between disaster relief and commercial chains. Fundamentally, the stakes are much higher in disaster relief: the relief manager's mandate is to quickly deliver relevant supplies and human support to people in need, often with life or death consequences. Due to the lack of event predictability and thus time for planning, the relief manager's job is also much more difficult. Demand for critical supplies is generally unknown until the moment of need, and supply sources, transportation methods and distribution networks must be finalized and executed in an ad hoc fashion. The key differences between disaster relief and commercial supply chains are summarized in Table 10.3, and described in detail below.

Forecasting

In the corporate world, the market is most likely stable and thus demand is typically forecast. In relief management, demand is difficult to predict and the delivery lead time is often zero. This is particularly true for rapid-response disasters such as earthquakes, tsunamis and floods. However, even slow-onset disasters, such as famine, can take victims and responders by surprise when they finally occur, especially if triggered by an unanticipated event. Disasters can also be worsened by human reaction to an event, e.g., riots.

Procurement

In the corporate supply chain, suppliers are often identified, evaluated and contracted with in a systematic way, stabilizing operations and the corporate budget. Alternatively, generic inputs for which there is ready supply can often be purchased from the spot market. In the relief chain, necessary supplies may

Table 10.2 **Recent Disasters and Lessons Learned**

Year	Disaster	Lesson
1988	December 7 Armenian Earthquake	Employ local. Armenia was part of the Soviet Union, but Moscow prohibited residents from working on rebuilding, causing political tension. Four years later, only 30 percent of necessary structures were finished.
1995	January 17 Kobe Earthquake	Communicate better, more often and more completely. A lack of timely and accurate information made it difficult for families to get needed services. For example, shelter locations were not well publicized, which delayed relief.
1999	August 17 Turkish Earthquake	Rebuild stronger. After quakes destroyed unsafe structures, rebuilding started quickly and without regulatory oversight or regard for the individual needs of each city—resulting in still-vulnerable infrastructure.
2003	December 26 Iranian Earthquake	Restore law and order quickly. Refugees from the countryside flooded the city in search of aid, but there was no system to support them. Several days of looting hindered distribution of supplies and threatened the overall recovery effort.
2004	December 26 Asian Tsunami	Basic provisions need to be regionally appropriate. Workers distributed non-halal food and built shelters inside Buddhist temples, so Muslims couldn't eat the food or use the shelters. Also, some donated goods weren't suitable for the climate.
2005	August 29 Hurricane Katrina	Deliver aid quickly, and with sensitivity. A fifth of aid recipients in Louisiana said assistance came too late and was delivered in an uncaring manner.
2005	October 8 Pakistani Earthquake	Medical care needs to be culturally appropriate. Few female doctors were deployed, and local religious beliefs restrict physical contact between men and women. Women were therefore under-served in the relief effort.
2006	May 27 Java Earthquake	Prepare. Areas where households had received some disaster training were better-equipped to handle the disaster.

Source: P. Duffy.

not have been recruited beforehand or may not be readily available, creating critical shortages that can make relief agencies susceptible to price gouging.

Some relief organizations try to avoid this problem by crafting purchasing contracts with suppliers that pre-negotiate pricing and allow them to secure capacity when needed. However, pre-negotiated contracts can be difficult to execute due to disaster variability and variability in purchasing environments; such contracts tend to work best for government-run disaster agencies that have

Table 10.3 **Commercial Supply Chains vs. Aid/Relief Supply Chains**

	Commercial Supply Chains	*Humanitarian Supply Chains*
Strategic Goal	To produce high quality products at a low cost; to achieve high customer satisfaction.	To minimize the loss of life and to quickly alleviate suffering.
Demand Pattern	Relatively stable and predictable; demand is typically generated from fixed locations in set quantities.	Demand is generated from random events that are unpredictable in terms of timing, location, type and size; demand requirements are estimated after they are needed, based on an assessment of disaster characteristic.
Lead Time	Lead time is determined by the various partners in the supply chain.	Likely zero lead time between event occurrence and demand; actual delivery time is still determined by supply chain partners.
Distribution Network Configuration	Well-defined methods exist to determine the number of distribution centers needed, and their optimal locations.	Challenging due to the range of unknowns (location, type and size of event, politics, culture) and the "last mile" considerations.
Inventory Control Method	Well-defined methods exist to determine inventory needs; lead time, demand and customer service goals come into play.	Inventory control is challenging due to variation in lead times, demand and demand locations.
Information System	Generally well-defined; uses advanced technology.	Information is often unreliable, incomplete or non-existent.
Performance Measurement	Traditionally focused on sales and efficient resource use, e.g., maximizing profit or minimizing costs.	Focus is on output performance measures, such as the time required to respond to the disaster or the ability to meet disaster needs.

Source: Adapted from Beamon and Balcik 2008.

established purchasing programs. Relief organizations in the field, particularly in the developing world, often end up buying needed supplies from stores or factories that are in close geographic proximity to the disaster area, sometimes paying market or above-market prices.

Transportation, Storage and Distribution

In corporate supply chains, transportation, storage and distribution activities are relatively predictable, and can even be optimized to serve as a company's distinctive competence. In relief supply chains, shipping, storage and distribution methods may need to be conceptualized and executed in an ad hoc manner. Even the best pre-disaster planning may not anticipate the level of devastation in an affected region, which can wipe out standard transportation routes and thus impact the utility of available equipment.

Communication

Good communication and information exchange is essential to both corporate and relief supply chains. However, relief chain information is usually spotty and sporadic, especially in the immediate aftermath of a disaster. Communication infrastructure may be damaged and thus, inoperable. Additionally, relief workers generally lack training in supply chain software, which can adversely affect the replenishment of critical supplies.

Resource Use and Performance Evaluation

Good financial performance is the main goal of most corporations. In contrast, relief chain managers are focused on quickly delivering goods and services to needy people. In fact, a relief organization may not even know its final operating budget until months after emergency aid has been delivered. Performance metrics in the field therefore often focus on reactionary activities, e.g., pounds of food delivered, number of children served, etc., that can be easily measured and reflect the fundamental scope of the organization.

While these metrics can accurately explain an organization's short-term actions, donors are increasingly asking for metrics that instead measure long-term impact. For example, instead of learning about the pounds of food delivered by an organization, a major donor may want to know how an organization improved a region's economic viability over the long term. Because donations are often tied to a particular activity or metric, this trend may free up funds for long-term development projects that have the potential for catalytic impact, such as infrastructure or technology improvements. However, accurately measuring the impact of one organization, when many relief agencies were likely involved in a relief effort and when many social and cultural factors are at play, is a challenge.

Technological advancements are enabling more sophisticated methods of measurement, so providing more robust data to donors is now plausible. Examples of robust performance metrics are provided in Table 10.4. Several agencies are also working on new criteria and sophisticated accounting procedures to assess the quality of an organization's humanitarian aid and relief work, from agricultural improvements to public health.

Coordination and Collaboration

Good coordination between all agents involved in a disaster relief effort is essential to a successful outcome. The typical agents in relief management are illustrated in Figure 10.5, including various relief agencies (international and

Table 10.4 **Possible Performance Metrics for Relief Efforts**

Resource Performance	*Output Performance*	*Flexibility Performance*
• Total cost of resources used • Overhead costs • Total cost of distribution, including transportation and handling costs • Inventory investment (the investment value of held inventory) • Inventory obsolescence and spoilage • Order/setup costs • Inventory holding costs/Cost of supplies • Number of relief workers employed per aid recipient • Number of "value added" hours (i.e., the number of direct hours spent on dispensing aid per total number of labor hours) • Dollars spent per aid recipient • Donor dollars received per time period	• Total amount of disaster supplies delivered to aid recipients • Total amount of disaster supplies of each type delivered to aid recipients • Total amount of disaster supplies delivered to aid recipients in each region • Amount of disaster supplies delivered to each individual recipient • Target fill rate achievement • Average item fill rate • Stock-out probability • Number of backorders • Number of stock-outs • Average backorder level • Average response time between occurrence of the disaster and the arrival of supplies • Minimum response time (minimum time between occurrence of disaster and first arrival of supplies)	• Number of individual units of Tier 1 supplies that an organization can provide in time period T_e • Minimum response time • Mix of different types of supplies that the relief chain can provide in a specified time period

Source: Beamon and Balcik 2008.

local), governments, militaries and even private industry. This section explains the dynamics of coordination and collaboration between these entities in the relief process and the relief supply chain.

Relief Agency Coordination

Despite the fact that different relief agencies have a common goal—helping people in need—they often have different mandates and thus varying priorities and needs. Due to limited resources, relief organizations are therefore often competing for cash, supplies and manpower. To help alleviate this situation, aid organizations may choose to work as a group—under an umbrella organization—just as donors sometimes choose to pool their contributions to maximize impact.

At the field level, relief personnel at a given location are often unfamiliar with one another. Each organization may also have its own supply chain,

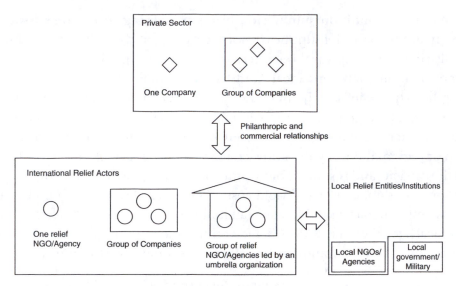

Figure 10.5 **Relief chain entities** (Source: Balcik et al. 2010).

managing transportation, procurement and warehousing activities independently. Their competition for critical resources can result in confusion. For
instance, after the 2004 tsunami in Sri Lanka, bottled water continued to arrive
long after local water services were restored. Not only was the water unnecessary
at that point, it clogged up supply routes that were desperately needed for
other goods. The "Battle of the Good Samaritans" is a common phenomenon
in disaster relief, illustrating the necessity of cooperation.

Joint procurement can reduce costs to relief organizations as collaboration
gives agencies collective bargaining power with suppliers. Sharing transportation resources can also yield cost savings and reduce transit time, particularly if
long-haul shipments to affected areas must clear customs. Using UNHRDs as
regional staging areas for in-kind donations in times of crisis can increase
efficiency in the supply chain. Off-site, regional staging enables relief agencies
to pull a targeted collection of goods to a disaster site, versus having to manage
a random selection of goods pushed to a site by well-intentioned donors.
Additionally, redundancies and blockages are reduced by the pull method of
sourcing, reducing lead times for critical items.

At the international level, most relief chain coordination is horizontal, so
resource sharing and joint decision making do occur. These collaborations
typically involve a single lead agency (a coordinating body, inter-agency
committee or an umbrella organization) that facilitates working together. For
example, the United Nations Joint Logistics Center (UNJLC), formally
established in 2002 to handle logistical issues, is hosted by the WFP. The UNJLC
collects and disseminates information, including infrastructure assessments,

transportation condition summaries, briefs pertaining to customs issues and maps. It also tracks relief supplies, prioritizes cargo and facilitates the rationing and distribution of logistical resources to individual organizations.

Coordination between local and international relief agencies greatly strengthens the relief supply chain. Local entities can be "home grown," with no international connection, or they can be franchises of international aid organizations that have had a long-term presence in and commitment to a given population or region. Blending the knowledge and cultural access of the local agency with the capacity and resources of the international agency can improve response time, prevent duplication and yield cost efficiencies. Working together can also increase bureaucracy and decrease flexibility, however. Nonetheless, the familiarity local agencies have with affected communities and regions usually justifies the tradeoffs of collaboration, especially in "last mile" distribution.

Government Collaboration

Good collaboration with local government is also critical to the success of an international disaster relief effort. Relief organizations are subject to the laws and customs of the countries in which they are working, which can impact relief delivery. For instance, religious beliefs in Pakistan restrict physical contact between men and women. Therefore, after the country's 2005 earthquake, many Pakistani women went without medical services due to a lack of female doctors available to deliver one-on-one medical services in the home, as is traditional in Pakistani culture. A government can halt a particular collaboration or international aid altogether if local concerns and customs are not being respected or addressed. In developing countries, cultural differences, suspicion about the motive of external relief organizations, corruption and, often, a lack of government efficiency can hamper relief work.

Government coordination problems do not just impact developing countries. For example, Hurricane Katrina demonstrated that the richest country is as vulnerable as the poorest when an administration is short on experience and know-how. An ice delivery debacle exemplified this. The US Federal Emergency Management Agency (FEMA) purchased 91,000 tons of ice before delivery destinations and routes were established for each load. As a result, truck drivers were redirected to numerous destination points across the nation, wasting time and money on unnecessary transportation and cold storage costs. One driver drove 20 tons of ice to five different destination points throughout the South before finally landing in Fremont, Nebraska with his load—a distance of over 4,000 miles. This example is just one among many in a relief effort characterized by inefficiency and confusion, with disastrous human consequences.

Military Assistance

Militaries frequently play a role in disaster relief efforts. They do this to protect the safety of relief workers and to facilitate emergency operations. The extent of military participation in disaster relief is variable and depends largely on how local governments use their military resources, and relief organizations' policies. For instance, the Red Cross, in order to protect its image as a neutral party, disallows its personnel and supplies to be transported or protected by any military, even UN peacekeepers.

When they are utilized, militaries often have the ability to move supplies and personnel when others cannot. They may also give relief agencies access to storage and mobile communication equipment, and give them logical and security support. The degree and type of cooperation between local and foreign militaries varies from situation to situation. While differences between militaries' missions, codes of conduct, cultures and operating procedures may create tension, success stories about collaboration do exist. During the ramp-up phase of the Haiti earthquake in 2010, for example, the United Nations Stabilization Mission and the US Air Force were vital in controlling riots, distributing goods and, eventually, getting a handle on air traffic so that relief flights could land at the nearly-devastated Port-au-Prince airport.

Private Industry Collaboration

Corporations choose to support and partner with large aid organizations as part of their corporate responsibility programs, and because corporate support helps with positive brand building. Corporate support is typically delivered via philanthropy, e.g., financial or supply donations. At times, corporations also donate manpower, through skilled or unskilled volunteers. When corporations' core competencies correspond to a relief organization's mission and needs, it is called integrative collaboration. An example of integrative collaboration is the partnership between the WFP and TNT, a large international logistics company. When TNT supports the WFP, the relief organization gains logistical expertise and support while TNT receives exposure in new markets.

Collaboration between private industry and the relief field has facilitated the adoption of new supply chain strategies in relief management in recent years. Concepts such as purchasing consortia, risk pooling and aggregation are examples of corporate procurement strategies that have benefited relief chain managers. Quick response, continuous replenishment, vendor managed inventory and warehouse standardization are examples of inventory management and distribution strategies that have benefited the relief sector. Because intrinsic differences between industry and relief chains exist, not all corporate supply chain mechanisms will work for all relief chains, but familiarity with industrial successes can help individuals in the relief field adapt their methods to enhance effectiveness.

Virtual Connections

The Internet is increasingly supporting collaboration and coordination in the relief management sector. Web-based collaboration tools include discussion groups, email lists, electronic libraries, distance learning and online seminars. The Internet can also directly connect agencies in need with resources. For instance, the Aidmatrix Network is a virtual "marketplace" connecting donors to development aid and disaster relief efforts worldwide. Recently, relief organizations have also started using global positioning system data from the UN and satellite images from Google to ascertain the location of homeless encampments and damaged infrastructure during disasters. MapAction is a UN-sponsored nongovernmental organization that provides geographic information and analysis support. Its information helps relief organizations gauge an area's real-time needs and coordinate efforts across the relief supply chain.

Most organizations today—including the UN, government agencies, relief organizations, charities and corporations involved in relief work—also use social networking tools, like Facebook and Twitter, to communicate about their activities generally and to give disaster relief updates. In this way, the Internet can facilitate public communication, as well as brand-building and fundraising. Relief agency homepages also explain agencies' missions and relay information about populations served, past performance metrics and preferred methods of philanthropic support.

Issue Analysis: The Southern Africa Drought

In February 2002, after experiencing the worst crop failure in nearly 50 years, Malawi declared a state of emergency. In April, when Lesotho and Zimbabwe made similar declarations, it became the worst food crisis in southern Africa in nearly a decade. Multiple factors complicated the crisis. Economic issues included long-standing financial and fiscal problems that reduced employment and purchasing power, and currency devaluation that was aggravated by inflation. Political problems also existed, including mismanagement of government-controlled supplies, destroyed food reserves and disagreement on initial assessments, which slowed NGO response. Demographic complications existed. Populations were scattered from the outset, and high HIV infection rates had reduced the work force and aggravated chronic malnutrition. Finally, environmental problems plagued southern Africa, including increasingly erratic weather patterns and crop mismanagement that had decimated the agriculture base.

This crisis loomed for years; the drought catalyzed its arrival. The WFP drew up a response plan and organized relief efforts. Once food distribution and delivery were in place, WFP learned that the food, mostly corn donated by the United States, was genetically modified. Several of the affected countries refused the food in part because of health concerns, but primarily because their subsistence economies depended on non-genetically modified grain. Since corn is wind-pollinated, genetically modified strains would invariably contaminate local corn if used as seed. This could in turn reduce indigenous biodiversity and limit the countries' future ability to export grain to the world market. Since genetically modified grain is patented and licenses must be purchased annually, the impoverished farmers would also not be able to afford the costs of production if GMO corn seed was to contaminate non-patented, non-GMO stock. Consequently, the genetically modified grain was not suitable. Long-term damage to the local economy outweighed immediate concerns about starvation.

The WFP respected this decision but faced a dilemma: stockpiles of food waiting in harbors and stalled in warehouses. They also faced the expense of replacing the genetically modified grain, and food relief would be delayed by as much as a month. A new strategy had to be devised. Ultimately, the organization decided to mill the genetically modified grain. However, plans for large-scale milling again forced unforeseen circumstances on the operation. WFP had to develop new methods for bagging, storing and distributing the milled product due to its modified nature. In Mozambique, for instance, where the genetically modified whole grain was rejected, deliveries could only travel if they were sealed to avoid spillage en route. This limited the transportation methods that could be used and increased logistical costs.

Nonetheless, the initial problem produced unforeseen benefits. Milling the corn meant that WFP could add vitamins and minerals to the grain to increase its nutritional value—a critical benefit for people weakened by HIV. It also reopened local mills that had stood empty for years, employing workers and encouraging local purchases, thereby stimulating the regional economy. The individuals served by WFP gained nutritional and economic benefits, and the WFP was able to make its effort successful while maintaining its reputation as an impartial humanitarian organization.

Discussion questions

1. From where is humanitarian food aid sourced? What concerns have been voiced about traditional food aid supplies?
2. How can long-term humanitarian aid hinder the economic strength of recipient countries or regions? If you were a development program manager, what strategies might you employ to avoid aid dependence?
3. What are the key phases in the disaster relief process, and what activities occur during these phases? How does the speed of a disaster impact the relief management process?
4. List the challenges that relief chain managers face in executing a successful, timely relief process. How might you address some of these challenges?

Additional Readings and Links

- The World Food Programme has a strategic plan (2008–2013) that articulates its recent shift away from a food aid agenda to a food assistance platform. The plan is available on WFP's website: http://www.wfp.org/about/strategic-plan
- The Fritz Institute is a nonprofit that is developing supply chain and technology solutions to improve disaster response. White papers on specific disaster relief topics are available on its website: http://www.fritzinstitute.org/index.htm
- MapAction is a nonprofit that maps disaster areas and activities to facilitate relief efforts. An interesting catalogue of recent maps is available for browsing on their website: http://www.mapaction.org/

11

THE FUTURE OF FOOD SUPPLY CHAIN MANAGEMENT

The viability of the sustainable food movement has been questioned in the past, and indeed, this book has surfaced a number of notable challenges to the concept—growing populations, increasing demand, the need for new farming and food distribution methods and the momentum of corporate consolidation. However, as this book has also illustrated, the need to do things differently in the food industry is pressing, and the chance to make a global transition to a more sustainable future presents many new and exciting opportunities for our world.

Sustainable agriculture and sustainable food systems can contribute to economic development and redevelopment in both urban and rural US locations. They can also contribute to economic enhancement internationally, in the developing world. Similarly, new food systems have the potential to mitigate environmental damage and climate change, and to contribute positively to society by reducing food-related health problems such as obesity and diabetes. They may also reinvigorate community connections in some places, through enhanced interactions with local farmers and food producers as part of an emerging food culture. The question for supply chain managers in the food industry is how to best facilitate this transition.

In this chapter, we review the social and environmental concerns that make the transition to a more sustainable food system a global imperative. We summarize the sustainability concepts and solutions that are emerging to address these challenges. We conclude with observations for food supply chain managers on how they can contribute to positive changes in the supply chains they manage.

Today's Concerns and Challenges

Maintaining the status quo of the existing food supply chain is problematic in several ways. Concerns include ensuring long-term food security, particularly for vulnerable populations in the United States and the developing world, to preventing ongoing degradation of the environment. Clearly, many of these problems are interrelated, thus potential solutions for one problem can positively affect other areas.

Food Security

Food security is widely understood as the circumstance in which all people have access to safe, sufficient and nutritionally adequate food at all times. Food resources have historically limited population sizes for all living creatures. With the introduction of agriculture and food storage 10,000 years ago, the human population has grown exponentially. Ironically, the agricultural system is at risk of no longer being able to support the population it helped generate. Consolidation in the industry is increasing risk.

Pests and disease can easily wipe out mono-crop farms. Reduced food supplies can in turn result in dramatic price increases, which in turn decrease food access. Instability in food supply systems and pricing is a known, significant driver of social unrest; food riots are, today, commonplace. In 2008, for instance, food price increases drove protestors to the streets from Mexico to Pakistan. Often the protests have turned violent. In several West African nations, rioters burned government buildings and looted stores, leaving dozens of people dead.

Thus, some politicians and policymakers are already being forced to consider the weaknesses of their current food systems and are considering policy changes to increase food security in their countries. While tactical approaches to stabilizing food prices vary, some approaches are common: increasing production with help from higher yields, stimulating trade and fighting food speculators who drive up market prices.

Rural Economic Decline in the US

In the United States, agricultural policy has traditionally focused on surpluses, not shortfalls. Programs such as price supports and acreage controls have never brought sustained prosperity to farmers. The total number of farms in America has declined from 6.5 million in 1935 to fewer than 2 million today. Most of this decline took place among midsized family farms. These farms have the unique ability to produce significant amounts of diverse regional food at a scale sufficient for regional retailers and institutions—the type of farm needed to support more sustainable food supply chain activities. Small farmers are able to generate higher margins by selling directly to restaurants and consumers via farmers' markets and other direct sales channels; typically these farmers do not rely on farming for the majority of their income. Midscale family farms on the other hand do rely on the farm's income, and struggle to compete against consolidated powerful large farm corporations with their mono-culture economies of scale. As a result, there is an increasing loss of crop diversity and farmer bankruptcy which has a spiraling effect of driving continual consolidation of farms and power.

Many argue that price supports and subsidies should be restructured to benefit the midsize family farms rather than large corporate farms which have institutional and government benefits already existing and do not need these additional monetary supports. The Farm Bill is the primary agricultural and food policy tool of the US Federal government. Intended as a safety net for farmers and ranchers, this comprehensive omnibus bill is passed about every five years by the US Congress, and deals with agriculture and related concerns. It has increasingly been put in the spotlight by those who seek to increase the presence of midsize farms in America. The status quo allows the largest commercial farms to receive the largest payments and even allows investors who do not farm or live on farmland to receive subsidies, leaving behind most farm families. Those interested in midsize farm preservation suggest limiting subsidies to $250,000, closing loopholes that get around that limit, and only allowing payments to those who actually farm or live on the land themselves.

Environmental Consequences: Pollution, Energy and Water

Meanwhile, nearly 50 million acres of agricultural lands are lost every year to soil erosion and degradation. The problem is worst in the poorest countries, where agricultural residue and animal dung compete for use as cooking fuel versus fertilizer, which could enrich depleted soil if applied to fields. Water is also needed for multiple purposes—drinking, irrigation, etc.—and is in limited supply. Irrigation also consumes energy and wastes water—as much as half of applied irrigation water can be lost to runoff or evaporation. As agriculture uses 70% of available fresh water worldwide, methods to reduce water use in agriculture are highly desirable.

Finally, the climate is changing. While marginally higher temperatures could increase crop yields, the accompanying decrease in rainfall would mitigate against potential benefits. Moreover, hotter, drier lands produce more wildfires. Burned land cannot hold water when seasonal rains arrive. Resulting floods erode topsoil, which in turn produces fewer crops. Climate change is also destabilizing prevailing weather patterns, increasing the severity of seasonal storms and droughts. Clearly our natural resources are diminishing as our population multiplies.

In the 1950s, 1960s and 1970s, technology transfers to developing countries created the "green revolution." New, drought- and pest-resistant plant cultivars increased land productivity. And mechanized cultivation and processing and technological advances such as irrigation, chemical fertilizers and pesticides brought much higher crop yields. In developing countries, labor is traditionally the major agricultural cost while in developed countries, the major costs are mechanization and fertilizers. During the green revolution, grain yields increased up to fourfold, but the increase was mostly attributed to fossil fuel energy inputs. Fossil fuel consumption in such industrialized food production cannot be sustained as the population continues to grow and requires the fuels for other uses.

Climate change and dietary transitions in developing countries are straining food production systems; populations are demanding more food and natural resources for its production. As the global population enters the middle class and changes to a high-energy consumption lifestyle, the pressures on food production systems and the environment will intensify.

Consequences in Developing Countries

Globalization and free trade agreements have not necessarily benefited all farmers in developing countries. The World Trade Organization (WTO) and North American Free Trade Agreement (NAFTA) created trade agreements that favored large western companies—for example, Monsanto in the United States, and Syngenta and Bayer CropScience in Europe—over traditional farmers. The WTO protects intellectual property, including engineered genes. When these genes are in crop seeds, farmers cannot retain part of one year's crop to sow the next. They must purchase seeds annually from the patent holder. While providing greater crop yields, the genetically modified crops may require companion herbicides, pesticides and/or fertilizers—frequently sold by the same agribusiness that sold the seeds. Local crop varieties, developed over centuries of natural selection for pest- and drought-resistance, are lost. Once a farmer has entered the GMO system, it is difficult to extricate him or herself, and agriculture is transformed from a way to produce food into a way to produce revenue.

Ten companies control 32% of the global seed market and all transgenic or genetically engineered seeds, also referred to as genetically modified organisms, or GMOs. These same companies also make and distribute the agrochemicals needed to grow GMO crops. Free trade agreements also often favor food exports to developing countries, further limiting local food production. In 1991, trade liberalization in India resulted in the introduction of cash crops, such as cotton, for export. These crops displaced food crops, with farmers buying seeds and chemicals on credit. When crops failed, the joint World

Bank/International Monetary Fund (IMF) project devastated many farms and the families who depended on them.

Concentration and Consolidation

All of the previous issues have been aggravated by the increasing trend toward consolidation in the food industry. As discussed in previous chapters, US agricultural policy favors large-scale farming and food processing which has resulted in a high level of agricultural and food industry concentration. This concentration and consolidation has led to a situation in which a handful of companies control the majority of agricultural production and food processing. This consolidation has multiple negative effects on a sustainable food system as outlined below.

First, with a handful of companies setting the prices for contracts with growers of produce and protein groups, the terms of the contracts are heavily tilted toward the companies. With such a power concentration, companies often abuse the situation by providing extremely low pricing, under-weighing products during sales, overestimating the weights of feed that they sell and providing marginal animal stock or feed. Farmers in effect become serfs to the company and, if they complain, can be blacklisted from future contracts. The previous sections have discussed the farmer's dilemma in getting tied to the GMO seed regime. Again, a dependency develops with companies with a highly inequitable power balance.

Second, as powerful players, consolidated food companies now have tremendous influence on US farm and food policy often working against consumer interests. For example, they have prevented GMO labeling on foods, thus allowing GMO products to enter the food chain without public consent. Also, they have altered organic standards to their benefit by allowing some nonorganic materials in products and now control several of the largest organic brands.

Third, from an environmental and social perspective, consolidated and concentrated production facilities have huge negative impacts. The large concentrated animal facilities not only struggle to manage the vast amounts of manure and effluent but contribute excess amounts of antibiotics and other pharmaceuticals drugs to the effluent stream, leading to major downstream health issues for everyone. Poor animal handling continues to plague the industry, with thousands of animals living in increasingly smaller spaces. From a social perspective, the facilities degrade the quality of life in the communities in which they operate by driving down wages, eliminating local smaller competitors and family businesses and destroying the environment.

Fourth, consolidation begets consolidation. As retailers consolidate, they require bigger, more organized suppliers to meet their demand. For example, retailers are most likely to supply their stores out of centralized warehouses which require full truck shipments from suppliers and cannot support deliveries from small farmers or producers. Even food service distributors, like Sysco, have high minimums on what they will stock in their warehouse; thus a restaurant that wants to support a local or sustainable product must get multiple other restaurants on board for that product before the distributor will carry it.

Finally, while consumers have benefited traditionally from the low pricing that comes from consolidation when power is left in the hands of a few players, this scenario could change. There have been recent incidents of price fixing on milk with large Chicago supermarket chains. And if worldwide supply cannot meet demand, the powerful players could potentially have a very different direction with pricing and greatly influence the political systems within their sphere.

Opportunities and Solutions

Many agree that the current system and trends have created a formidable force against the emergence of alternative food systems—particularly one that considers economic, environmental and social attributes simultaneously. A desirable food supply chain would provide food security (adequate nutritious food for consumers) and not harm society or the environment in the pursuit of profit. It would fairly compensate and provide for the welfare of stakeholders at every level of the chain—from farm workers to processors to distributors and grocers. It would be environmentally sustainable, whether that means organic production or the responsible use of minimal amounts of chemical fertilizers and pesticides. And it would treat animals raised for food humanely.

When considering alternative food supply chains, the technology of the green revolution stands in opposition to more recent environmentally friendly alternatives regarding poverty, famine and economic development not only in developing nations but in the United States. The green revolution relied on biotechnology and genetic engineering. Today's experts consider organic and sustainable farming and local knowledge to come up with new solutions. Table 11.1 contrasts the competing approaches between conventional and alternative systems. The future food system will have to resolve the tension between these two competing models. Regional food systems offer one solution for supply chain managers and policy makers to explore sustainable alternatives. Another is to use trade policy to encourage the development of appropriate institutions and activities. The following sections look at these approaches.

Regional Production

While there are many reasons for "buying local"—supporting local economic development, reducing transportation, building supply chain links with traceability,

Table 11.1 **Key Elements of the Competing Agricultural Paradigms**

Conventional Agriculture	*Alternative Agriculture*
Centralization	**Decentralization**
• National/international production, processing and marketing • Concentrated control of land, resources and capital	• More local/regional production, processing and marketing • Dispersed control of land, resources and capital
Dependence	**Independence**
• Large, capital-intensive production units and technology • Consumerism and dependence on the market	• Small, low-capital production units and technology • More personal and community self-sufficiency
Competition	**Community**
• Farm traditions and rural culture outdated • Farming is a business only • Primary emphasis on speed, quantity and profit	• Preservation of farm traditions and rural culture • Farming is a way of life as well as a business • Primary emphasis on permanence and quality
Domination of nature	**Harmony with nature**
• Humans are separate from and superior to nature • Human-made systems imposed on nature • Highly processed, nutrient-fortified food	• Humans are part of and subject to nature • Natural ecosystems are imitated • Minimally processed, naturally nutritious food
Specialization	**Diversity**
• Most plants grown in monocultures • Separation of crops and livestock • Standardized production systems	• More plants grown in polycultures • Integration of crops and livestock • Locally adapted production systems
Exploitation	**Restraint**
• Short-term benefits outweigh long-term consequences • Based on heavy use of nonrenewable resources • High consumption to maintain economic growth	• Short-term and long-term outcomes equally important • Based on renewable resources; nonrenewable resources conserved • Consumption restrained to benefit future generations

Source: Adapted from C.E. Beus and R.E. Dunlap.

etc.—consumers and retailers have begun to understand that it is almost impossible to have all food produced within a 100-mile radius of where they live. As a result, the concept of a regional food system has emerged. Regional food systems have four dimensions: food supply and demand, sustainability of resources, economic development, and diversity. Regional food supply chains aim for self-reliance. Ideally, a food region would supply as much of its own food as possible without degrading resources. Food regions, therefore, may include metropolitan areas, geographic features, states, provinces or entire countries.

Another key focus of a regional system is social and environmental sustainability. Farmland, marine systems, rainfall and other natural resources cross manmade boundaries, and demand regional approaches. Stakeholders—local, state and federal agencies, interest groups, NGOs—can work together to craft appropriate land use policy, negotiate water rights, and develop resource conservation and economic growth plans. A regional food system offers diversity; it reflects the need to produce a variety of foods to meet cultural and culinary demands. This diversity also creates resiliency within a regional food system, allowing it to adapt to climate change, policy change and evolving resource issues.

Economic development and sustainability, the third dimension of regional food systems, retains profits in the region. All supply chains require infrastructure, distribution networks, processing facilities and regional markets to sell products. The regional supply chain concept addresses issues related to economies of scale, capacity utilization and overall efficiency. A regional food system also allows producers to profit from regional and global trade. This implies that food regions overlap; consumers and marketers determine boundaries over time.

Regional food systems challenge the prevailing food system. They require diverse agricultural production, small-scale processing, small-scale distribution and environmental responsibility by all participants. They will often demand a higher price in exchange for healthy food and social and environmental sustainability. On the other hand, a regional food system ideally would not drive protectionism against other regions or countries, nor favor one economic group over others. Rather, they are value chains designed to include conservation, human rights and opportunity. These values focus on healthy food, a healthy environment, food security and social and economic equity. Many regional food proponents voice skepticism towards transnational firms and their energy-intensive infrastructures. By creating jobs and profits while emphasizing social and ethical values, regional food supply chains typically emphasize the importance of communities, fair wages, trustworthy relationships and equitable power structures.

Typically, localized production creates production clusters as we have seen in the US wine and grass-fed beef industries. Regional growers and processors benefit from using local industries' production outputs (byproducts and waste) as inputs. They can also share resources—production methods, distribution channels, capital equipment or warehouses—to enhance the overall regional food system.

As a viable alternative, regional food systems need to reach a certain scale of production, distribution and markets. The question for supply chain managers is how to leverage (and re-scale) large system resources to accommodate smaller scales. Regional food systems focus on the value chain, with the goal of allowing customers to understand the energies—human and mechanical—spent in food production. The idea is that the product cost reflects the true cost of production and that the consumer will choose to support farmers and growers.

One question remains: can everyone within a region afford food, or is a regional food system simply another means of exclusivity? This issue is as pertinent a topic in sub-Saharan Africa as it is in middle America. The interplay of regulation, voluntary corporate initiatives, and private and government research will decide the answer to this question. An alternative food supply chain will undoubtedly incorporate aspects of both industrial scale production and local environmental and societal concerns.

International Trade Policy

In as much as ecological maladies do not respect borders, international cooperation is essential to protect the environment. An environmentally friendly agriculture system would de-emphasize industrialized production and channel research toward resilient, low-input systems that minimize greenhouse gases and other destructive emissions. Today, government policies support sustainable agriculture minimally relative to industrial agriculture. Sustainable agricultural policies could redirect investment from patented seed and crop technology toward traditional plant breeding, livestock husbandry and farming systems. Energy and trade policies, currently slanted to favor solely economic interests, could also be modified to consider their impact on sustainable agricultural development. Priorities in establishing a sustainable food supply chain should include transparency, measurement systems that assess impacts on food security, the environment, biological diversity and rural welfare.

Current international negotiations on climate issues and carbon markets often consider environment and trade as bargaining chips. To avoid these tradeoffs, separate treaties (multilateral environmental agreements) would be preferable. Since a weak environment or poor enforcement can create artificial advantages, agricultural agreements should consider environmental standards.

These agreements could provide technical assistance to developing countries to comply with health and safety standards.

Toward a Sustainable Food Supply Chain

Food and non-food supply chains differ in fundamental ways; food is personal and intimate. It is something we consume: "we are what we eat." The uniqueness of food presents challenges and opportunities when considering economic, social and environmental issues in food production and food supply chain management. Food connects directly to cultural heritage and evokes deep memories of childhood and family. Across cultures, food connotes hospitality and friendship; it also communicates identity and values. For the same reasons, our approaches to food politics, production and consumption reflect our economic, cultural and political beliefs. Different from other products, this connection influences how we consider values surrounding the food supply chain.

Throughout this chapter, our objective has been to highlight the food supply chain challenges and accentuate the progress that has been made as food supply chain professionals seek solutions to these challenges. Food product development is driven by disparate social and technical dynamics. New nonfood products are a result of scientific advancement and market demand. For food products, production methods, regulation and legislation play a larger role in creating new products. As we have seen throughout previous chapters, large agricultural businesses, both growers and retailers, play an important role in shaping the social and technological landscape and influencing the worldwide food supply chain.

This book leaves a big question for food supply chain managers. How can managers position themselves to take advantage of changes in the food supply chain? It's not a question of whether or not sustainability issues will have to be faced by their company but how quickly and which issues will dominate their sector. Supply chain managers will encounter many challenges as they confront economically, socially and environmentally sustainable food systems and products. Understanding of regional food systems, supply chain traceability and transparency, food security and justice, certification of agricultural practices and products, humane animal handling, food safety regulation and imminent climate-related legislation and trade treaties will be essential for a supply manager to carry out his or her job. An effective food supply chain manager will need in-depth knowledge of the social and political contexts of food and food production systems. He or she will need astute sensitivity to food trends and innovative practices. Most importantly, he or she will need to fulfill their social responsibility in making business decisions that help build supply chains that benefit multiple stakeholders, including the natural environment.

Discussion Questions

1. What key concerns does sustainable agriculture seek to address?
2. What are the values underlying the notion of a regional agriculture food system? From a supply chain management point of view, how is a regional agriculture food system different from an industrial food supply chain?
3. Consider the region where you reside, and assess how the regional food system concept applies. What might be the system's boundaries, and why? What major agricultural products would the system produce? How would food processing, manufacturing, retailing and food service activities and vendors be integrated into the system? What is the system's primary value proposition and competitive advantage? What opportunities and challenges exist with regard to sustaining the system?
4. Please identify and discuss an emerging sustainability issue(s) for a particular type of food product or food production system. What is the nature of the issue? What market opportunities does the issue present for the entrepreneurial food company (e.g. retailer, producer, processor)?

REFERENCES

AccuWeather. "New USDA Offers In-Depth Look at Organic Farming." Accessed September 22, 2010. http://www.accuweather.com/blogs/outdoor/farming/26847/new-usda-data-offers-indepth-l.asp.

Advameg, Inc. 2010. "Flour. How Products Are Made." Accessed May 5, 2010. http://www.madehow.com/Volume-3/Flour.html.

Agricultural Cooperative Service. 1978, Revised 1990. "Fruit and Vegetable Cooperatives: Farmer Cooperatives in the United States." *Cooperative Information Report 1, Section 13.* United States Department of Agriculture.

Agricultural Marketing Service. 2007. *Supply Chain Basics: Niche Agricultural Marketing—The Logistics.* United States Department of Agriculture, Marketing Services Program.

Agriculture Marketing Service. 2009. "Farmers Markets and Local Food Marketing." United States Department of Agriculture. Accessed January 15, 2011. http://www.ams.usda.gov/AMSv1.0/FARMERSMARKETS.

Agricultural Statistics Board. 2009. *Overview of the United States Hog Industry.* United States Department of Agriculture, National Agricultural Statistics Service.

American Egg Board. "Egg Industry." Accessed July 18, 2010. http://www.aeb.org/egg-industry.

The Associated Press. September 13, 2010. "Whole Foods to Post Seafood Sustainability Ratings." Accessed September 18, 2010. http://www.ap.org.

Balcik, Burcu, Benita M. Beamon, Caroline C. Krejai, Kyle M. Muramatsu, and Magaly Ramirez. 2010. "Coordination in Humanitarian Relief Chains: Practices, Challenges and Opportunities." *International Journal of Production Economics.* 126(1): 22–34.

Baldwin, Cheryl. 2010. "Principles of Sustainability for Food Products." Accessed January 7, 2011. http://www.impomag.com/scripts/ShowPR.asp?RID=15158&CommonCount=0.

Ball, Charles. 1998. *Building the Beef Industry.* Saratoga: Saratoga Publishing Group.

Bantham, Amy, Courtney Oldham. May 2003. "Creating Value through Traceability Solutions: A Case Study." *Food Origins.*

BBMG. 2007. "Conscious Consumers are Changing the Rules of Marketing: Are You Ready?" *BMG Conscious Consumer Report.*

Beaman, Jill A. and Aaron J. Johnson. December 2006. "Food Distribution Channel Overview." EM 8921. Accessed December 23, 2010. http://extension.oregonstate.edu/catalog/html/em/em8921/index.html#t1.

Beamon, Benita M. and Burcu Balcik. 2008. "Performance Measurement in Humanitarian Relief Chains." *International Journal of Public Sector Management.* 21(1): 4–25.

Benbrook, Charles. 2009. "Impacts of Genetically Engineered Crops on Pesticide Use in the United States: The First Thirteen Years." Accessed August 22, 2010. http://www.organic-center.org.

Bernstein, Lee. 2010. "Correctional Dining." Accessed January 6, 2011. http://www.edible-communities.com/hudsonvalley/summer-2010/on-the-line.htm.

Bernstein, Sharon. August 21, 2010. "US Restaurants Starved for Business." *Los Angeles Times.*

Beuerlein, Jim. 2001. "Classes and Uses of Wheat." *Ohio State University Fact Sheet – Horticulture and Crop Science*. Accessed September 9, 2010. http://ohioline.osu.edu/agf-fact/0146.html.

Beus, C. E. and R. E. Dunlap. 1990. "Conventional versus Alternative Agriculture: The Paradigmatic Roots of the Debate." *Rural Sociology*. 55(4): 590–616.

Bickel, Ulricke, and Jan M. Droos. 2003. "The Impacts of Soybean Cultivation on Brazilian Ecosystems." World Wildlife Fund. Accessed September 9, 2010. http://assets.panda.org/downloads/impactsofsoybean.pdf.

Blackburn, Joseph and Gary Scudder. 2009. "Supply Chain Strategies for Perishable Products." *Production and Operations Management*. 18(2), pp.129–137.

Blanton, Bruce. 2008. "The State of U.S. Transportation: Implications for the U.S Fruit & Vegetable Industries." United States Department of Agriculture, Agricultural Marketing Service.

Bowersox, Donald, David Closs, and Bixby M. Cooper. 2009. *Supply Chain Logistics Management*. McGraw-Hill/Irwin Series Operations and Decision Sciences. New York: McGraw Hill Higher Education.

Boyd, W. and M. Watts. 1997. "Agro-industrial Just-in-time." In Goodman, D. and M. Watts (Ed.) *Globalizing Food: Agrarian Questions and Global Restructuring*. London, Routledge.

Boyer, Kenneth and Thomas Hult. 2005. "Extending the Supply Chain: Integrating Operations and Marketing in the Online Grocery Industry." *Journal of Operations Management*. 23: 642–661.

Bryson, Lee. 2007. "In Search of Beer's Big O." Accessed September 22, 2010. http://www.portfolio.com/views/columns/first-draft/2007/08/17/Organic-Craft-Beer/index.html.

Bureau of Economic Analysis. 2010. "US Economic Accounts." United States Department of Commerce.

Burt, Steve, Kurt Davies, John Dawson, and Leigh Sparks. 2008. "Categorizing Patterns and Processes in Retail Grocery Internationalisation." *Journal of Retailing and Consumer Services*. 15(2): 78–92.

California Department of Public Health, Food and Drug Branch. August 2008. "San Joaquin County, All Hazards Workshop." Accessed January 24, 2011. http://www.sjgov.org/ems/files/CaliforniaDepartmentofPublicHealthFoodAndDrugBranch.ppt.

The Carbon Trust. "The Label." Accessed December 14, 2010. http://www.carbon-label.com/the-label.

Carr, Austin. Oct 5, 2010. "Frito-Lay Bags Its Green Chip Packaging: Not Worth the Noise." *Fast Company*. Accessed December 12, 2010. http://www.fastcompany.com/1693162/frito-lay-green-packaging-not-worth-the-noise.

Cattlemen's Beef Board and National Cattlemen's Beef Association. 2009. "Modern Beef Production; Fact Sheet." Accessed July 20, 2010. http://www.explorebeef.org.

Center for Science in the Public Interest. 2009. "The Ten Riskiest Foods Regulated by the U.S. Food and Drug Administration." Accessed January 15, 2011. http://www.cspinet.org/new/pdf/cspi_top_10_fda.pdf.

Centers for Disease Control and Prevention. 2009. "Morbidity and Mortality Weekly Report." Accessed January 6, 2011. www.cdc.gov/mmwr/preview/mmwrhtml/mm5804a4.htm.

Centers for Disease Control and Prevention. 2009. "Timeline of Infections: Multistate Outbreak of Salmonella Infections Associated with Peanut Butter and Peanut Butter-Containing Products." Accessed January 4, 2011. www.cdc.gov/salmonella/typhimurium/salmonellaOutbreak_timeline.pdf.

Centers for Disease Control and Prevention. 2011. "Justification of Estimates for Appropriation Committees; Fiscal Year 2011." Accessed January 22, 2011. http://www.cdc.gov/fmo/topic/Budget%20Information/appropriations_budget_form_pdf/FY2011_CDC_CJ_Final.pdf.

Cochrane, Willard W. 2003. *The Curse of Agricultural Abundance: A Sustainable Solution*. Lincoln, NE: University of Nebraska Press.

Code of Federal Regulations. "Current Good Manufacturing Practice in Manufacturing, Packing or Holding Human Food." Title 21, Part 110.

Compassion in World Farming. "Food Chains and Farm Animals." Accessed December 20, 2010. www.ciwf.org.

Congressional Research Service. "Fruit and Vegetable Trade." *U.S. International Trade Commission's Trade DataWeb Database* (Version 2.8.4).

Cook, Karla. February 25, 2009. "Peanut Recall's Ripples Feel Like a Tidal Wave for Some Companies." *The New York Times*.

Cook, Roberta. 2000. "The Fresh Fruit and Vegetable Value Chain Faces New Forces for Change." Accessed January 15, 2011. http://www.farmfoundation.org/news/articlefiles/94-cook.pdf.

Cook, Roberta A. 2009. "The US Fresh Produce Supply Chain." Department of Agriculture and Resource Economics, University of California.

Czarnezki, Jason. 2010. "The Future of Food Eco-labeling: Organic, Carbon Footprint, and Environmental Life-cycle Analysis." *Vermont Law School - Environmental Law Center, Working Paper*.

Dairy Farming Today. "Life on the Farm: All About Cows." Accessed July 18, 2010. http://www.dairyfarmingtoday.org.

Dairy Herd Management. 2009. "Culling Dairy Cattle for Reproduction." Accessed July 20, 2010. http://www.dairyherd.com.

Davis, Christopher and Bing-Hwan Lin. 2005. *Factors Affecting United States Beef Consumption*. United States Department of Agriculture, Economic Research Service.

Davis, Sharon. "The Natural History of Wheat." Food & Culture Encyclopedia. Accessed September 14, 2010. http://www.answers.com/topic/the-natural-history-of-wheat.

DeLaval Dairy Knowledge. 2007. "Cow Comfort: 15) Milking." *Milk Production* library article. Accessed July 20, 2010. http://www.milkproduction.com.

Department of Economic and Social Affairs, Population Division. 2006. "World Population Prospects." United Nations. Accessed January 30, 2011. http://www.un.org/esa/population/publications/wpp2006/WPP2006_Highlights_rev.pdf.

Department of Justice, Office of Public Affairs. November 29, 2010. "D.C. Fish Wholesaler ProFish Ltd. Owner and Employee Sentenced for Purchasing Illegally Harvested Striped Bass."

Dimitri, Carolyn and Catherine Greene. 2002. *Recent Growth Patterns in the U.S. Organic Foods Market*. United States Department of Agriculture, Economic Research Service.

Diop, N. and S. Jaffee. 2005. "Fruit and Vegetables: Global Trade and Competition in Fresh and Processed Product Markets." in Aksoy, M. A. and J.C. Beghin. *Global Agricultural Trade and Developing Countries*. Washington, D.C: World Bank.

Earthbound Farm. "About Us." Accessed January 15, 2011. http://www.ebfarm.com.

East Africa Dairy Development. 2010. "Innovation Technology for Smallholder Farmers: The Pulverizer Feed Mill." Accessed December 8, 2010. http://eadairy.wordpress.com under appropriate technology, Feeds, Fodder.

Easterly, William. 2006. *The White Man's Burden: Why the West's Effort to Aid the Rest Have Done So Much Ill and So Little Good*. New York: Penguin Press.

Ecolabel Index. 2010. "Ecolabels." Accessed November 14, 2010. http://www.ecolabelindex.com.

Economic Research Service. 2010. *Briefing Rooms: Rice*. United States Department of Agriculture.

Economic Research Service. 2010. "Rapid Growth in Adoption of Genetically Engineered Crops Continues in the US." United States Department of Agriculture.

Economic Research Service. 2009. *Briefing Rooms: Food Marketing System in the U.S.: Food Service*. "Food Expenditure Data Series." United States Department of Agriculture.

Accessed November 27, 2010. http://www.ers.usda.gov/Briefing/FoodMarketingSystem/foodservice.htm.

Economic Research Service. 2009. *Organic Briefing Room*. United States Department of Agriculture.

Economic Research Service. January 13, 2011. "Data Sets: Foreign Agricultural Trade of the United States, Monthly Summary." Accessed January 30, 2011. http://www.ers.usda.gov/data/fatus/monthlysummary.htm.

Encyclopedia of the Nations. 2010. "Technical Cooperation Programs – World Food Program." Accessed November 20, 2010. http://www.nationsencyclopedia.com/United-Nations/Technical-Cooperation-Programs-WORLD-FOOD-PROGRAM-WFP.htmlixzz15qdAZBi5.

Environmental Protection Agency. 2010. "Pollution Prevention Act of 1990." Accessed January 7, 2011. www.epa.gov/p2/pubs/p2policy/act1990.htm.

Environmental Protection Agency. March 24, 2010. "Food Waste." Accessed December 14, 2010. www.epa.gov/foodrecovery.

Environmental Working Group. 2010. "Farm Subsidy Database." Accessed September 9, 2010. http://farm.ewg.org/region.php?fips=00000.

EurActiv. 2010. "Growing Demand for Soybeans Threatens Amazon Rainforest." Accessed September 9, 2010. http://www.euractiv.com/en/cap/growing-demand-soybeans-threatens-amazon-rainforest/article-188566.

Fairtrade Labeling Organizations International. 2010. "Facts and Figures." Accessed November 14, 2010. http://www.fairtrade.net/facts_and_figures.html.

Falkenstein, Drew. February 2010. "Revisited: Salmonella Saintpaul Outbreak Linked to Alfalfa Sprouts." *Food Poison Journal*.

Farm Sanctuary Report. 2009. "The Truth behind the Labels: Farm Animal Welfare Standards and Labeling Practices."

Farm to School. "National Farm to School Network." Accessed January 6, 2011. www.farmto-school.org/.

Fassler, Joe. September 16, 2010. "Timeline of Shame: Decades of DeCoster Egg Factory Violations." *Atlantic Monthly*.

Fast Company Staff. 2010. "The World's Most Innovative Companies." *Fast Company*. Accessed January 6, 2011.

FIAN International. 2009. "International Responses to the Food Crisis." Accessed January 30, 2011. www.fian.org/resources/documents/others/international-responses-to-the-food-crisis/pdf.

Finch, Julia. April 16, 2008. "Tesco labels will show products' carbon footprints." *The Guardian*.

First Research. 2005. "Grocery Stores and Supermarkets Industry Profiles." Accessed January 15, 2011. www.firstresearch.com/Industry-Research/Grocery-Stores-and-Supermarkets.html.

First Research. 2010. "Food Distributors Industry Profile." Accessed December 14, 2010. http://www.firstresearch.com/industry-research/Food-Distributors.html.

Fishman, Charles. December 1, 2003. "The Wal-Mart You Don't Know." Fast Company.

Flynn, Dan. 2009. "Ingredient-Based Recalls Used To Prevent Outbreaks." *Food Safety First Research*. 2005. "Grocery Stores and Supermarkets Industry Profiles." Accessed January 15, 2011. www.firstresearch.com/Industry-Research/Grocery-Stores-and-Supermarkets.html.

Food Alliance. "A History of Food Alliance." Accessed November 14, 2010. http://foodalli-ance.org/about/history/.

Food and Agricultural Organization of the United Nations. March 3, 2003. "New Report on Diet and Chronic Diseases Released." Accessed January 15, 2011. http://www.fao.org/english/newsroom/news/2003/14683-en.html.

Food and Agriculture Organization of the United Nations. 2009. "Food Outlook Global Market Analysis." Accessed September 9, 2010. http://www.fao.org/docrep/013/al969e/al969e00.pdf.

Food and Agriculture Organization of the United Nations. "Hunger: Global Hunger Declining, but Still Unacceptably High." Accessed January 30, 2011. http://www.fao.org/hunger/en/.

Food and Agriculture Organization of the United Nations. "Table 9.1: World Calories, Developed Countries." Accessed January 30, 2011. http://www.fao.org/economic/ess/chartroom-and-factoids/chartroom/en/.

Food and Agriculture Organization of the United Nations. "Table 9.2: World Calories, Developing Countries." Accessed January 30, 2011. http://www.fao.org/economic/ess/chartroom-and-factoids/chartroom/en/.

Food and Drug Administration. 2010. "Importing Food Products into the United States." United States Department of Health and Human Services. Accessed January 7, 2011. www.fda.gov/Food/InternationalActivities/Imports/default.htm.

Food and Drug Administration. February 26, 2009. "Inspection Report, Peanut Corporation of America, Plainview, Texas." Form 483.

Food and Nutrition Service Agency. 2010. "School Programs: Meal, Snack and Milk Payments to States and School Food Authorities." United States Department of Agriculture. Accessed January 14, 2011. http://www.fns.usda.gov/cnd/governance/notices/naps/nsl10-11t.pdf.

Food and Nutrition Service Agency, Team Nutrition. "Approach 2 Influence Food and Beverage Contracts." United States Department of Agriculture. Accessed January 14, 2011. http://www.fns.usda.gov/tn/resources/g_app2.pdf.

Food Processing Environmental Assistance Center. "Clean Water Act (CWA)." Accessed January 7, 2011. http://www.fpeac.org/cwa.html.

Food Processing Environmental Assistance Center. "Resource Conservation and Recovery Act." Accessed January 7, 2011. www.fpeac.org/rcra.html.

Foodprocessing.com. 2009. "Food Business Mergers & Acquisitions Fall 30.4% in 2009." www.foodprocessing.com/articles/2010/top100foodbusiness_ma.html.

Foodprocessing.com. 2010. "Food Processing's Top 100." Accessed January 3, 2011. http://www.foodprocessing.com/top100/index.html.

Food Safety and Inspection Service. 2010. "Irradiation and Food Safety." United States Department of Agriculture, Food Safety and Inspection Service. Accessed January 7, 2011. ww.fsis.usda.gov/Fact_Sheets/Irradiation_and_Food_Safety/index.asp

Foreign Agricultural Service. 2005. " NAFTA Agriculture Fact Sheet: Corn." Accessed September 9, 2010. http://ffas.usda.gov/itp/policy/nafta/corn.html.

Freedonia Group. June 2010. "US Produce Packaging Industry." Accessed January 15, 2011. http://www.reportlinker.com/p091957/US-Produce-Packaging-Market.html.

Fresco, Louise and Wilfried Baudoin. 2002. "Food and Nutrition Security Towards Human Security." *Proceedings of the International Conference on Vegetables* (ICV-2002), 11–14 November 2002, Bangalore, India. Accessed January 15, 2011. http://www.fao.org/AG/AGp/agpc/doc/reports/ICV02e90SPE.pdf.

Friends of the Earth. 2005. "Illegal Genetically Engineered Corn Found in Shipments to U.S. Largest Grain Importer." Accessed August 25, 2010. http://www.foe.org.

Fulmer, Melinda. August 22, 2002. "Bagged Greens Toss in Profits; Salad Days For Lettuce Growers." *The Los Angeles Times.*

Gatignon, Aline, Luk Van Wassenhove, and Charles Aurelie. 2010. "The Yogyakarta Earthquake: Humanitarian Relief Through IFRC's Decentralized Supply Chain." *International Journal of Production Economics* 126: 102–110.

Ghemawat, Pankaj. September 2001. "Distance Still Matters: The Hard Reality of Global Expansion." *Harvard Business Review*, pp. 137–147.

Gibson, C. E. Ostrom and T. Ahn. 2000. "The Concept of Scale and the Human Dimensions of Global Change: A Survey." *Ecological Economics.* 32(2):217–239.

Gibson, Lance and Garren Benson. 2002. "Origin, History and Uses of Corn." Iowa State University, Department of Agronomy. Accessed September 9, 2010. http://www.agron.iastate.edu/courses/agron212/Readings/Corn_history.htm.

GMO Compass. 2008. "Crops: Soybeans" Accessed September 9, 2010. http://www.gmo-compass.org/eng/grocery_shopping/crops/19.genetically_modified_soybean.html.

Goodman, David, Bernardo Sorj, and John Wilkinson. 1987. *From Farming to Biotechnology: a Theory of Agro-industrial Development.* Oxford: Blackwell.

Gosselin, Maggie. 2010. *Beyond the USDA: How Other Government Agencies Can Support a Healthier, More Sustainable Food System.* Minneapolis, MN: Institute for Agriculture and Trade Policy.

Greene, C., E. Slattery, and W. McBride. 2010. "America's Organic Farmers Face Issues and Opportunities." *Amber Waves.* United States Department of Agriculture, Economic Research Service.

Gunderson, G. W. 2008. "The National School Lunch Program: Background and Development." United States Department of Agriculture, Food and Nutrition Service.

Halweil, B. 2002. "Home Grown – The Case for Local Food in a Global Market." Paper 163. Washington D.C.: Worldwatch Institute.

Hembree, Brandon. 2009. "Harvesting, Storing Corn." Delta Farm Press. Accessed September 9, 2010. http://deltafarmpress.com/corn/harvesting-storing-corn.

Hoovers. 2010. "Canned and Frozen Fruits and Vegetables." Accessed January 15, 2011. http://www.hoovers.com/industry/canned-frozen-fruits-vegetables/1353-1.html.

Hoovers. 2010. "Industry Overview." Accessed September 14, 2010. http://www.hoovers.com/grain-milling/–ID__376–/free-ind-fr-profile-basic.xhtml

Horovitz, Bruce. November 22, 2010. "Table for Two? More Americans Chose to Eat Out." *USA Today.*

Howard, Philip. 2008. "Organic Industry Structure." Michigan State University Department of Community, Agriculture, Recreation and Resource Studies.

Howard, Philip. 2009. "Consolidation in the North American Organic Food Processing Sector, 1997 to 2007." *International Journal of Sociology of Agriculture and Food.* Volume 16, Issue 1.

IBIS World. 2010. "Frozen Food Production." U.S. Industry Report. Accessed January 7, 2011. http://www.ibisworld.com/industry/default.aspx?indid=236.

Interagency Agricultural Projections Committee. 2010. *USDA Agricultural Projections to 2019.* United States Department of Agriculture, World Agricultural Outlook Board.

International Assessment of Agricultural Knowledge, Science and Technology for Development. "Towards Multifunctional Agriculture for Social, Environmental and Economic Sustainability." Accessed January 30, 2011. agassessment.org/docs/10505_Multi.pdf.

International Food Service Distributors Association. "About Efficient Foodservice Response." Accessed January 14, 2011. http://www.ifdaonline.org/webarticles/anmviewer.asp?a=540&z=71.

Iowa Department of Public Health, Center for Acute Disease Epidemiology. 2006. *The Foodborne Outbreak Investigation Manual.*

IRI Information Resources, Inc. 2007. "CPG 2007 Year in Review." *Times and Trends: A Snapshot of Trends Shaping the CPG Industry.*

James, C. 2000. "Global Status of Commercialized Transgenic Crops: 1999." ISAAA Briefs No. 17. Accessed September 9, 2010. http://www.isaaa.org/resources/publications/briefs/17/default.html.

Johnson, Rachel. 2010. *Livestock, Dairy, and Poultry Outlook.* United States Department of Agriculture, Economic Research Service.

Jones, Keithly and Mathew Shane. 2009. *Factors Shaping Expanding United States Red Meat Trade.* United States Department of Agriculture, Economic Research Service.

Jones, Nicola, Harry Jones, Liesbet Steer, and Ajoy Datta. 2009. "Improving Impact Evaluation Production and Use." Overseas Development Institute (ODI). Working Paper 300.

Kenner, R. (Producer) and Schlosser, E. (Co-producer). 2009. *Food, Inc.* (Motion Picture). United States: Participant Media, River Road Entertainment and Magnolia Pictures.

Key, Nigel and William McBride. 2007. *The Changing Economics of United States Hog Production.* United States Department of Agriculture, Economic Research Service.

Kilman, Scott, Liam Pleven, and Gregory Zuckerman. August 5, 2010. "Russian Export Ban Raises Global Food Fears." *Wall Street Journal.*

Lee, Hau L., V. Padmanabhan, and Seungjin Whang. 1997. "The Bullwhip Effect in Supply Chains." *Sloan Management Review* 38 (3): 93–102.

Lee, H., So Kut, and Christopher Tang. May 2000. "The Value of Information Sharing in a Two Level Supply Chain." *Management Science* 46 (5): 626–643.

MacDonald, James. 2008. *The Economic Organization of the United States Broiler Production.* United States Department of Agriculture, Economic Research Service.

McDonald's. 2009. "Sustainable Supply Chain: Animal Welfare, Specific Animal Welfare Practices." *Values in Practice Report.* Accessed December 14, 2010. http://www.aboutmc-donalds.com/mcd/csr/report/sustainable_supply_chain/animal_welfare/specific_animal_welfare_practices.html.

Magical-Cruise-Ships.com. 2009–2010. "Disney Cruise Line Chef Jobs." Accessed November 27, 2010. http://www.magical-cruise-ships.com/disney-cruise-line-chef-jobs.html.

Mara, Andrew and Lynn McGrath. 2009. *Defending the Military Food Supply: Acquisition, Preparation, and Protection of Food at U.S. Military Installations.* National Defense University, Center for Technology and National Security Policy. Available through http://www.ndu.edu/ctnsp/publications.html.

Market Ventures. April 5, 2007. "A Study on the Development of a New York City Wholesale Farmers' Market." City Hall Briefing. Accessed January 15, 2011. http://www.market-venturesinc.com/download/NYC-WFM-ExecSum-Phase-1.pdf.

Martinez, Steve W. 2007. "The US Food Marketing System: Recent Developments, 1997–2006." Report Number 42. United States Department of Agriculture, Economic Research Service.

Mattson, B. and U. Soneson. 2003. "Environmentally Friendly Food Processing." *Woodhead Publishing in Food Science and Technology.* Cambridge, UK.

Meizer, Eartha J. March 31, 2010. "GOP Budget Calls for Privatizing Prison Food Service." *The Michigan Messenger.*

Murphy, Andrew. 2007. "Grounding the Virtual: The Material Effect of Electronic Grocery Shopping." *Geoforum* 38: 941–953.

National Chicken Council. "About the Industry." Accessed June 20, 2010. http://www.national-alchickencouncil.com/aboutIndustry.

National Corn Growers' Association. 2008. "Key Issues." Accessed August 28, 2010. www.ncga.com.

National Restaurant Association. 2010. "Facts at a Glance." Accessed November 27, 2010. http://www.Restaurant.org/research/facts/.

National Soybean Research Laboratory. "Soy Benefits." Accessed September 9, 2010. http://www.nsrl.uiuc.edu/soy_benefits.html.

Newman, L. and A. Dale. 2009. "Large Footprints in a Small World: Toward a Macroeconomics of Scale." *Sustainability: Science, Practice, & Policy.* 5(1):9–19.

Norkus, Gregory and Elliot Merberg. June 3, 1994. "Food Distribution in the 1990s." *The Cornell Hospitality & Restaurant Administration Quarterly.* Vol. 35, No. 3.

North American Millers' Association. 2010. "Wheat Milling." Accessed September 14, 2010. http://www.namamillers.org/ci_products_wheat.html.

Oberholtzer, Lydia, Carolyn Dimitri, and Catherine Greene. 2005. "Price Premiums Hold on as U.S. Organic Produce Market Expands." United States Department of Agriculture, Economic Research Service.

Office of the Federal Register. July 19, 2010. "Department of Agriculture, Food and Nutrition Service; National School Lunch, Special Milk, and School Breakfast Programs, National Average Payments/Maximum Reimbursement Rates." Volume 75, Number 137.

Olive-Drab. "Military Food Supply, General." Accessed January 6, 2011. http://www.olive-drab.com/od_rations_general.php.

Organic Trade Association. 2010. "Industry Statistics and Projected Growth." Accessed September 20, 2010. http://www.ota.com/organic/mt/business.html

Ortmann, F., J.H. Van Vuuren, and J.H. Van Dyk. 2006. "Modelling the South African Fresh Fruit Export Supply Chain." Department of Mathematical Sciences, University of Stellenbosch, South Africa.

Paarlberg, Philip, Michael Boehlje, Kenneth Foster, Otto Doering, and Wallace Tyner. 1999. "Structural Change and Market Performance in Agriculture: Critical Issues and Concerns about Concentration in the Pork Industry." West Lafayette, Indiana: Purdue University, Department of Agricultural Economics.

Padel, S., A. Jasinska, M. Rippin, and D. Schaask. 2008. "The European Market for Organic Food in 2006." *The World of Organic Agriculture*, pp. 131–139.

Pagh, Janus D. and Martha C. Cooper. 1998. "Supply Chain Speculation and Postponement Strategies." *Journal of Business Logistics*. 19(2): 13–33.

Palermo, William. *Casino Restaurants: Maximizing Their Impact*. Accessed November 28, 2010. http://casinodev.com/revisedsiteworkBUBUBU/Articles/restaurantnewsletter.pdf.

Palitza, Kristin. 2009. "Poor Nutrition in Food Aid Triggers Malnutrition." Inter Press Service. Accessed February 26, 2009. http://www.ipsnews.net/news.asp?idnews=45872 accessed November 20, 2010.

Park, Kristen. 2008. "Estimates of Produce Sales through Retail, Foodservice, and Wholesale Channels." Food Distribution Research Society Annual Meeting.

Perosio, Debra J., Edward W. McLaughlin, Sandra Cuellar, and Kristen Park. 2001. "Supply Chain Management in the Produce Industry." *Fresh Track 2001*. Cornell Food Industry Management, Department of Agricultural, Resource and Managerial Economics.

Philp, John. March 7, 2008. "From Ice Blocks to Satellite Technology, Perishable Foods Transportation Has Come a Long Way." Accessed January 15, 2011. http://www.uprr.com/newsinfo/releases/service/2008/0307_reefers.shtml.

Pimentel, D. R., R. Doughty, C. Carothers, S. Lamberson, N. Bora, and K. Lee. 2008. "Energy Inputs in Crop Production in Developing and Developed Countries" in *Food, Energy and Society*. CRC Press.

Pimentel, D. and M. Giampietro. 1994. "Food, Land, Population, and the US Economy." Carrying Capacity Network. Executive Summary Accessed January 30, 2011. http://www.carryingcapacity.org/resources.html.

Pincus, Walter. January 11, 2010. "U.S. Food Delivery Contracts in Middle East Worth Billions." *The Washington Post*.

Pollack, Andrew. August 9, 2010. "Canola, Pushed by Genetics, Moves into Uncharted Territories." *The New York Times*.

Produce Marketing Association. May 2004. "RFID in the Produce Supply Chain." Accessed January 14, 2011. http://www.pma.com/resources/supply-chain-efficiencies/automated-data-capture/rfid-radio-frequency-identification.

Public Citizen. 2010. "NAFTA Truth and Consequences: Corn." Accessed September 9, 2010. http://www.citizen.org/trade/article_redirect.cfm?ID=11330.

Pullman, Madeleine, Robin Fenske, and Wayne Wakeland. 2009. "Food Delivery Footprint: Addressing Transportation, Packaging, and Waste in the Food Supply Chain." Oregon Transportation Research and Education Consortium.

Pullman, Madeleine, Greg Stokes, Price Gregory, Mark Langston, and Brandon Arends. 2010. *Portland Roasting Direct: Farm Friendly Direct*, Oikos Sustainability Case Collection, http://www.oikos-international.org/projects/cwc.

Ramos, Juan. October 15, 2010. "Worldwide Consumption of Fruits and Vegetables Too Low." Accessed January 15, 2011. http://www.suite101.com/content/worldwide-consumption-of-fruits-and-vegetablestoo-low-a297263#ixzz14iZn1kK0.

Rankin, Bill. 2009. "Agriculture." Radical Cartography. Accessed June 20, 2010. http://
    radicalcartography.net/.

Ravana, Anne. May 8, 2008. "Maine Bread Company Bashes U.S. Fuel Policy." *Bangor Daily
    News.*

Reardon, Thomas, Peter C. Timmer, Christopher B. Barrett, and Julio Berdegue. 2003. "The
    Rise of Supermarkets in Africa, Asia, and Latin America." *American Journal of Agricultural
    Economics.* 85(5): 1140–1146.

ReportLinker. March, 2010. "Flour Milling Industry in the U.S. and its International Trade."
    Accessed June 14, 2010. http://www.reportlinker.com/p0185654/Flour-Milling-Industry-
    in-the-U-S-and-its-International-Trade-March-2010.html.

Rice, Andrew. September 2, 2010. "The Peanut Solution." *New York Times Magazine.*

Rice, Judy. May 2010. "Fruit Packer Conquers Producer Traceability Initiative Challenge."
    Packing World Magazine. Accessed January 15, 2011. http://www.packworld.com/
    casestudy-29675.

Roberts, Michael. 2006. "Role of Regulation in Minimizing Terrorist Threats against the
    Food Supply: Information, Incentives, and Penalties." *Minnesota Journal of Law, Science &
    Technology.* 8(1):199–223.

Rosenthal, Elizabeth. October 22, 2009. "To Cut Global Warming, Swedes Study Their Plates."
    The New York Times.

Roth, Alenda V., Andy Tsay, Madeleine Pullman, and John Gray. 2008. "Unraveling the Food
    Supply Chain: Strategic Insights from China and the 2007 Recalls." *Journal of Supply
    Chain Management.* 44(1).

Ruhf, K. and K. Clancy. 2010. "It Takes a Region...Exploring a Regional Food Systems
    Approach, A Working Paper." Accessed January 31, 2011. http://api.ning.com/files/
    7hD2ixX*sgFIRP2q*2Il100sJiUh2NPf56GlUeHruNV1nd5sp6WDeNvHd3EXGeJKoxvo
    B9KFPUm1RXgZjKueaeg-JlISDAWz/NESAWGRegionalFoodSystemFINALSept2010.
    pdf.

Schlosser, Eric. 2001. *Fast Food Nation: The Dark Side of the All-American Meal.* New York:
    Houghton Mifflin.

Seafood Source. 2010. "Public Awareness of MSC Eco-label Growing." Accessed November 14,
    2010. http://www.seafoodsource.com/newsarticledetail.aspx?id=4294999338.

Shiva, V. 2000. *Stolen Harvest: The Hijacking of the Global Food Supply.* Cambridge, Massachusetts:
    South End Press.

Simchi-Levi, David, Philip Kaminsky, and Edith Simchi-Levi. 1999. *Designing and Managing the
    Supply Chain: Concepts, Strategies and Cases.* McGraw-Hill/Irwin.

Smith, Bruce D. 1998. "The Emergence of Agriculture." *Scientific American Library.* New York:
    HPHLP.

Smith DeWaal, Caroline and Kristina Barlow. 2004. "Outbreak Alert! Closing the Gaps in
    Our Federal Food-Safety Net." Center for Science in the Public Interest. Accessed
    January 6, 2011. www.cspinet.org/new/pdf/outbreakalert2004.pdf.

Smithfield Foods. 2009. *Smithfield Foods' Corporate Social Responsibility Report 2008/2009.* Accessed
    July 20, 2010. http://www.smithfieldfoods.com/PDF/smi_csr_0809.pdf.

Socyberty. 2010. "Trends in Stadium Food Service." Accessed November 28, 2010. http://
    socyberty.com/society/trends-in-stadium-food-service/#ixzz16bbSH5k2.

Specter, Michael. February 25, 2008. "Big Foot." *The New Yorker.* Accessed January 7, 2011.
    http://www.newyorker.com/reporting/2008/02/25/080225fa_fact_specter.

Sperber, William and Richard R. Stier. January 2010. "Happy Birthday to HACCP: Retrospective
    and Prospective." *Food Safety Magazine.*

Spurlock, Morgan. 2004. *Super Size Me.* Samuel Goldwyn Films. Roadside Attractions.
    New York: Hart Sharp Video.

Stadler-Olson, Birgitte. March 2007. IFRC presentation. ifrc.org.

Starling, Shane. 2009. "Soyfood sales resist recession to top $4bn." Accessed September 9,
    2010. http://www.nutraingredients-usa.com/Industry/Soyfood-sales-resist-recession-to-
    top-4bn.

Stockwell, Ryan. 2009. "Sweden Begins Labeling Food for Carbon Footprint." Centered on Sustainability. Accessed November 15, 2010. http://minnesotaproject.wordpress.com/2009/10/30/sweden-begins-labeling-food-for-carbon-footprint/.

Taha, Fawzi. 2007. *How Highly Pathogenic Avian Influenza Has Affected World Poultry-Meat Trade.* United States Department of Agriculture, Economic Research Service.

Tauxe, Robert. V. 2009. "Molecular Epidemiology and the Transformation of Public Health." PulseNet/OutbreakNet Annual Meeting, Snowbird, Utah.

Thomas, Anisya. 2004. "Humanitarian Logistics: Enabling Disaster Response." Fritz Institute Report. Accessed May 24, 2011. http://www.fritzinstitute.org/PDFs/ InTheNews/2004/AidandTrade_0104.pdf.

Thomas, Anisya. 2004. "Elevating Humanitarian Logistics." *International Aid and Trade Review.*

Thompson, James, Gordon Mitchell, Tom Rumsey, Robert Kasmire, and Carlos Crisosto. 1998. "Commercial Cooling of Fruits, Vegetables, and Flowers." University of California, Davis. DANR Publication 21567.

Todd, Jessica, Lisa Mancino, and Lin Biing-Hwan. 2010. "The Impact of Food Away From Home on Adult Diet Quality." Report No. ERR-90. United States Department of Agriculture, Economic Research Service.

Tondel, Fabien and Timothy Woods. 2006. "Supply Chain Management and the Changing Structure of U.S. Organic Produce Markets." American Agricultural Economics Association Annual Meeting, Long Beach, California, July 23–26.

Trivedi, B. 2008. "Dinner's Dirty Secret." *The New Scientist.*

Trostle, Ronald. 2008. "Fluctuating Food Commodity Prices." *Amber Waves,* Vol. 6. *United States Department of Agriculture,* Economic Research Service.

Tyson Foods, Inc. "Live Production: Pork." Accessed July 18, 2010. http://www.tyson.com/Corporate/AboutTyson/LiveProduction/Pork.aspx.

Tyson Foods, Inc. 2009. *Fiscal 2009 Fact Book.* Accessed June 18, 2010. http://www.tyson.com/Corporate/Factbook/2009.

UNICEF. November, 2009. "Tracking progress on child and maternal nutrition – a survival and development priority."

United States Department of Agriculture. June 30, 2008. "Food Safety Rules of Practice." Accessed January 24, 2011. http://www.fsis.usda.gov/PDF/ROP_Module.pdf.

Upton, David M. and Virgina A. Fuller. 2004. *The ITC eChoupalIinitiative.* Harvard Business School. Case number 9-604-016.

US Census Bureau. 2008 (Based on Census 2000 Data). "Table 1. Projections of the Population and Components of Change for the United States, 2010–2050." Accessed January 30, 2011. http://www.census.gov/population/www/projections/summarytables.html

US Wheat Associates. "Wheat Land Use." Accessed July 24, 2010. www.uswheat.org.

van Donk, Dirk Pieter. 2001. "Make to Stock or Make to Order: The Decoupling Point in the Food Processing Industries." *International Journal of Production Economics.*

Van Wassenhove, Luk N. 2006. "Humanitarian Aid Logistics: Supply Chain Management in High Gear." *Journal of the Operational Research Society.* 57: 475–489.

Vegas, Pete. "Rice 101." Accessed September 9, 2010. http://www.sagevfoods.com/MainPages/Rice101/.

Visual Economics. July 12, 2010. "What are We Eating? What the Average American Consumes in a Year." Accessed January 30, 2011. http://www.visualeconomics.com/food-consumption-in-america_2010-07-12/.

Vrechopoulos, Adam P., Robert M. O'Keefe, Georgios I. Doukidis, and George J. Siomkos. 2004. "Virtual Store Layout: An Experimental Comparison in the Context of Grocery Retail." *Journal of Retailing.* 80:13–22.

Wallace, Scott. 2010. "Farming the Amazon." National Geographic. Accessed September 9, 2010. http://environment.nationalgeographic.com/environment/habitats/last-of-amazon.htmlpage=1Walt, Vivienne. February 27, 2008. "The World's Growing Food-Price Crisis." Time Magazine.

Walt, Vivienne. February 27, 2008. "The World's Growing Food-Price Crisis." *Time Magazine.*

Wellener, Paul and Tanay Shah. 2010. "Entering the Federal B2G Marketplace in Six Steps." Accessed December 8, 2010. http://manufacturing.net/Articles/2010/08/Entering-The-Federal-B2G-Marketplace-In-Six-Steps/.

Wendy's. "Wendy's Animal Welfare Program." Accessed December 14, 2010. http://www.wendys.com/about_us/animal_welfare.jsp.

Wheat Harvest, Drying and Storage. "Management of Soft Red Winter Wheat. Integrated Pest Management." Accessed September 9, 2010. http://extension.missouri.edu/explorepdf/agguides/pests/ipm1022_Pp33-37.pdf.

Wolverton, Troy. October 30, 2001. "Seeking relics amid Webvan's ruins." Cnet News. Accessed December 3, 2010. http://news.cnet.com/2100-1017-275181.html.

Working Villages International. 2010. "Our Development Model: Village Self Reliance." Accessed November 21, 2010. http://www.workingvillages.org/our-development-model.html.

World Food Programme. "Quantity Reporting." Accessed November 28, 2010. http://www.wfp.org/fais.

World Food Programme. "About: WFP in Numbers." Accessed January 16, 2011. http://www.wfp.org/wfp-numbers.

World Food Programme. "WFP's Partners." Accessed January 16, 2011. http://one.wfp.org/aboutwfp/partners/governments.asp?section=1&sub_section=4.

World Health Organization. 2008. "Terrorist Threats to Food: Guidance for Establishing and Strengthening Prevention and Response Systems." Accessed January 25, 2011. www.who.int/foodsafety/publications/general/en/terrorist.pdf.

World Health Organization. "Availability and Changes in Consumption of Animal Products." Accessed August 8, 2010. http://www.who.int/nutrition/topics/3_foodconsumption/en/index4.html.

INDEX

profit **7**, 188, 204, **240**, 254–6; coffee 141, 142, 144, 165, 169, 173, 177, 181, 188; commodities 65, 67, 81, 91–2; food service 165, 169, 173, 177, 181; foreign aid 231, 232, 233; profit margins 142, 184, 210, 213, 216; retail 210, 211, 213–16
promotions, sales 143, 199, 212, 215, 224 *see also* marketing
protectionism, trade 83, 86, 256
protein 25, 31, 33–5, 50, 51, 54, **125**, 167, 177, 188, 253; in commodity crops 74–5, 77, 79, 80
Public Health Information System 17
pullet farms 47–9
pulsed electric field processing 187
pulsed-field gel electrophoresis 18
PulseNet **15**, 18, 29
purchasing consortia 245

quality assurance 20–6, 31, 40, 47, 113, 127; continuous improvement 21, 33, 54, 134, **136**; ISO 127; Six Sigma 20–1; Six Ts 20, **21**, 22, 32; Total Quality Management 20
quaternary packaging 197
quotas: coffee 133, 146; grains 86 *see also* trade, international

radio frequency identification 10, 23, 51, 108, 196, 213, 214, 223 *see also* traceability
railways: and beef 36; and commodities 71, 75, 80, 84; and cross-docking 212; drawbacks of 195; and food safety 198; and fruits and vegetables 96, 106; and warehousing 196
rainforest 88
Rainforest Alliance 127, 139, 146, **147**, 149–50, 158
ranchers *see* cow/calf operators
raspberries 101, 112, 117–18, 180, 202–3
ready-to-eat meals 105, 162; Meals Ready to Eat 170
recalls 12, 15, 17, 19, 24, 29–32, 51
recession, global 86–7, 164
recycling 88, 157–8; food waste 178–9, 183; packaging waste 104–5, 191
Red Cross: American 228, **230**; IFRC 237, 245
Red Jacket Orchards 116–21
refiners 74
refrigeration 10, 26, 40, 102–3, 192, **221**, 224; and transportation 36, 96, 106
refugees 230, 232, **239**

regional food systems 114, 116, 179, 222, 250, 254–7
regulations 15–20, 26, 27, 45, 51, 124–5, 168; and calorie information 178; environmental 191, **192**; European Union 72, 90, 131; and food security 257–8; Japan 131, 135, 151; labor 106; organic **61–2**, 128–31, 139, 148, 150, 158, 202, 225 *see also* Agriculture, Department of; Environmental Protection Agency; Food and Drug Administration
regulatory traceability 23
religion 44, 200, **239**, 244
Rembrandt Enterprises 48–9
replenishment (inventory) 196, 211–13, 219, 226, 236, 241; continuous 245
Request for Proposals 166
Request for Quotations 166
respiration 100, 102–4, 118
restaurants **6**, 161–5; and dietary patterns 161, 164, 177, 209; food safety 12, **14**, 16; National Restaurant Association 164; nutritional labeling 177–8 *see also* fast food; food service
retail, food **2, 6**, 206–10; allocation 210–11; assortment 210–11, 226; "buy local" 113, 120, 213, 215–16, 220, 225; consolidation 210, 222–3, 226; convenience 206–9, 213–14, 216; distribution 207, 209, 210, 216, 219, 222; food safety 27, 30, 50–1; fresh format 215; information management 213; international retailing 220–2; inventory management 207, 209, 210–14, **221**, 223, 225, 226; loyalty cards 219; mass merchandisers 207–9; online 206, 209, 213, 218, 220; organic selections 111, 130, 207, 213, 215–16, 219; perishability 207, 211, 213–14, 222; private label 81, 202, 219; retail strategy 213–20; specialization 215, 222, 223, 232; stockouts 212; store layout 213, 216–18, 222, 226; supercenters 207, **208**, 213, 215, 217; technological innovation 213, 220, **221** *see also* supermarkets
reusable plastic containers 104–5
RFID *see* radio frequency identification
rice **14**, 65, 67–9, 81–7, 134, 232; paddy pools 84
Rice, Robert 150
Riceland cooperative 84
Richey's Market 222–6
riots: disaster-related 233, 238, 245; food 87, 250, 168